GDALENÆ
NOSTRA
Honoratissimo et Nobilissimo
ROBERTO D.no BROOKE Baroni
de Beauchamps-Court in Comi:
Warwici. Regiæ Majestatis in
Agro Staffordiæ Locumtenenti
& hujus Collegij olim Con
victori. D.D.C.Q.
D. Loggan.
A. Capella
B. Bibliotheca
C. Refectorium
D. Præsidis Hospitium
F. F. pedes 297
A
C
F

THE MAGDALEN METAPHYSICALS

THE MAGDALEN METAPHYSICALS

Idealism and Orthodoxy at Oxford 1901-1945

BY

JAMES PATRICK

MERCER

ISBN 0-86554-145-0

The Magdalen Metaphysicals

Printed in the United States of America

All books published by Mercer University Press are produced on acid-free paper that exceeds the minimum standards set by the National Historical Publications and Records Commission.

Library of Congress Cataloging in Publication Data

Patrick, James, 1933-
The Magdalen metaphysicals.
Bibliography: p. 171
Includes index.
1. Philosophy, English—20th century. 2. Webb, Clement Charles Julian, 1865-1954. 3. Smith, J. A. (John Alexander), 1863-1939. 4. Collingwood, R. G. (Robin George), 1899-1943. 5. Lewis, C. S. (Clive Staples), 1898-1963. 6. Magdalen College (University of Oxford)—History—20th century. I. Title.
B1615.P33 1985 192 84-20751
ISBN 0-86554-145-0

•CONTENTS•

Not all of Isis flows under Folly Bridge or meanders about the shoals of Seacourt Stream. And (if I must drag my parable to light) not all her philosophies are philosophies of negation and despair; she is fed by secret streams. . . .

Ronald Knox
The Hidden Stream, 1952

•ABBREVIATIONS•

BLW Bodleian Library, Department of Western Manuscripts

CBP(1) *Contemporary British Philosophy*, series 1, ed. J. H. Muirhead

CBP(2) *Contemporary British Philosophy*, series 2, ed. J. H. Muirhead

CBP(3) *Contemporary British Philosophy*, series 3, ed. H. D. Lewis

CPB Collingwood Papers, BLW

CUM W. J. van der Dussen, "Collingwood's Unpublished Manuscripts"

DNB *Dictionary of National Biography*

HAS W. J. van der Dussen, *History As a Science: The Philosophy of R. G. Collingwood*

HJ *Hibbert Journal*

LCSL *Letters of C. S. Lewis*

LJ Journals of C. S. Lewis, quoted in the Lewis family history, LPW

LPW Lewis Papers, Marion E. Wade Collection, Wheaton College

LJRRT *Letters of J. R. R. Tolkien*, ed. Humphrey Carpenter

JTS *Journal of Theological Studies*

PAS *Proceedings of the Aristotelian Society*

PBA *Proceedings of the British Academy*

SPM J. A. Smith Papers, Magdalen College Library

SPB	J. A. Smith Papers, Balliol College Library
WJB	Clement Webb Journals, BLW

•PREFACE•

Four Philosophers

While the Oxford realists—Cook Wilson and his disciples H. A. Prichard and H. W. B. Joseph—celebrated their increasingly frequent victories over the ghost of Thomas Hill Green, other Oxford philosophers, having tried Wilson's realism, quietly returned to the work of renewing classical metaphysics and clarifying the relation between theology and philosophy that the Neo-Hegelian followers of Green had obscured and the realists denied.

My aim in this book is to give an account of the thought of four of these rebels against what by 1918 was clearly the fashionable philosophy, and to document their existence as a community of philosophic opinion at Oxford. They were not a movement or a school, but they shared certain convictions rooted in classical metaphysics and transmitted to them by the great teachers of the late nineteenth century, especially Green and Richard Nettleship. They also shared a time, the years between the wars; a place, Oxford, "towery city and branchy between towers" in Hopkins's words; and a college, Magdalen, its deer park circled by the Cherwell, its face dusty from the traffic of the London road. Founded originally in 1448 for the study of philosophy and theology by the bishop of Winchester, William of Waynflete, Magdalen boasted Joseph Addison in the seventeenth century; Gibbon in the eighteenth; and great academics like Henry Longueville Mansel, the first Waynflete professor, and Martin Joseph Routh, the founder of patristic studies at Oxford, under Victoria. Of Magdalen as it had been about 1910, one of its sons wrote, "We lived on loyalties this age disowns," and yet "the place was liberal, believed in learning."[1]

Of the four, Clement Charles Julian Webb (1865-1954) came to Magdalen first, in 1889, where he was a fellow until 1922 and an honorary fellow from 1938 until his death. He inhabited for many years Holywell Ford, a medieval mill house across the water walks from Magdalen. John Alexander Smith (1863-1939) became a fellow on his election to the Waynflete professorship, a university chair associated with the college by statute, in 1910, and lived at the top of stairwell three, New Buildings, until his retirement in 1935. Clive Staples Lewis (1898-1963), finally elected to the fellowship he longed for in May 1925, kept his college rooms until his election to the professorship of medieval and Renaissance literature at Cambridge in 1954. Robin George Collingwood (1889-1943) succeeded to the Waynflete professorship, and to the Magdalen fellowship annexed, on Smith's retirement in 1935.

Among Webb, Smith, Collingwood, and Lewis there were friendships that proved significant both personally and intellectually, although only J. A. Smith was closely acquainted with each of the others. Smith had probably known Clement Webb during their undergraduate years, 1884-1887, when Smith had been at Balliol and Webb at Christ Church. Certainly they were acquainted by 1891, when Smith returned to Oxford from Edinburgh, becoming by his appointment at Balliol, like Webb, a philosophy tutor. Webb and Smith were both members of the Aristotelian Society, a dozen scholars who met on Monday evenings in Ingraham Bywater's rooms to discuss Aristotelian texts; the Synthetic Society, the London club founded by Arthur Balfour, Wilfrid Ward, Charles Gore, and E. S. Talbot in 1896 to promote the discussion of the relation between philosophy, faith, and science;[2] the Oxford Philosophical Society, organized by F. C. S. Schiller about 1898 to encourage consideration by tutors and professors of current philosophical topics;[3] and the smaller Deipnosophic, which, as its name suggests, existed as a forum for the

---

[1]James Matthew Thompson, *My Apologia* (Oxford: Alden Press, 1940) 67.

[2]On the Synthetic Society, see Oliver Lodge, *Past Years: An Autobiography* (London: Hodder and Stoughton, 1931) 172; John David Root, "The Philosophical and Religious Thought of Arthur James Balfour (1848-1930)," *Journal of British Studies* (Spring 1980): 131-37; Gwendolyn Stephenson, *Edward Stuart Talbot 1844-1934* (London: S.P.C.K., 1936) 128-29.

[3]C. C. J. Webb, "Autobiography," 71.

discussion of classical metaphysics.[4] After hearing Smith's speech on the occasion of his admission to Magdalen in 1910, Clement Webb praised his colleague's remarks in his journal, and for twenty years, until Webb's retirement in 1930, a week in term seldom passed without Webb's noting that he had met J. A. to discuss university business or philosophy. J. A. came to the Webbs for tea, "full of good stories," accompanied by Mrs. Caird or another friend, and wrote Clement Webb long philosophical letters; together Webb and Smith planned and executed the visit of the famous Italian idealist Benedetto Croce to England in 1923, and when the Edinburgh *Scotsman* wanted an account of Smith's life and importance, they naturally turned to Webb.[5]

By 1916 both Clement Webb and J. A. Smith knew Robin Collingwood, a young philosophy tutor at Pembroke, and both came over time to consider him the best philosopher of his generation. Webb called him "brilliant" and "all-accomplished." Although Webb was twenty-four years Collingwood's senior, there was close acquaintance, and visits were exchanged between the Webbs at Old Marston and the Chantry, the Collingwoods' house in North Moreton.[6] Webb reviewed Collingwood's first book and his last, and was one of the few Oxford philosophers who saw in the young Collingwood the significance even those who disliked him would discover after 1925.[7] Webb's journals note his reading of Collingwood's books, and his interest in Collingwood's standing in the uni-

---

[4]F. C. Carritt, *Fifty Years a Don* (Oxford: The Author, 1960) 29; Clement C. J. Webb, *Religious Experience*, ed. L. W. Grensted (Oxford: University Press, 1945) 18; W. D. Ross, "Clement Charles Julian Webb, 1865-1954," *PBA* 41 (1955): 342.

Webb consistently gives this society the name Deipnosophic, and it is probably to be identified as that small society of older men over which J. A. Smith presided, into which Collingwood was invited in 1921. See Collingwood to de Ruggiero, 20 March 1921, quoted in *HAS*, 22. See WJB, 5 June, 11 October 1924 [MS.Eng.misc.e. 1167]; 16, 29 January, 11 June 1925 [MS.Eng.misc.d.1117]; 6 March 1930 [MS.Eng.misc.d.1122].

[5]WJB, 12 September 1910 [MS.Eng.misc.e.1156]; 26, 27 June 1923 [MS.Eng.misc.d.1115]; 29 May 1924 [MS.Eng.misc.d.1116].

[6]WJB, 18, 21 January 1924 [MS.Eng.misc.d.1115]; 11, 25 May 1925 [MS.Eng.misc.d.1117].

[7]C. C. J. Webb, Review of *Religion and Philosophy*, by R. G. Collingwood, *Oxford Magazine*, 1 June 1917, 281-82; Review of *The Idea of Nature*, by R. G. Collingwood, *JTS* 46 (1945): 248-51.

versity.[8] For J. A. Smith, Collingwood was that rarest of creatures, a young philosopher of obvious promise who shared Smith's interests in history, Aristotle, and most important of all, in Croce. Smith praised Collingwood's translation of Croce's *Philosophy of Giambattista Vico* in 1916, and Smith's sponsorship was instrumental in Collingwood's appointment to the Waynflete professorship in 1935.[9] Collingwood, who was fortunate in his philosophical friendships outside Oxford, with men like Samuel Alexander at Manchester and Guido de Ruggiero at Rome,[10] but had few such close friendships in his own university, repaid his sponsors with loyalty, praising Webb's work, and treating Smith as a revered mentor.

C. S. Lewis, who came to Magdalen in 1925, caught Smith at his zenith. Lewis accompanied J. A. on walks around the Magdalen garden, and basked in the great professor's notice. Lewis soon became an almost filial companion, who breakfasted with Smith daily and sat up late philosophizing with his increasingly lonely, ever ebullient elder.[11] Lewis numbered Smith and Webb among the five great Magdalen men who had enlarged his very idea of the learned life.[12]

---

[8]WJB, 15 December 1923 [MS.Eng.misc.d.1115]; 14-20 November 1924 [MS.Eng.misc.e.1167]; 5 May 1925 [MS.Eng.misc.d.1117]; 11 March 1926 [MS.Eng.misc.d.1118]; 31 October 1939 [MS.Eng.misc.e.1176].

[9]J. A. Smith, Review of *The Philosophy of Benedetto Croce: The Problem of Art and History*, by H. Wildon Carr, *HJ* 16:3 (1916): 505; E. W. F. Tomlin, "The Philosophy of R. G. Collingwood," *Ratio* 1 (1958): 117.

[10]Six letters of Collingwood to Alexander are in BLW. See *HAS*, 451. On Collingwood's friendship with de Ruggiero, see R. G. Collingwood, *An Autobiography* (Oxford: Clarendon Press, 1939) 99. The Collingwood-de Ruggiero correspondence, 36 letters written between 1920 and 1938, are in BLW [*HAS*, 451].

[11]C. S. Lewis to Arthur Greeves, 1 June 1930, Walter Hooper, ed., *They Stand Together: The Letters of C. S. Lewis to Arthur Greeves (1914-1963)* (New York: Macmillan, 1979) 355-56; Adam Fox, "At the Breakfast Table," in James T. Como, ed., *C. S. Lewis at the Breakfast Table and Other Reminiscences* (New York: Macmillan, 1979) 90-92, 93.

[12]C. S. Lewis, *Surprised by Joy: The Shape of My Early Life* (New York: Harcourt Brace, 1956) 216. The others were Clement Webb, Frank Edward Brightman (1856-1932), a liturgiologist and ecclesiastical historian, and editor of the *Journal of Theological Studies* (1904-1932); P. V. M. Beneke (1871-1944), who was Lewis's tutor in 1920, an organist of great ability, and as Oxford was fond of pointing out, the grandson of Mendelssohn. C. T. Onions (1873-1965) was professor of English, founder and editor of *Medium Aevum*. See Lewis's description of Beneke in his letter to his father, 21 January 1921, *LCSL*, 52. Beneke's papers are in the Magdalen College Library.

Although Lewis and Collingwood each occasionally mentioned the other's work, journals and letters have left no evidence of friendship between them. Lewis recommended Collingwood's essays on Roman Britain, and Collingwood cited *The Allegory of Love*.[13]

The philosophy shared by Webb, Lewis, Smith, and Collingwood would without hesitation have been identified by their university contemporaries as idealism—this despite Lewis's affection for Aristotle and neglect of Kant;[14] despite Collingwood's attempts to create a new realism and his vehement rejection of the title idealist after about 1930;[15] and despite J. A. Smith's reliance on classical sources and Benedetto Croce rather than Hegel.[16] In a broad but fundamental sense, Smith and Webb, Collingwood and Lewis were the heirs of the greatest nineteenth-century English idealist, Thomas Hill Green, and of John Ruskin. That patrimony was interpreted, at least by Smith and Collingwood, in the light of the thought of the seventeenth-century Italian philosopher Giambattista Vico and his modern disciples Croce and Giovanni Gentile. Webb's father was Benjamin Webb, a follower of Pugin and later Ruskin in matters architectural and aesthetic, and at Christ Church Webb had learned philosophy from Cook Wilson while Wilson was still in the mainstream of Victorian idealism. Smith's tutor at Balliol had been Richard Nettleship, Green's successor and literary executor, and Collingwood's father (through his tutor Bernard Bosanquet) had been a disciple of Green and of Ruskin in the 1870s. The elder Collingwood finally moved to Coniston to be near Ruskin, and there Robin Collingwood

---

[13]R. G. Collingwood, *The New Leviathan* (Oxford: Clarendon Press, 1942) 57; C. S. Lewis, "Psycho-Analysis and Literary Criticism," *Selected Literary Essays*, ed. Walter Hooper (Cambridge: University Press, 1969) 298; Lewis to I. O. Evans, 26 September 1945, *LCSL*, 207.

[14]Lewis wrote in June 1924 that he was not a Kantian. [LJ, 8:245]. In 1931 he was at work developing a neo-Aristotelian aesthetic. See Lewis to T. S. Eliot, 2 June 1931, Roger Lancelyn Green and Walter Hooper, *C. S. Lewis: A Biography* (New York: Harcourt Brace Jovanovich, 1974) 223.

[15]Collingwood, *Autobiography*; Collingwood to Ryle, 9 May 1935, CPB. After his rejection of the realism of Cook Wilson and Carritt about 1917, Collingwood continued to seek a philosophical synthesis, writing a "Fragment on Neo-Realism" (1922-1923); and an "Experiment in New Realism" (1935), as well as a manuscript of 125 pages entitled "Realism and Idealism" (1936). See *HAS* 446, 449, 450.

[16]J. A. Smith, "Philosophy as the Development of the Notion and Reality of Self-Consciousness," *CBP* (2):228.

grew up in an atmosphere formed by the idealistic pursuit of unity between thought and action.[17] Lewis was drawn into the milieu established at Magdalen by Smith and Webb as his own thought developed toward an appreciation for history and classical metaphysics and away from the realism of his philosophy tutor E. F. Carritt.

Systematically the philosophy shared by the Magdalen metaphysicals was a development of four convictions: (1) an interest in classical sources typified by the revival at Oxford of Aristotelian studies and by the persistence of the influence of Plato's *Republic*; (2) participation in the revival of historical studies, especially interest in classical and medieval texts, and in the status and character of history as a discipline; (3) the belief that philosophy was essentially literary, with affinities to poetry; and (4) the conviction that religion, though it might begin with experience, was finally a matter of truth. From Victorian idealism they borrowed their rejection of the realist epistemology, which held that knowledge was caused by the immediate intuition of facts or objects. Each would have defended the idealist axiom that knowledge leaves neither knower nor known unchanged,[18] but they were more dedicated to idealism as the defense of the possibility of thought than as a means of establishing the existence of cosmic mind or of the Absolute. Taking seriously the possibility that thinking yields real knowledge, convinced of the significance of the perennial moral and metaphysical questions, confident of the relation between the intellectual and moral life, and more disposed to revere than to neglect their predecessors, they saw themselves as grateful heirs of the tradition established by Plato, perfected by Descartes and Kant, and represented in Oxford's recent past by Thomas Hill Green, Richard Nettleship, Francis Herbert Bradley, and Edward Caird. None of the four was antiquarian in matters intellectual, but there was among them something of the spirit displayed by Ronald Knox's remark that Edward Caird on Plato "was alone worth all the vaporings of

---

[17][R. G. Collingwood], "Mr. W. G. Collingwood: Artist, Author, Antiquary," *Times*, 3 July 1932; "Autobiography," 148-51.

[18]Smith, "Philosophy," 230; Collingwood, *Autobiography*, 44-46; C. S. Lewis, *The Pilgrim's Regress: An Allegorical Apology for Christianity, Reason and Romanticism* (London: Geoffrey Bles, 1933) 68-69. Harold H. Joachim, *The Nature of Truth* (Oxford: Clarendon, 1906) 37.

the moderns."[19] J. A. Smith wrote of his own philosophy in 1924:

> Novelty or originality I do not claim for it, but rather disdain. On the contrary, it appears to me something which has slowly formed itself in the great orthodox or Catholic succession of modern philosophy, and it had confirmed and strengthened myself in the renewal of reverential discipleship to the great classics of Modern, Medieval, and Ancient Philosophy.[20]

Above the bickering of the philosophical sects, wrote Collingwood, "is a melody sung in unison by the spirits of the spheres, which are the great philosophers," a *philosophia quaedam perennis*, "a living thought whose content, never discovered for the first time, is progressively clarified by every genuine thinker."[21]

Collingwood and Lewis both called their philosophy romantic, though romantic was a word neither Webb nor Smith used often. In *Speculum Mentis*, the philosophic summa Collingwood wrote at midcareer, he claimed only "to be working out the tradition founded a century ago by the great men of the Romantic Movement," and to Collingwood that meant "a renewed medievalism, some new interpretation of Christianity."[22] In *Pilgrim's Regress*, written in 1932, C. S. Lewis argued that the business of life, and hence of thought, is the recovery of the unity that ought to exist between joy, reason, and virtue; between past and present, and between Israel and the Greeks—all unities perceived historically, and understood most fully according to the one genuinely consistent and revelatory account of Mother Kirk.[23] The search for unity, the unity of man and nature and of the natural and the supernatural, was itself a romantic project; and in the 1943 preface to *Pilgrim's Regress*, Lewis took as the key to this search for unity "a particular recurrent experience," an intense longing whose ultimate object is nothing in this world. Yet this longing—unlike Nietzschean fury or Schleiermacher's feelings of dependence—was legitimized and satisfied only by its object,

---

[19]Ronald A. Knox, *A Spiritual Aeneid* (London: Longmans, 1918) 62.

[20]Smith, "Philosophy," 233.

[21]R. G. Collingwood, *Speculum Mentis* (Oxford: Clarendon Press, 1924) 13.

[22]Ibid., 38.

[23]Lewis, *Pilgrim's Regress*, 160-73.

directed by reason, and capable of issuing in happiness among those who developed in themselves the life of virtue. The romanticism of Collingwood and Lewis, and the idealism of Webb and Smith, were all attempts to develop the metaphysical tradition central to the Greats curriculum and to Western thought from Plato to Edward Caird.

Characteristically the Magdalen metaphysicals believed that philosophical questions often provoked theological answers. This was true even of the vaguely modernist Smith, whose earliest published writings were skeptical notes on analogy and on the creed; and Webb, Collingwood, and Lewis each devoted part of careers begun as professional philosophers to the exposition or defense of some aspect of the Christian religion. Lewis will be remembered best for his literary apologies on behalf of Christianity. From the publication of his first book, *Religion and Philosophy*, in 1916 to his defense two years before his death of the necessity of Christianity for philosophy, Collingwood never philosophized apart from Christian belief.[24] Three of the four, Webb, Collingwood, and Lewis, were arguably orthodox in the sense presupposed by Lewis's "mere Christianity," believing that truths regarding God's existence and nature, his actions on man's behalf, and human duty and destiny, truths partly understood by philosophy, are revealed to human beings by means with respect to which the Fathers, Newman, and Charles Gore would have agreed. In the thought of the Magdalen four, philosophy enjoyed an integral relationship to orthodoxy thus defined, and throughout their Oxford careers they were interested in various projects for restating the Christian religion and clarifying the relation between faith and reason. Before 1914 this interest made Smith, Collingwood, and Webb sympathetic toward Modernism, anxious to conciliate the claims of supernatural religion and modern science. But, Smith excepted, the drift of their thought, unlike the drift of English academe generally, was toward the distinctively orthodox presuppositions of Lewis's *Pilgrim's Regress* (1933); Webb's *The Historical Element in Christianity* (1935); and Collingwood's *New Leviathan* (1942). While much of scholarly Oxford was hard at work unraveling the traditional relation between philosophy

---

[24]See especially Collingwood's "Fascism and Nazism," *Philosophy* 15 (1940): 168-76, perhaps his clearest statement of the impossibility of European civilization apart from Christianity.

and theology, a project encouraged by the manifest decadence of the "spiritual" philosophies of the pre-1914 period, the Magdalen metaphysicals seemed impelled toward belief by their philosophic interests.

I have called the philosophers whose thought is the subject of this book "metaphysicals" because their philosophy tends deliberately toward poetry, complementing the achievement of the seventeenth-century metaphysical poets from within the purely intellectual discipline of philosophy. Donne, Cowley, Crashaw, and Herbert wrote poetry to which a background of philosophic notions gave a distinctive form, displaying their emotions by means of images formed around metaphysical affirmations and questionings. Webb, Lewis, Smith, and Collingwood, each in a distinctive way, wrote as though philosophy were a literary genre, and Lewis developed a form for which no name exists, writing story after story in which ideas dominate narrative and diction. All four shared the conviction that language, and hence poetry, is a kind of truth, a philosophic strain running in English letters to Coleridge and on the Continent to Vico. This conviction, reinforced in the Magdalen metaphysicals by their reading of sources as disparate as Aristotle and Croce, became a dominant theme setting them apart in an Oxford in which poetry and language were increasingly considered too irrational or vague to be of much use philosophically.

Since the four were a community of acquaintances sharing common interests, who never (with the exception of the half-serious alliance Smith and Collingwood formed in the 1930s against the minute philosophers) conceived of themselves self-consciously as a philosophic school, their existence as a group is best understood by means of the definition their relationships with contemporary intellectual movements suggest. Three movements whose memberships and ideals overlapped the Magdalen metaphysicals were the classicism of Eliot and the *Criterion*, the new idealism of the 1920s, and Modernism. Not one of the four was part of all of these three movements, and the relationship of the Magdalen metaphysicals to each was characterized by some tension as well as by broad sympathies.

Clement Webb and J. A. Smith were both too full of years and distinction to write reviews for a stylish and somewhat radical literary journal when the *Criterion* began in 1922, and after 1927 there was between Webb and Lewis and Eliot's magazine the matter of Neo-Scholasticism, which Webb disapproved and Lewis distrusted, but to which Eliot acknowledged intellectual debts. Given this obvious and important tension, there was still a distinct sympathy between Webb, Collingwood, and Lewis, and the young American philosopher-poet who signed himself T. Stearns Eliot. In 1917 Eliot welcomed Webb's refutation of Durkheim's theory that religion might be a group illusion and praised Collingwood's *Religion and Philosophy*, in which the intellectual content of theology was defended.[25] The conviction that Christianity was true, not merely satisfying, distinguished the thought of Webb, Collingwood, and Lewis, and the intellectualism it presupposed was set forward persistently by the *Criterion*. This belief in reason was of course rooted in the philosophers of the Greats curriculum that Eliot had known only during a brief period of graduate study in 1916 and 1917, but the American seemed to see its import with a clarity reserved for brands snatched from the fires of Russell's positivism. Generally, T. S. Eliot used the *Criterion* to encourage philosophers and philosophy of a traditional bent. Hastings Rashdall, an able idealist of Smith's generation who had died accidentally and prematurely in 1924, won Eliot's approval: "His philosophy is Greats philosophy. Of such was the salt of Oxford."[26] Eliot reviewed Collingwood's first book favorably—the only other favorable notice was Clement Webb's—and saw to it that reviews by Collingwood and reviews of Collingwood's books were published in the *Criterion*. By 1938 Eliot and Collingwood had become advocates of one another's work.

Sympathy between Eliot and Lewis was complicated by Lewis's undergraduate dislike of "Eliotic" verse, and interrupted by a misunderstanding to which Lewis responded with overzealous disapproval of Eliot's Neo-Scholasticism. In 1925 Lewis and his literary friends had plotted to submit parodies of Eliot's verse to the *Criterion*, hoping that Eliot might publish these as serious poetry.[27] But as Lewis grew close to Christianity, he apparently developed a tentative interest in Eliot despite

---

[25] T. Stearns Eliot, Review of *Group Theories of Religion and the Religion of the Individual*, by C. C. J. Webb, *International Journal of Ethics* 27:1 (October 1916): 115-17; Webb, Review of *Religion and Philosophy*. Collingwood published nine book reviews in the *Criterion*.

[26] Review of *Ideas and Ideals*, by Hastings Rashdall, *Criterion* 8 (1928-1929): 757.

[27] Lewis, *Selected Literary Essays*, xv-xvi.

his misgivings about Eliot's poetic form. In 1930 Lewis, acting for the Michaelmas Club, invited Eliot to speak and offered the hospitality of his college rooms, and the next year Lewis submitted "The Personal Heresy in Criticism" to the *Criterion*.[28] There the friendship stalled. Eliot kept the essay too long and finally suggested that it be published in a scholarly journal. Lewis was piqued by the implication that his essay lacked popular appeal, and during 1931 and 1932 was acerbic about Eliot's Neo-Scholasticism, suggesting in both *Pilgrim's Regress* and in correspondence that Eliot's advocacy of Jacques Maritain represented a tendency to turn Christianity into a highbrow fad.[29] Lewis's mistrust of Eliot, which had probably faded somewhat when Eliot was helpful in the publication of the *Festschrift* for Charles Williams in 1943, was rekindled by a meeting in 1945, at which Eliot opened conversation with the comment that Lewis looked older than his photographs.[30] Later there would be mutual service on the Prayer Book commission, and finally the flowering of the friendship for which Lewis had perhaps hoped in 1931. Lewis told Walter Hooper that when he finally came to know Eliot, "I loved him at once."[31]

The aim of Eliot's *Criterion*, the purpose of Collingwood's philosophy, and the motive of Lewis's apologies were nearly identical. Lewis, Collingwood, and Smith shared with Eliot a concern for the unity of the European mind and the European past, and a conviction that Christianity should either be judged true and followed or condemned as false. Eliot disliked romanticism because he thought it affirmed the innate perfectibility of human nature, and rendered life inglorious and impossible by denying original sin. By romanticism Eliot meant the historicist myth of progress, with its irrationalism and exaltation of emotion. About 1930 Lewis and Collingwood probably meant by romanticism what Eliot meant by classicism: the one tradition of the West in its in-

---

[28]Lewis to Eliot, 21 May 1930, 19 April, 2 June 1931, LPW. See Humphrey Carpenter, *The Inklings: C. S.Lewis, J. R. R. Tolkien, Charles Williams, and Their Friends* (Boston: Houghton Mifflin, 1979) 192-93, 197, 246.

[29]Lewis to Bede Griffiths, ? June 1931; Lewis to Sr. Madeleva, 7 June 1934, LPW; Lewis, *Pilgrim's Regress*, 10, 100; *Screwtape Letters* (New York: Macmillan, 1945) 84.

[30]Green and Hooper, *C. S. Lewis*, 223.

[31]Hooper, ed., *Selected Essays*, xxi.

tellectual, moral, and psychological unity. Eliot's classicism was romanticism purged of the affectivities that so easily beset the dark, Hegelian side of the Romantic movement. In attacking romanticism, Eliot attacked men like William Morris whose poetry Lewis loved, but even in the 1930s the two were unwitting allies. In 1935, perhaps still anxious to demonstrate that unity of purpose he had sensed between Eliot and himself in 1930, Lewis began his essay "Shelley, Dryden, and Mr. Eliot" with the claim that he would show Eliot that Shelley was not only a better but a more classic poet than Dryden.

The author of "Prufrock" had discovered both Webb and Collingwood by 1918. That Eliot and Lewis failed to realize their intellectual alliance in the 1930s was a mistake encouraged by their differing strategies for confronting the common enemy. Eliot probably never trusted sweet desire or saw in it, as Lewis plainly did, a guide toward truth and God, but both poets defended reason and tradition against the world for three decades.

A second intellectual movement whose path the Magdalen four crossed and with which they are sometimes associated was the new idealism of the 1920s. The title, almost inevitable in an environment already graced with the new realism, the new theology, and the new psychology, appears occasionally in journals for about a decade, and was an attempt to describe philosophers who were neither realists nor disciples of the great idealists Bradley and Bosanquet. There was, Collingwood noted, "no ready-made class into which you could put a philosopher who, after a thorough training in 'realism' had revolted against it and arrived at conclusions of his own quite unlike anything the school of Green had taught."[32] The new idealism differed from the old in its moderation of the Hegelianism of Green and Bradley in favor of a renewed interest in Kant; in its acknowledged debt to the Italian idealists Benedetto Croce and Giovanni Gentile; and in its interest in history and the philosophy of history. The interest in Croce, perhaps the most distinctive characteristic of the new idealism, was acknowledged by Croce and his English followers. In his memoir of Collingwood, Croce implied that Collingwood and Smith were his English disciples, and both did profess admiration for Croce's thought—Smith publicly, Collingwood in

---

[32]Collingwood, *Autobiography*, 56.

correspondence with Croce.[33] Webb also paid a good deal of attention to Croce in the period after 1918, though when he visited Oxford in 1923 Webb noted in his journal (7 June) that because Croce knew little English and spoke French in a way Webb found hard to follow, he "had not made much of Croce."[34] Occasionally dependence on Croce's thought was immediate, but for Collingwood, Webb, and Smith, Croce's method, style, and interests were probably as important as any particular doctrine, and Croce was always only the most recent in a succession that included Plato, Aristotle, Vico, and Kant. The appeal to Croce was an appeal to an established continental authority who stood above the epistemological wars of Oxford and whose writings stressed the unity of the European mind, the importance of history as a form of knowledge, and the fecundity of the metaphysical tradition. Even Croce's passage from literary criticism to philosophy probably appealed to Collingwood, who considered philosophical writing a kind of literature,[35] and to Smith, who never lost his early interest in language, and who considered literature the repository of the significant content of Western philosophic tradition.[36]

The new idealism never existed as a school having well-defined authorities and membership. Smith, an almost slavish follower of Croce, called his own philosophy absolute idealism. G. Dawes Hicks assumed

---

[33]Benedetto Croce, "In Commemoration of an English Friend, A Companion in Thought and Faith, R. G. Collingwood," trans. Lionell Rubinoff, from Benedetto Croce, ed., *Quaderni della "Critica,"* 2 (1946): 60-63, in L. M. Palmer and H. S. Harris, eds., *Thought, Action, and Intuition: A Symposium on the Philosophy of Benedetto Croce* (Hildesheim: Georg Olms Verlag, 1975) 49-65. For J. A. Smith's dependence on Croce, see his "Philosophy," 230-31; W. D. Ross, "John Alexander Smith (1865-1939)," *DNB*, 1931-1940, 819. See also Smith's preface to Benedetto Croce, *An Autobiography*, trans. R. G. Collingwood (Oxford: Clarendon Press, 1927) 5-18. Much of the Collingwood-Croce correspondence is reproduced in Croce's "In Commemoration of an English Friend," 48-65.

[34]Clement C. J. Webb, *God and Personality* (London: George Allen and Unwin, 1919) 157-59, 161, 176, 196-202.

[35]R. G. Collingwood, *An Essay on Philosophical Method* (Oxford: Clarendon Press, 1933) 199-220.

[36]J. A. Smith, "The Nature of Mind and the Reality of Genuine Intercourse Between Minds," *Proceedings of the Sixth International Congress of Philosophy*, ed. E. S. Brightman (New York: Longmans, Green, 1927) 128-36.

in 1939 that this was the same thing as the new idealism and that Smith had been its founder.[37] Collingwood fought free of the title idealist, but as late as 1934 Martin D'Arcy thought it impossible to read Collingwood's *Essay on Philosophical Method* "in abstraction from the metaphysical background of the Italian idealists." The positivist Gilbert Ryle angered Collingwood in 1935 by calling his essay on the ontological argument the work of an idealist.[38] Lewis was deeply influenced by the residual idealism he found at Magdalen, but he was never a member of what he called the Italian school, and on more than one occasion expressed disapproval of Croce.[39] Smith, Webb, and Collingwood—even had all three been willing to identify themselves publicly as new idealists—would still have constituted only part of a larger movement that included H. J. Paton, G. R. G. Mure, H. Wildon Carr, Alfred Hoernlé, and, until his death in 1924, Hastings Rashdall.[40] The new idealism now seems ephemeral, but in 1921 Bernard Bosanquet considered the recrudescent idealism developed from the thought of Croce no less a danger

---

[37]G. Dawes Hicks considered Smith the founder of the New Idealism in the obituary notice he provided in the *Hibbert Journal* 38 (1939-1940): 401-402. Bernard Bosanquet called Croce's English followers Neo-Idealists; see his *The Meeting of Extremes in Contemporary Philosophy* (London: Macmillan, 1921). In their symposium of 1923, "Can the New Idealism Dispense With Mysticism?" Evelyn Underhill and Collingwood assumed that the movement existed. See *PAS*, suppl. 3 (1923): 161-75. See also H. Wildon Carr, "The New Idealist Movement in Philosophy," *The Scientific Approach to Philosophy* (London: Macmillan, 1924) 27-50.

[38]Martin D'Arcy, Review of *Essay on Philosophical Method*, by R. G. Collingwood, *Criterion* 13 (1933-1934): 503. Collingwood was angered by Gilbert Ryle's somewhat condescending remark, "Mr. Collingwood is presumably to be classified, for what such labels are worth, as an Idealist . . . " in "Mr. Collingwood and the Ontological Argument," *Mind* 44 (1935): 137. Collingwood's reply is in CPB.

[39]See Lewis to Eliot, 2 June 1931, quoted in Green and Hooper, *C. S. Lewis*, 126.

[40]Herbert Wildon Carr (1857-1921) came to philosophy after a successful career on the exchange, becoming professor of the University of London in 1918, president of the Aristotelian Society 1916-1918, and later professor at the University of Southern California. See "Biographical," *CBP* (1) 102-105. R. F. Alfred Hoernlé (1880-1943) had been a lecturer under Bosanquet in St. Andrew's (1905-1907), then taught at Durham (1912-1914), Harvard (1914-1921), and Johannesburg. See "Biographical," *CBP* (2) 131-44. Geoffrey Reginald Gilchrist Mure (1893-1979) was a tutor in philosophy at Merton College, Oxford, later a university lecturer and after 1947 Warden of Merton. H. J. Paton (1887-1969) was tutor at Balliol, then professor at Glasgow (1927-1937), and White's Professor of Moral Philosophy at Oxford until 1952.

to philosophy than realism.[41] Bosanquet's reservations regarding the new idealism were reciprocated by a distrust of Bosanquet's philosophy, especially his philosophy of religion, on the part of Webb, Lewis, and Collingwood.[42]

A third movement whose history intersected the work of the Magdalen Metaphysicals was Modernism, although Modernism in England was as various as the stance the four took toward it. Smith was a modernist of a rationalizing bent who doubted that the intellectual formulations historically given Christian faith were either true or defensible. Although Smith supported von Hügel and the continental modernists, he considered the modernist attempt to unite a positivist view of history and criticism with a mystical understanding of the Church inconsistent.[43] Webb, who came under the influence of von Hügel about 1896, and who remained von Hügel's closest confidant among Oxford philosophers until the baron's death in 1925, was sympathetic both to the critical and the mystical insights of Catholic Modernism. But Webb was by temperament no radical, and when the Modernist crisis touched Oxford in 1911, he refused to offer unambiguous support to the offending priest, J. M. Thompson, Magdalen's dean of divinity, who had gone further than his bishop would tolerate by suggesting that miracles should be explained psychologically. Webb, who throughout his life was likely to append long, somewhat tortured qualifications to sentences that finally came down firmly on the side of the historicity of Christian sources, wrote that although the miracles were not of primary importance to his

---

[41]Bosanquet, *Meeting of Extremes*, 52-60, 180-85.

[42]Collingwood, "Can the New Idealism Dispense With Mysticism?" 165; Lewis, *Pilgrim's Regress*, 132-33; Smith, "Philosophy," in which the reference to "extremes" that "meet" is to Bosanquet's book; Clement C. J. Webb, "Bosanquet's Philosophy of Religion," *HJ* 22 (1923-1924): 75-96. See also Eliot's criticism of Bosanquet's philosophy of religion in "A Prediction in Regards to Three English Authors," *Vanity Fair* 21:6 (February 1924): 24; and A. E. Taylor's unfavorable comparison of Bosanquet to von Hügel in his review of *Baron Friedrich von Hügel*, ed. Bernard Holland, *HJ* 25 (1926-1927): 751: "With all its high qualities, how 'thin' is the conception of 'soul-making' which pervades Bosanquet's Gifford Lectures by the side of that which stands revealed in these letters."

[43]J. A. Smith, "Study of a Revolt from Christianity," SPM 1:2, "Modernism," SPM 1:27.

own religion, he was loathe to support a sweeping attack on the credibility of the Bible.[44] Both Webb and Smith, sharing the Kantian axiom that knowledge is or at least must begin with experience, preferred religious experience to dogmatism, but they were still anxious that the historicity of Christianity, and indeed of other religions, not be decanted to some idealistic residue. Both supported Tyrrell in England and Loisy and Sabatier in France not so much because they agreed with all their conclusions, but because they considered attempts to suppress Modernism attacks on the principle of freedom in the Church that both cherished.[45] When von Hügel brought the modernist bishop of Albi, Monsignor E. I. Mignot, to Oxford in 1904, the list of those who sponsored the visit was a catalog of philosophic lights that included J. A. Smith, Clement Webb, Edward Caird, and Hastings Rashdall.[46] Smith and Webb were members of the Synthetic Society, which also included among its members von Hügel, George Tyrrell, and the modernist vicar of Paddington Green, A. L. Lilley.

In 1910 modernist sentiment coalesced at Oxford in the formation by Burnett Hillman Streeter, a fellow of Queen's College, of a group of dons that met weekly to discuss theological topics. Ronald Knox knew it in 1911 as "a sort of Eranos, eight Oxford fellows who met in each other's rooms on Fridays throughout the term, for Sext, luncheon, and None." It included several of the dons who would publish the modernist manifesto *Foundations* in 1912, and it or some undergraduate predecessor may have been the Eranos before whose members Collingwood read his essay "The Devil" in 1908. Knox called it "a sort of Eranos" because it was an

---

[44]Webb to Thompson, 16 May 1911 [MS.Eng.lett.d.181]. See also John D. Root, "Roman Catholic and Modernist Interaction, 1896-1914," *The Historical Magazine of the Protestant Episcopal Church* 49 (1980): 144-45.

[45]Webb called Cyril Emmet's death in 1923 "a great loss to religious freedom" [WJB, 24 June 1923 (MS.Eng.misc.d.1115)]. He had written Thompson on 12 April 1914 to say that he sympathized with the Modern Churchman's Union "in so far as it supports the general policy of freedom and comprehension within the Church" [MS.Eng.lett.d.182].

[46]Alec Vidler, *A Variety of Catholic Modernists* (Cambridge: University Press, 1970) 30, 111, 273. At von Hügel's suggestion, Mignot wrote to the Oxford men who had welcomed the archbishop. See Mignot to Hastings Rashdall, 1 December 1904 [MS.Eng.lett.346 (212)].

Oxford imitation of the Greek meal to which each present contributed his share, and its informality was such that even after a minute book was begun in 1910, its members called it simply The Group, or the theological group.[47] The dons who attended typically had close associations with the Modern Churchman's Union and with a wider circle of intellectuals that included Lily Dougall, Cyril Emmet, and, in the 1930s, Joseph Needham.[48] Webb attended The Group with some regularity from 1910 until 1930. Collingwood published his first theological essay in Lily Dougall's *Concerning Prayer* (1916), and was himself occasionally in attendance until 1935. Webb, though careful to specify that his support for the Union was simply support for "the general policy of freedom and comprehension within the Church," and insistent that the *Modern Churchman* did not speak for him "in the least,"[49] occasionally published both in the *Churchman* and the *Hibbert Journal*, the other modernist periodical. Collingwood published in the *Hibbert Journal* in the 1920s, his

---

[47]Ronald Knox, *Some Loose Stones, Being a Consideration of Certain Tendencies in Modern Theology Illustrated by Reference to the Book Called "Foundations"* (London: Longmans, Green, 1913) viii; F. A. Iremonger, *William Temple, Archbishop of Canterbury: His Life and Letters* (Oxford: University Press, 1948) 89. The Group was founded 1 October 1910, and included B. H. Streeter, R. Brook, R. G. Parsons, W. H. Moberly, N. S. Talbot, A. E. J. Rawlinson, James Moffatt, G. K. A. Bell, W. A. Pickard-Cambridge, R. A. Knox, and N. P. Williams. Clement Webb and Collingwood attended regularly in the 1920s and 1930s. The original minute book is in BLW. See also J. M. Thompson, "Oxford Modernism, 1910-1914," *Oxford Magazine* 68:3 (28 October 1948). After the Thompson crisis in 1911, membership in The Group was apparently more carefully defined. Thompson no longer attended.

[48]Lily Dougall (1858-1923) was a novelist and apologist, who during the last twenty years of her life lived near Oxford and cooperated with Cyril Emmet and B. H. Streeter in the publication of essays stating the modernist position. See Webb's account of her funeral in WJB, 13 October 1923 [MS.Eng.misc.e.1167]. Cyril Emmet (1875-1923) was vicar of West Hundreds, Berkshire, and after 1918 examining chaplain to the bisop of Oxford. He wrote *The Eschatological Question in the Gospels* (1911) and *Conscience, Creeds, and Critics* (1918) as well as contributing to collections edited by Lily Dougall. Joseph Needham, born in 1900, became a distinguished biochemist, and was as well during the 1930s an active supporter of modernist projects. Needham was later (1956-1961) president of Gonville and Caius College, Cambridge.

[49]WJB, 22 November 1923 [MS.Eng.misc.d.1115]; 13 November 1924 [MS.Eng.lett.e.1167] 6 March 1930 [MS.Eng.misc.d.1122]; 8 May 1930 [MS.Eng.misc.d.1122]; Webb to J. M. Thompson, 12 April 1914 [MS.Eng.lett.d.182].

books were sometimes reviewed there, and Smith occasionally wrote reviews for the *Hibbert Journal*.[50]

Smith was a straightforward rationalist who thought nothing less than radical revision could render Christianity intelligible and convincing, believing as he did that Protestantism had failed and that Catholicism was impossible.[51] The relation of both Collingwood and Webb to the movement was more complex. Webb was never a wholehearted modernist, certainly not after the Thompson crisis in 1911, although he did adhere to the modernist claim that truth arises from experience, and despite his willingness to strain out the gnat of the miraculous while swallowing the camel of orthodox theism. Both Webb and Collingwood probably saw Modernism as a serious attempt to commend faith on rational grounds, which at its best combined an antiobscurantist theme with a genuine religious interest. The litmus test for Modernism was Charles Gore, editor in 1889 of *Lux Mundi*, founder of the Community of the Resurrection, and from 1911 to 1919 bishop of Oxford. Dogmatic modernists like A. L. Lilley and Hastings Rashdall profoundly distrusted Gore, who by 1905 had become a defender of traditional Christian beliefs.[52] Webb, who had been influenced by Gore as an undergraduate, praised him, and Collingwood called his work impressive.[53] The Modernism of Webb and Collingwood was at least in part a religious quest that drew Webb not to Tyrrell but to von Hügel, and

---

[50]Collingwood read "The Church" before The Group on 29 April 1920 [*HAS*, 446], and a paper on effective symbols on 8 May 1929 [WJB (MS.Eng.misc.d.1122)]. He appeared with Joseph Needham and Streeter in a series entitled "Science, Religion, and Civilization" at Coventry Cathedral late in 1930 [*HAS*, 447].

[51]Smith, in the words of Adam Fox, "had no great opinion of the church," and as his paper read before the Synthetic Society shows, believed theology was philosophy misunderstood. See Fox, "At the Breakfast Table," 93; J. A. Smith, "On Proving the Existence of God," *Papers Read Before the Synthetic Society* (1896-1908) (London: Spottiswoode, 1909) 414-20; "On Religious Sympathy," *Papers Read Before the Synthetic Society*, 556-60. See also "Modernism," SPM 1:26. Blanshard recalled, "I once heard him [Smith] speak deprecatingly of the establishment of Webb's chair in the philosophy of the Christian religion; I believe he considered that there was no such discipline" (Brand Blanshard to the author, 31 May 1984). See also SPB, e, 4.

[52]Vidler, *Catholic Modernists*, 30, 111, 273.

[53]Webb, *Religious Experience*, 17; R. G. Collingwood, Review of *The Philosophy of the Good Life*, by Charles Gore, *Criterion* 10 (1930-1931): 560-62.

pulled Collingwood from the Streeter circle toward beliefs his biographer found inexplicably dogmatic. Absent from the writings of Webb and Collingwood were two themes of Modernism: rage against the Church and certainty that revelation in something of the classic sense did not exist. That Collingwood could contribute so successfully both to the *Hibbert Journal* and to the *Criterion* is an index to the complexity of his thought. In the end he moved closer to Lewis's orthodoxy and away from the religion of the Streeter group. Finally Collingwood became, intellectually, a catholic, willing to denounce Protestantism and utilitarianism to defend monasticism, and to consider the Athanasian Creed the fundamental presupposition of Western civilization.[54]

Lewis, who returned in 1931 to the practice of the Anglicanism into which he had been born, knew Modernism only as a memory. He had gone through a period of pious, philosophic Hegelianism, but Lewis never confused this with Christian theology, and when he became a practicing Christian, he was an unabashed believer in the supernatural. Lewis seems superficially to have taken nothing from Modernism, from Eliot, or from the new idealism, but this is an illusion encouraged by scholarly neglect of his intellectual development between 1919 and 1930. Lewis was not a modernist because he was not a Christian until Modernism was moribund, and because he, like Collingwood, finally rejected the modernist claim that revelation is philosophy misunderstood. Lewis was not a new idealist—in part because he resisted by nature every enthusiasm; in part because he preferred other sources the new idealists shared, especially Aristotle and Berkeley, to Croce; in part because he gave no name to the idealism that influenced him when he came to Magdalen in 1925. Lewis never supported the *Criterion*, partly because he disapproved of Eliot, partly because he had been unable to secure Eliot's interest. In the long run Lewis, like Webb, Smith, and Collingwood, cannot be understood apart from the contemporary movements that sought to rejoin, however haltingly, faith and reason, to perpetuate traditional metaphysics, and to recover the unity of the European mind. At Oxford in the 1920s this meant Modernism, the new idealism, and sympathy, at least, for the *Criterion*.

---

[54]R. G. Collingwood, *The First Mate's Log of a Voyage to Greece in the Schooner Yacht Fleur de Lys in 1939* (Oxford: University Press, 1940) 151-53; *An Essay on Metaphysics* (Oxford: Clarendon, 1940) 213-20.

Almost nothing has been written about these four dons that represents them as a community of philosophic interest, although Collingwood and Lewis have been the subjects of several studies, nor have the specifically theological aspects of their thought been given much consideration. Only one systematic study of Lewis's theology has been published,[55] and nothing about his philosophy as such. Only one recent philosophical writer, Lionel Rubinoff, has taken more than passing interest in the importance of the Christian religion for Collingwood's thought.[56] John Alexander Smith is more or less completely forgotten, and I know of only one recent work that recognizes Webb's importance.[57] If these great men did make a movement, unself-conscious and informal though it was, and if in following the principles and interests of that movement they mounted a metaphysical rebellion against the then-dominant realism in favor of traditional philosophic thought and—J. A. Smith excepted—in favor of Christian theology, the story certainly bears telling.

Warnings are in order. No one's thought is explained exhaustively by his intercourse with other minds. Ideas are not necessarily caused in others by antecedent events, even by long friendships and frequent conversation. Every intellect has its originality and its own distinction, and above all, its own experience of itself and the world. Certainly nothing that the Magdalen Metaphysicals thought was simply taken over from their predecessors or from one another. Furthermore, by arguing that they influenced one another, I do not intend even to raise the question of originality and authorship as it is now usually conceived. The claim of originality in ideas presupposes that ideas are subject to ownership. Since the four philosophers whose work these chapters discuss would have passionately opposed that opinion, the suggestion that they learned from one another represents nothing more than the claim that each was

---

[55]John Randolf Willis, *Pleasures Forevermore* (Chicago: Loyola University Press, 1983).

[56]Lionell Rubinoff, ed., *Faith and Reason in the Philosophy of Religion of R. G. Collingwood* (Chicago: Quadrangle Press, 1968); "The Relation Between Philosophy and History in the Thought of Benedetto Croce," Palmer and Harris, eds., 9-47.

[57]Thomas A. Langford, *In Search of Foundations: English Theology 1900-1920* (New York: Abingdon Press, 1969) 67-68, 73-77, 79, 271-73.

driven by a love of truth, and found in the conversation of his fellows many things of value. Collingwood thought the copyright law should be repealed because he did not believe ideas were property.[58] Lewis thought creation a misleading term: "There is not a vestige of real creativity *de novo* in us."[59] Originality, Smith wrote, I do not claim.

One codicil: To the degree that this book presupposes the customary life of Oxford, I write as an outsider, and there may be misunderstandings of the use and language that give the university and its colleges their character. For these I apologize. I have been interested chiefly in the ideas of Oxford's distinguished sons. Since they and their work cannot be understood apart from their university, I have trespassed on ground I can never comprehend with native intuition.

The subjects of this study are for the most part men whose work lies in the breach between the obvious and public importance of their careers and the realistic appreciation of their intellectual achievements. Manuscripts and letters have therefore been an important source, and I am indebted to the libraries and copyright holders who have made the use of the necessary materials possible. In citing letters and other archival material, I have usually given the source that is most accessible, preferring published collections whenever these existed. The Bodleian shelfmark has been given for manuscripts in that collection whenever possible. This book could not have been written without the assistance of three librarians: Vincent Quinn of Balliol, and F. W. J. Scovil and G. L. Harriss of Magdalen. Mr. Quinn graciously made me aware of additions to the Smith Papers as these came into Balliol. Mr. Scovil did as much at Magdalen, made me at home while I worked my way through the Smith Papers, and kindly answered my queries and requests. Dr. Harriss, one winter morning, delayed his preparation for an imminent lecture to give me access to the Magdalen archives so that my time in Oxford would not be lost.

I thank the Bodleian for permission to quote the letters of F. S. Marvin, Hastings Rashdall, and J. A. Smith in its collection. I am indebted to Mr. Ian Ross-Smith, the master and fellows of Balliol, and the president and fellows of Magdalen for permission to quote the Smith papers

---

[58]R. G. Collingwood, *The Principles of Art* (Oxford: Clarendon Press, 1938) 325-26.

[59]C. S. Lewis to Sister Penelope, 20 February 1943, *LCSL*, 203.

in the Balliol and Magdalen libraries; to the late Mrs. K. F. Collingwood, to Mrs. Douglas Smith, to the Bodleian Library, and to the president and fellows of Magdalen for permission to quote the Collingwood papers in the Bodleian and at Magdalen; to the Bodleian for permission to quote the journals and letters of Clement Webb, to the provost and fellows of Oriel College for permission to quote Clement Webb's manuscript autobiography; and to Wheaton College, C. S. Lewis PTE Ltd, and Elizabeth Stevens of Curtis Brown for permission to cite the Lewis letters and to quote from his philosophy lectures of 1924. Nellie D. Kendall kindly permitted me to quote the published works of Willmoore Kendall, his letters, and the letters of R. B. McCallum in the Kendall Collection. Mrs. Margaret McCallum consented to my using the letters of R. B. McCallum in the Kendall Collection; Mrs. Diana Blunt allowed me to quote correspondence of G. R. G. Mure; Andrew Know allowed me to cite a letter of Sir Malcolm Knox; and Miss Janet Gnosspelius permitted me to quote from the diary of Barbara Collingwood Gnosspelius. I also thank Professor Brand Blanshard of Yale for sharing his memories of Oxford and allowing me to quote his correspondence. Both Clyde Kilby and the Reverend Walter Hooper were helpful at the beginning of this project, and I am also grateful to the many librarians in England and Scotland who kindly provided me with sources and information.

I thank William Collins Ltd. for permission to quote C. S. Lewis, *Pilgrim's Regress* (Geoffrey Bles, 1943); Harcourt Brace Jovanovich, Inc. for permission to quote excerpts from W. H. Lewis, editor, *Letters of C. S. Lewis* (Harcourt, Brace & World, Inc., 1966); lines from the poem "Reason" in *Poems* (Harcourt Brace Jovanovich, 1964), copyright © 1964 by the executors of the estate of C. S. Lewis; and excerpts from *Surprised by Joy* (Harcourt Brace Jovanovich, 1956), copyright © 1955 by C. S. Lewis; the Macmillan Company Ltd., London, for permission to quote from R. G. Collingwood, *Religion and Philosophy*; Macmillan Publishing Company, New York, for permission to quote excerpts from *They Stand Together: The Letters of C. S. Lewis to Arthur Greeves (1914-1963)*, edited by Walter Hooper (Copyright © 1979 by the estate of C. S. Lewis); Oxford University Press for permission to quote R. G. Collingwood, *Speculum Mentis* (Clarendon Press, 1924), *An Essay on Philosophical Method* (Clarendon Press, 1933), *The Principles of Art* (Clarendon Press, 1938), *An Essay on Metaphysics* (Clarendon Press, 1940), *The First Mate's Log of a Voyage to Greece in the Schooner Yacht "Fleur de Lys" in*

1939 (Oxford University Press, 1940), *The New Leviathan* (Clarendon Press, 1942), *The Idea of Nature* (Clarendon Press, 1945), *The Idea of History* (Clarendon Press, 1946); The Society for Promoting Christian Knowledge for permission to quote Austin Farrer's essay "Poetic Truth" in *Reflective Faith*, edited by Charles C. Conti (1972); and W. J. van der Dussen and Martinus Nijhoff for permission to quote from *History As a Science: The Philosophy of R. G. Collingwood* (The Hague, 1981).

This book is the result of intellectual debts happily accrued through two decades. I would never have been interested in the influence of Kant in twentieth-century philosophy without the guidance of the memorable Robert S. Hartman of the University of Tennessee and the encouragement of Richard W. Peltz of the University of Wisconsin at Milwaukee. It is a hard thing to be a grown man before one has the grace to have a senior professor shout in anger that language is not communication. Charles Harrison of the University of the South did that for me. I am also indebted to several Americans who represented broadly the theory of language the Oxford idealists presupposed. Allen Tate and Louise Cowan raised for me the question of imagination as a way of knowing, and Donald Cowan represented ably in the office of university president the ideal of knowledge as transformational and of the curriculum as the form of learning. The roots of these things run to the men and ideas of which this book is an anamnesis. I also owe much to several students who became colleagues as we discussed the ideas in this book, and who will remember these ideas and the pleasures of sharing them.

Finally, I thank Jeri Guadagnoli, who typed this manuscript and the studies that led to it over many years; Canon Howard Buchner, who twice read and criticized these chapters; and the visitors and fellows of the Saint Thomas More Institute, Fort Worth, whose encouragement, together with the indispensable sponsorship of Mr. and Mrs. Donald Grantges and Mr. and Mrs. Charles Clinton Booth, made the writing of this book possible.

"Parents worship their children, as Christians can never forget," Collingwood wrote; this book is dedicated to my son Michael.

James Patrick
Dallas
5 July 1984

• A MAGDALEN ALBUM •

Clement Charles Julian Webb. Sepia drawing by Sir William Rothstein, 1933.
(Courtesy of the president and fellows of Magdalen College, Oxford.)

John Alexander Smith. Pencil drawing ca. 1930. (Courtesy of the president and fellows of Magdalen College, Oxford.)

Clive Staples Lewis. Photographed by Warren H. Lewis at Stonehenge, 8 April 1925. (Courtesy of the Marion E. Wade Collection, Wheaton College.)

J. A. Smith and H. H. Joachim. Photographed walking by the Cherwell by W. S. Chang, ca. 1917.

Willmoore Kendall, ca. 1935. (Courtesy of Nellie D. Kendall.)

Sir Malcolm Knox. Painting by N. Andrew Firth, 1966. (Courtesy of Andrew Knox.)

Geoffrey Reginald Gilchrist Mure, ca. 1940. (Courtesy of Mrs. Diana Blunt.)

·CHAPTER I·

Edwardian Idealism

When I say that Green's school at this time obsessed Oxford philosophy, what I mean is that the work of that school presented itself to most Oxford philosophers as something that had to be destroyed. . . .

R. G. Collingwood,
An Autobiography

With a rare display of sympathy between the calculations of the calendar makers and the inflexible particularities of history, Queen Victoria died in the first month of the first year of the new century. Her demise made way at last for Edward VII, and for a decade of overmellow opulence characterized by magnificence, the decay of British power, the posturing and misappraisals that would result in the 1914 war, constitutional crisis, and a degree of social unrest unknown since the Chartist movement of the 1840s and the corn laws. The novelist typical of the period was Thomas Hardy; design was organized around the open, indeterminate line of Art Nouveau; and in music there was Elgar, glorious and a little banal.

In 1901 the University of Oxford was an academic jewel set in the glittering crown of Victorian empire, distinguished by its colleges, which placed the undergraduate in a compact community of varied and intense scholarly interests; its curriculum, laboriously reformed throughout the nineteenth century; its method of instruction, chiefly tutorial; and by a professorial body that in recent times had included men as brilliant and diverse as John Ruskin, E. B. Pusey, and Benjamin Jowett. The college tutors and the most distinguished undergraduates were all, or almost all, products of the Honour School of *Literae Humaniores*, which in 1830 was defined as including "Greek and Latin Language and History, Rhetoric and Poetics, the Moral and Political Sciences, with ancient writers illustrated from the moderns, as well as Logic." The philosopher most important for the Greats curriculum was Plato, the *Republic* the most important text. There had been many Platos in late-Victorian England, but the Edwardians probably knew best the Plato of Benjamin Jowett, T. H. Green, and Richard Nettleship, a moral philosopher and social critic whose thought was cited in defense of the personal ideals of self-sacrifice and duty and in support of a political settlement based on communitarian, cooperative principles.[1]

Aristotle had been less important for the Victorians, but by 1850 the study of his works, unpopular since Bacon had condemned him as obscurantist and unscientific in the early seventeenth century, was again common in the colleges. The *Ethics* was especially important to T. H. Green, who discovered in Aristotle support for liberal values inherited from liberal Christianity. Others, Thomas Hughes in particular, considered the *Ethics* morally important to the Victorian state.[2] By 1885, thanks largely to Ingraham Bywater, the critical study of Aristotle had been revived and the Oxford Aristotelian Society founded.[3] In 1906 the Oxford Aristotle, intended to include finally translations of the entire corpus, was begun with J. A. Smith and W. D. Ross as editors. In 1910 Professor John Burnet of St. Andrews recommended Smith for the

---

[1]Webb, *Religious Experience*, 36.

[2]On the philosophical texts important in Greats, see G. R. G. Mure, "Oxford and Philosophy," *Philosophy* 12 (1937): 291-301; Mark Pattison, "Philosophy at Oxford," *Mind* 1 (1876): 82-97. For the Victorian interpretation of Plato, see Pattison, *Essays*, ed. Richard Nettleship (Oxford: Clarendon Press, 1889) 1: 463-65.

[3]On Green's interpretation of Aristotle, see Frank M. Turner, *The Greek Heritage in Victorian Britain* (New Haven: Yale University Press, 1981) 359-65. For Bywater's biography, see Robert William Chapman, "Ingraham Bywater (1840-1918)," *DNB* 1912-1921, 81-82. The Oxford Aristotelian Society met in Bywater's rooms on Monday evenings in term from the early 1880s. J. A. Smith succeeded Bywater as president in 1908. See Webb, *Religious Experience*, 18.

Waynflete Chair by calling him an excellent representative of Oxford Aristotelianism. H. H. Joachim was reputed to know the *Ethics* by heart, and both Collingwood and Lewis would display more interest in Aristotle than Plato.

Modern philosophers had begun to appear in the examinations in the 1860s: first Kant, then a special question on his philosophy in 1875, and in 1876 a paper on Hegel. Kant was by 1880 probably the modern philosopher most important in *Literae Humaniores*. Clement Webb, William Temple, and R. G. Collingwood all found their vocations in philosophy by reading Kant as adolescents, and J.A. Smith remarked in 1924 that Kant still provided the only certain framework for ethics.[4] After Kant, the modern philosopher most influential in the Oxford of 1900 was probably Hegel, although firsthand knowledge of his works was by no means universal among the philosophers whom historians would call Oxford neo-Hegelians. Neither Smith nor Webb read much of Hegel, though Joachim, Collingwood, and G. R. G. Mure became distinguished students of the Hegelian texts.[5] The influence of Hegel, strong enough by 1880 to color the Greats curriculum with certain broad Hegelian themes, maintained its vigor into the 1930s.

The Greats curriculum directed students to a common body of texts, placed these texts at the center of a conversation that went on in tutorials and common rooms, and required that philosophy and history be studied with equal seriousness. Though the connection was seldom spelled out, the assumption was Benjamin Jowett's: knowledge was to issue in action; the Edwardians' criticisms of the Athenian constitution would

---

[4]Clement C. J. Webb, "Biographical," *CBP* (2) 338; William Temple, "Biographical," *CBP* (1) 412; Collingwood, *Autobiography*, 4; Smith, "Philosophy," 229.

[5]J. A. Smith thought he was the last don who remembered that Hegel had been introduced to Oxford by Jowett (Geoffrey Faber, *Jowett: A Portrait with Background* [Cambridge MA: Harvard University Press, 1957] 182 n.2). On knowledge of Hegel ca. 1900, see Smith, "Philosophy," 229; Webb, "Biographical," 338; G. R. G. Mure, *Idealist Epilogue* (Oxford: Clarendon, 1979) 171.

After Hegel and Kant, the philosopher most influential at Oxford about 1900 was probably Hermann Lotze. See A. S. L. Farquharson, ed., *Statement and Inference with Other Philosophical Papers by John Cook Wilson* (Oxford: Clarendon Press, 1926) 1: xxvii; Clement C. J. Webb, *Problems in the Relations of God and Man* (London: Nisbet, 1911) 133, 267, 274; *God and Personality*, 18-20, 52-56, 106-108.

promote political and social prosperity in the twentieth century.[6] Studies at Oxford were to produce men well grounded in the classics, knowledgeable in history, at least the history of Greece and Rome, and capable of running the courts, churches, and mercantile enterprises of the empire. Knowledge and action formed a unity; so did past and present. When an Oxford graduate of the period 1901-1914 spoke of philosophy, what he most often meant was the tradition that began with Plato and Aristotle as it had been developed by Kant and Hegel and perfected by his own teachers. By "doing Greats" he meant mastering a body of texts by examining and questioning them. Collingwood would later give that method formal status, but what he called the logic of question and answer was in one sense a commonplace of Oxford undergraduate life. John Brett Langstaff, whose tutor was the memorable F. E. Brightman, one of Lewis's five great Magdalen men, wrote in 1914,

> The English method would seem to be to inspire you to ask questions related to your subject, and then through tutorial conferences and occasional lectures to indicate to you how you might find the answer to your own question.

The practical meaning of the idealist axiom that knowledge left neither knower nor known unchanged was implicit in Langstaff's addendum:

> It is his [Brightman's] idea that going to lectures and accumulating facts is all very well for reference, but they need to be referred to and made part of one's self. I am trying to do this under his direction.[7]

Education was primarily what Langstaff called making facts part of one's self, the incorporation of knowledge in a pattern of wisdom and duty. Though their hegemony would soon end, for about four decades, roughly since 1860, that party in the university that considered teaching the chief scholarly task had been ascendant. The pressure from the sciences, whose professors often considered knowledge cumulative, objective bodies of information to which new facts might be added, was

---

[6]In Victorian England there was, as Turner points out (*Greek Heritage*, 340-42), a historicist interpretation of the Greek philosophers; its exponents located the thought of Plato and Aristotle in its fourth-century context and refused to admit the relevance of the ancients for the nineteenth century. This nascent positivism never kept men like Jowett and Green from finding in Aristotelian and Platonic texts principles for their own age.

[7]John Brett Langstaff, *Oxford 1914* (New York: Vantage Press, 1965) 52, 130.

increasingly difficult to ignore, and research was an increasingly important part of professorial duties. But in 1910 those responsible for the Greats curriculum still considered it their duty to give students the opportunity to engage and question historical and philosophic texts, and to relate these to their own moral and political actions. Ronald Knox, Collingwood's exact contemporary, wrote of his Balliol years:

> A first in Greats left me neither a professional philosopher nor a professional historian; but it left me with a fierce love of sifting evidence, and the power of not being fascinated into acquiescence when superior persons talked philosophy at me.[8]

There had never in the history of Oxford been a tutor who won the friendship and loyalty of his pupils as deeply as had Thomas Hill Green of Balliol. When Green died in 1882, having held the Whyte professorship of moral philosophy only four years, it seemed that his distinctive idealism—Plato interpreted by Kant, Hegel, and Lotze—would become a permanent and dominant influence in the university. Henry Scott Holland described what Green had meant. When he became a tutor in 1873, "Oxford lay abjectly imprisoned within the rigid limits of Mill's logic. Individualistic sensationalism held the field. There was a dryness in the Oxford air. . . . Out there in the huge and hideous cities, the awful problem of industry lay like a bad dream." But through his teaching, Green "broke for us the sway of . . . sensationalism"; he "gave us back the language of self-sacrifice, and taught us how we belonged to one another." And philosophy began to change the world: "We were startled and kindled by seeing the great intellectual leader give himself over to civic duties."[9] Collingwood recalled that his father, who entered the University College in 1872, had been caught up in the philosophical movement of T. H. Green, and W. G. Collingwood's tutor, Bernard Bosanquet, was influenced by Green to leave Oxford for a career in social work in Lon-

---

[8]Knox, *Spiritual Aeneid*, 63. On the intrauniversity conflict between teaching and research, see Sheldon Rothblatt, *Tradition and Change in English Liberal Education* (London: Faber and Faber, 1976) 169-70.

[9]Percy Dearmer, ed., *Lombard Street in Lent* (London: Robert Scott, 1911) x; James Brice Bryce, *Contemporary Studies in Biography* (London: Macmillan, 1920) 85-89.

don.[10] J. A. Smith knew the tradition of Green through Green's disciple, Richard Nettleship, of whom Smith wrote:

> What I think struck us most was the width and variety of his sympathies: he was interested in so many things, yet without distraction or dissipation, catholic, not eclectic, sometimes almost startlingly tolerant. He approached almost everything with great openness and deep simplicity of mind and heart. Above all he was utterly sincere. Philosophy was nothing worth except as the outcome of personal experience.[11]

To have been at Oxford during the 1870s or 1880s was to be touched by Green's philosophy, but the power of the school was too much his own and soon after his death circumstances conspired to weaken his influence. His successor to the Whyte chair of logic was William Wallace (1844-1897) of Merton, competent, sympathetic to Green's idealism, but nevertheless only a great disciple. Bernard Bosanquet, who might reasonably have been expected to perpetuate idealism in the university, had left Oxford for London in 1881, and in 1883 J. R. Illingworth, perhaps the most able clerical representative of the school, exchanged his Keble fellowship for a country rectory. Francis Herbert Bradley, whose *Appearance and Reality* (1893) made him the most important intellect among the idealists, was partly by disposition, partly for reasons of health, a recluse. Collingwood, whose house was a few hundred yards from Bradley's for sixteen years, never saw him, and J. A. Smith recalled that Bradley, "though he lived among us for so long, never lectured or taught in any way."[12] In 1897 William Wallace was killed in a cycling accident near Oxford.

---

[10][R. G. Collingwood], "W. G. Collingwood," *Times*, 3 July 1923; Melvin Richter, "T. H. Green and His Audience: Liberalism as a Surrogate Faith," *Review of Politics* 18:4 (October 1956): 431.

[11]Smith, "Lectures on Nineteenth Century Philosophy," SPM 2:13 (117).

[12]Collingwood, *Autobiography*, 16; Smith, "Lectures," 124. Webb never spoke to Bradley (*Religious Experience*, 34). Brand Blanshard recalled that Bradley had once lectured for Wallace, and had concluded that he did not understand undergraduates (Paul Arthur Schilpp, ed., *The Philosophy of Brand Blanshard* [La Salle IL: Open Court Press, 1981] 74). Yet Bradley was willing to talk with those who sought him out. Smith wrote that he had "enjoyed little personal intercourse with him [Bradley] until I sought him out—and that diffidently—during the years of the war. By that time his eminence was so recognizably great, that younger men were somewhat deterred from approaching him" ("Lectures," 124). One who was not deterred was Brand Blanshard (Schilpp, 76).

Students who came up to Oxford in the first year of the new reign found three great teachers, Thomas Case (1844-1925), Waynflete professor since 1889, John Cook Wilson (1849-1915), whose career had begun in 1874, and Edward Caird, a Scot who had returned to his college, Balliol, as master in 1893. Of these men, the most influential was probably Cook Wilson, Wykeham professor of logic since 1889, talented in mathematics as well as history and philosophy. By 1890 Wilson had abandoned the idealism of Green and Hermann Lotze in favor of an increasingly independent critical position that had much in common with the empiricism of Hume and Mill and with the pluralism of the Aristotelian text. John Passmore has called Wilson a historian's nightmare, for both personally and intellectually he combined seemingly contradictory characters.[13] His passion for philosophy was evinced in a single-minded willingness to begin anew and to follow wherever any question led. He was the champion of patient inquiry and the foe of all philosophical pretension, though his patience sometimes seemed dilatory and his definition of presumption broad. His mathematical skill was such that he could challenge C. L. Dodgson, though not always successfully. Wilson was a source of personal inspiration to younger men like H. A. Prichard (1871-1947) and H. W. B. Joseph (1867-1943), who followed his lead in philosophy. But combined with these good qualities was a temper naturally adversarial, even vindictive, dedicated as much to the destruction of his enemies as to their conversion. "Workers in the same vineyard," A. S. L. Farquharson wrote, "except personal friends, he regarded with instinctive, almost childish, rivalry."[14] And Wilson as his posthumous essays portray him was atypically narrow for an Oxford man of the 1880s. His love for philosophy was lifelong, but there is little in Cook Wilson's writings that betrays an interest in history. Unity was not his passion. "His primary philosophical principle," Metz noted, "was the conviction that there was no such first principle at all."[15]

---

[13]John Passmore, *A Hundred Years of Philosophy* (London: Gerald Duckworth, 1957) 242.

[14]Farquharson, *Statement and Inference*, 1:xlv.

[15]Rudolf Metz, *A Hundred Years of British Philosophy*, trans. J. W. Harvey, T. E. Jessop, and Henry Sturt (New York: Macmillan, 1938) 519.

Cook Wilson's rebellion, a matter not of years but decades, was hardly complete before 1900; indeed, his pupils believed that his thought had matured only in the last years of his life. But by 1900 certain specific themes of Wilson's thought had made him the bulwark of Oxford realism and the archopponent of idealism. Knowledge he considered unanalyzable, staunchly denying that the act of knowing changed known or knower and convinced of the objectivity of experience. Logic was to be "kept free of psychology, free from all dependence on the subjectivity of the thinker"; indeed, it was in Wilson's view "incompatible with the idea of knowledge that the subject should exercise any kind of activity on the object."[16] Wilson was the sworn foe of the term *judgment*, which he felt presupposed the combination of knowledge derived from sense experience with something which was not knowledge.[17] Religious belief he held to be the working of a poetic faculty.[18] Cook Wilson became "more and more the leader of an opposition which did not try utterly to destroy idealism by opposing to it an equally comprehensive world view, but tried to shake it by a series of shrewdly aimed separate strokes."[19]

Thomas Case, Waynflete professor from 1889 until 1910 and president of Corpus Christi from 1905 until 1921, was a clearer and better-tempered thinker than Cook Wilson, and it was probably his *Physical Realism*, published in 1888, that gave realism its name. Opposed alike to Herbert Spencer's evolutionary pragmatism and to the idealism of Green, Case believed that the task before philosophy was the completion of the reform begun by Bacon in the seventeenth century.[20] Case, no dogmatist, having carefully analyzed both idealism and realism, had concluded that both had certain defects. Idealism could deal neither with matter nor with the mutual impenetrability of bodies, while realism

---

[16]Metz, *British Philosophy*, 522.

[17]Ibid., 524.

[18]Farquharson, *Statement and Inference*, 2:865. This judgment need not be invidious, but in context Wilson did mean that religion had much to do with feeling, little with thought.

[19]Metz, *British Philosophy*, 521.

[20]Thomas Case, *Physical Realism, Being an Analytical Philosophy from the Physical Objects of Science to the Physical Data of Sense* (London: Longmans, 1888).

could give no account of origins of bodies, consciousness, or of bodies' becoming good for conscious beings. But in Case's view idealism contained two further errors: "the arbitrary hypothesis of a sense of sensation or of ideas, and the intolerable neglect of logical inference."[21] What Case meant by "the arbitrary hypothesis of sensation" is clear enough. He would have agreed with Wilson that knowledge is unanalyzable and immediate, requiring none of the epistemological hypotheses put forward by the school of Green. By the idealists' neglect of logical inference, Case meant their neglect of induction, and hence of science. Though he lacked the fervor for the destruction of idealism that marked Cook Wilson's later career, Case worked tirelessly to move Oxford philosophy beyond idealism and toward a new, physical realism.

The third great teacher of the 1890s was Edward Caird, ten years older than Case, Green's contemporary as much as his disciple. In 1866, the year Green accepted a Balliol tutorship, Caird returned to the chair of moral philosophy at Glasgow. His career in Scotland was one of unbroken success, and his interpretations of Kant and Hegel were well received. Then upon the death of Benjamin Jowett in 1893, Caird was elected Master of Balliol, a post that he accepted after long consideration because in it he would have "his hand on the heart of England."[22] Caird was the antitype of Cook Wilson, as dedicated to the Hegelian-Kantian tradition as Wilson was opposed. He was also a faithful communicant in his college chapel, a student of Dante and Shakespeare, convinced that philosophy, theology, history, and literature were inextricably related.

In addition to these three giants, there were somewhat younger men newly appointed who were beginning by 1901 to earn their reputations as teachers. The disciples who would perpetuate the spirit of Wilson's realism had been elected to fellowships during the 1890s, Joseph at New College in 1891[23] and Prichard at Hertford in 1895.[24] A third young phi-

---

[21]Thomas Case, "Metaphysics," *Encyclopaedia Britannica*, 11th ed. (Cambridge: University Press, 1911) 249.

[22]On Caird, see *DNB* 1901-1911; Henry Jones, *The Life and Philosophy of Edward Caird* (Glasgow: MacLehose, 1921).

[23]On Joseph, see Clement C. J. Webb, "Horace William Brindley Joseph (1867-1943)," *DNB* 1941-1950, 439-40. Joseph was the brother of Webb's wife Eleanor.

[24]On Prichard, see W. D. Ross, "Harold Arthur Prichard (1871-1947)," *DNB* 1941-1950, 697-98.

losopher who was generally sympathetic to Cook Wilson's realism was John Alexander Smith (1863-1939), a Balliol man, a Scot like Caird, who returned to his college in 1891. Smith, a fascinating lecturer and a profoundly sensitive teacher, was in the 1890s firmly committed to no school, but pursued his tutorial responsibilities in a Socratic spirit, questioning everything and encouraging his pupils to do so. It was the fashion, Ronald Knox wrote, having followed Bradley in his destruction of all previous logicians, to destroy Bradley in one's essays: "Professor Cook Wilson and Professor J.A. Smith were the venerated heroes of our campaigning."[25]

Besides Smith, Prichard, and Joseph—all realists or, in the case of Smith, eclectic—there were three newly appointed fellows who promised to carry on the idealist tradition. Hastings Rashdall (1858-1924), elected to a fellowship at Hertford in 1888, would tutor in philosophy for twenty-seven years, representing consistently during most of that period the personalist critique of Bradley's absolute idealism.[26] C. C. J. Webb (1865-1954) was appointed in 1889 at Magdalen where he would over the course of more than three decades produce a steady stream of books and articles on philosophy and philosophy of religion, as well as important studies and translations of medieval thinkers.[27] The third young idealist, and by far the most critical intellect, was Harold H. Joachim (1868-1939), who returned in 1894 to Balliol, where he tutored in philosophy with J. A. Smith for three years before moving to Merton, succeeding there to Wallace's post.[28] Of the younger men only J. A. Smith was a match for Cook Wilson. By 1901 Smith had won a reputation as perhaps the best teacher in the university, but Smith had no philosophy of his own. Apart from Caird, who devoted himself to the administration of Balliol; Rashdall, who had developed a philosophy dependent more on

---

[25]Knox, *Spiritual Aeneid*, 62.

[26]P. E. Matheson, *The Life of Hastings Rashdall* (London: Humphrey Milford, 1928) 221.

[27]On Webb, see "Biographical," *CBP* (2) 336-40; F. M. Powicke in *DNB* 1951-1960; Webb, *Religious Experience*; and W. D. Ross in *PBA* 41 (1955), 338-47.

[28]G. R. G. Mure, "Harold Henry Joachim (1868-1938)," *DNB* 1931-1940, 486-87; H. W. B. Joseph, "Harold Henry Joachim, 1868-1938," *PBA* 24 (1938): 396-422.

Berkeley than Green; and the reticent Joachim, idealism was without a voice at Oxford.

That the idealism of Green had faded so quickly on its home ground is hardly surprising. There had never been a philosophic orthodoxy in the university; philosophies and philosophers had come and gone. Witnesses differ regarding the lingering influence of the tradition of Green between 1900 and 1918. Collingwood believed that the school, or rather its destruction, obsessed most Oxford philosophers, but in 1919 idealism still seemed to C. S. Lewis to be an official philosophy powerful enough to justify undergraduate rebellion.[29] H. J. Paton thought that even in the heyday of Cambridge realism, when G. E. Moore's essays rocked idealism year after year, Bradley had still been the most revered philosophical mind in England.[30] Certainly while Bradley lived, idealism remained imposing. But, in fact, while idealism lived out its triumphant public existence, drawing year by year on its ever-decreasing fund of scholarly originality, younger men quietly began abandoning it. The philosophy of the Absolute was impressive; it persisted as a presence long after its force was spent; and, as Lewis wrote, it went down like the Bastille.[31] When the war was over in 1918 it was, at least in the form given it by Green and Bradley, moribund. In 1922 J. H. Muirhead scoured England and Scotland for philosophers fit and willing to be included in his *Contemporary British Philosophy*, an anthology of personal statements. The first series contained a contribution from only one Oxford philosopher, the pragmatist F. C. S. Schiller. The second series, published in 1924, included contributions by Webb and Smith. There were not many philosophers of the first rank at Oxford; only one or two Oxford philosophers stood unambiguously in the succession of Green.

The signs of the end had been evident earlier. When William Wallace died in 1897, Edward Caird stood for the Whyte professorship, but was unaccountably not appointed. In 1900 the venerable Henry Sidgwick, whose career at Cambridge had begun in 1859, came to Oxford to read a paper before the Philosophical Society on the thought of T. H. Green.

---

[29]Collingwood, *Autobiography*, 19; Lewis, *Surprised by Joy*, 209.

[30]H. J. Paton, "Fifty Years of Philosophy," *CBP* (3), 343.

[31]C. S. Lewis, "Modern Theology and Biblical Criticism," *Christian Reflections*, ed. Walter Hooper (Grand Rapids MI: William B. Erdmans, 1967) 162.

That Sidgwick should have brought the attack on Green from Cambridge was appropriate: he was an elder statesman of the Cambridge Apostles, a powerful undergraduate society into which promising undergraduates like G. E. Moore, Lytton Strachey, John Maynard Keynes, and Ludwig Wittgenstein were clected, and whose best-known members often combined—at least in the years before 1920—brilliance with an aestheticism that sometimes erupted into virulent pacifism or desultory homosexuality. Sidgwick's career had represented those abilities that made the Apostles a natural intellectual leadership at Cambridge, and in the nation.

His criticism of Green was the last paper the old man would read, and in it he argued that Green's idealism and his spiritualism—his Kantian belief that all reality is thought and his Hegelian conviction that finite relations presuppose some transcendent or transhistorical spiritual reality—were at odds with one another.[32] Then in 1903 Sidgwick's pupil G. E. Moore published "The Refutation of Idealism" in *Mind*, ridiculing the idealist belief that every being was in some sense "spiritual," and raising to an art the twentieth-century philosophic style that combined an aggressive diffidence with well-mannered insinuation that the opponents' positions were intellectually hopeless.

"The Refutation of Idealism," with the *Principia Ethica*, which Moore had published with Bertrand Russell in 1900, enshrined the realist doctrine that the world we know consists of unalterable facts having no necessary relation to the knower, other beings, or God. H. H. Joachim attacked Moore and Russell in *The Nature of Truth* (1906). The new philosophy was, Joachim wrote, really an "extreme Occasionalism without the *Deus ex machina* to render Occasionalism plausible." If "experience makes no difference to the facts," it then followed either that the world was utterly unknowable, or that our knowledge was radically subjective, our own *simpliciter*, a critique of realism the idealists considered both obvious and irrefutable.[33]

---

[32]Henry Sidgwick, "The Philosophy of T. H. Green," *Mind* 10 (1901): 18-29. See also Henry Scott Holland, *A Bundle of Memories* (London: Wells Gardner, Darton, 1915) 121-31; Bertrand Russell, *Portraits from Memory* (New York: Simon and Schuster, 1951) 63-65.

[33]Joachim, *The Nature of Truth*, 35-63.

Russell answered Joachim sharply in his review of *The Nature of Truth* in *Mind*. In the same year, 1906, J. A. Smith's conversion to the realist camp was rumored,[34] and H. W. B. Joseph, tutor at New College since 1895, published his *Introduction to Logic*, which was a criticism of the traditional logic. When Edward Caird died in 1908 there was every reason to believe that the Aristotelian pluralism of Cook Wilson, reinforced by the skepticism of the Cambridge Apostles, Russell, Moore, and their followers, would displace the idealism of Jowett, Caird, and Bradley. As though to drive the point home, H. A. Prichard published in 1909 *Kant's Theory of Knowledge*, which attacked idealism by attacking Kant, and in 1912 wrote "Does Moral Philosophy Rest on a Mistake?" which undercut traditional moral philosophy at Oxford much as Moore's work had at Cambridge. By then Prichard himself had distinguished pupils, among them E. F. Carritt, who had already sent Collingwood to the realists' lectures, and who would, after 1919, attempt to recruit another promising young philosopher, C. S. Lewis, into the realist camp.[35]

The decay of idealism was encouraged by intramural doubts and its inherently paradoxical character. Bradley's *Appearance and Reality* had described a world in which ordinary experience was mostly appearance, while reality itself belonged to the Absolute, which comprehended all time and place and within which neither error nor contradiction existed. The business of the individual was then, as C. S. Lewis later wrote, to multiply the experience of the Absolute, though each person was condemned to see his own life as largely illusory.[36] This heavily Hegelian construct could not, of course, be reconciled with Christian theology, and Bradley never tried, bravely denying both theism and the resurrection.[37] But Bradleian idealism also violated the personalism inherent in Kant's insistence on the primacy of the categories of thought. As a re-

---

[34]Bernard Bosanquet to Alfred Hoernlé, 1 January 1906, in J. H. Muirhead, ed., *Bernard Bosanquet and His Friends: Letters Illustrating the Sources and Development of His Philosophical Opinions* (London: Allen and Unwin, 1935) 104.

[35]Collingwood, *Autobiography*, 22-23.

[36]Lewis, *Surprised by Joy*, 222-23; *Pilgrim's Regress*, 138-41.

[37]Francis Herbert Bradley, *Appearance and Reality*, 2d rev. ed. (London: Swan and Sonnenschein, 1897) 448, 453.

sult, by 1890 many of the followers of Green, among them a good number of the philosopher-theologians, had become personal idealists, maintaining that experience was not correlative with the knowledge of the Absolute—if indeed the Absolute could be said to *know* anything—but with the knowledge of the individual, and that individuality and hence personality were real. The defense began with Andrew Seth Pringle-Pattison's *Hegelianism and Personality* (1887). In 1894 Illingworth gave his Bampton Lectures on the subject *Personality Human and Divine*, and by 1900 Webb had written on the importance of the use of the term *personality* with reference to God.[38] Bradley had made personality appearance; the personal idealists made personal experience reality. Both were of course unsatisfactory, and the conflict provided grist for the mills of Cook Wilson's new realism.

To the difficulties of intramural discord was added the pressure that the rising interest in science brought upon the philosophic tradition and the Greats curriculum. Henry Sturt, recalling his undergraduate days, remarked in 1906 that in the 1880s "no open-minded student . . . was quite at ease about the attitude of the Oxford idealists to modern science," though the philosophers themselves seemed content to ignore it.[39] Thomas Case, the Waynflete professor, was an exception. Case took the method of physics as the model for philosophic inquiry, and attempted to reform logic along lines first developed by John Venn at Cambridge in the 1880s.[40] Venn had created a system of symbols that functioned analytically, so that logic could be considered a matter of deductive validity without reference to any fact. This double move, toward induction that could justify its conclusions no better than Hume, and toward an abstract logic that claimed no contact with reality, cut at the root of the very concept of judgment, rendered the synthetic *a priori* moot, abrogated the

---

[38]Clement C. J. Webb, "The Idea of Personality as Applied to God," *JTS* 2 (1900-1901): 49-65.

[39]Henry Sturt, *Idola Theatri: A Criticism of Oxford Thought and Thinkers from the Standpoint of Personal Idealism* (London: Macmillan, 1906) 2; J. H. Muirhead, "Past and Present in Contemporary Philosophy," *CBP* (1), 320.

[40]John Venn (1834-1923) undertook to rationalize and perfect Boole's theories. See J. A. Venn, "John Venn (1834-1923)" in *DNB* 1922-1930, 869-70. His most important works were *Symbolic Logic* (London: Macmillan, 1881) and *The Principles of Empirical or Inductive Logic* (London: Macmillan, 1889).

traditional belief that the operations of logic reflected reality, and denied the possibility of any real relation between psychology and valid reasoning. And if psychology had little or nothing to do with truth or reality, the psyche might all too easily become the repository of the unconscious and irrational. If induction were the great model for knowledge, then expertise, knowledge of matters particular, was wisdom. Reason as it had been classically conceived, as a cosmic rationality in which personality participates, was hard to reconcile with the new psychology, the new logic, or the new science.

In its relation with theology, Edwardian idealism was no more fortunate than it had been with physics. The alliance had never been without its tensions. Whether T. H. Green had actually believed in the Christian God was a matter much debated,[41] but Bradley did not and Bosanquet's allegiance to Christianity was tenuous and highly abstract.[42] By 1901 most Oxford idealists had passed from the conviction of Edward Caird that religion was a necessary form of human experience and Christianity the highest form of religion to the view that the highest religion was philosophy, the Christian religion was outworn and narrow, and theology was a confusion that only philosophy could clarify. The papers J. A. Smith read for the Synthetic Society in 1903 and 1908 were respectively pleas for a creed that transcended the narrowness of any particular religion and a realist attack on the possibility of analogy.[43] At the same time, perhaps in imitation of Caird, Smith tried (in his own

---

[41]Green, the first lay tutor in the university, believed in his spiritual principle, and his addresses to students on religious topics were memorable. But his faith was always highly philosophic and somewhat rationalizing. "God is forever reason," he wrote, "as taking a body from and giving life to the whole system of experiences which makes the history of man." Such testimonies to the cosmic reason were not matched by an emphasis on the historical and dogmatic content of Christianity. See T. H. Green, *The Witness of Faith* (London: Longmans, Green, 1883) 22.

[42]See Webb, "Bernard Bosanquet's Philosophy of Religion." Webb doubted that Bosanquet "did full justice to such individuality as belongs to any man or woman." In 1893 Bosanquet had quoted Turgenev, "My faith is civilization, and I require no other creed." (*The Civilization of Christendom and Other Studies* [London: Sonnenschein, 1893] 63).

[43]J. A. Smith, "On Proving the Existence of God"; "On Religious Sympathy," *Papers Read Before the Synthetic Society*, 414-20, 556-60.

judgment unsuccessfully) to lecture on the philosophy of religion.[44] Where Christianity was concerned, the philosophers, even Rashdall and Webb, were for the most part on the side of reason and experience and against superstition and particularity. When Baron von Hügel, a lifelong friend of Webb and Smith, brought the modernist bishop of Albi, Monsignor Mignot, to Oxford in July 1904, J. A. Smith entertained the party at Balliol. Von Hügel later indicated to Mignot that not only Smith, but Webb, Caird, and Hastings Rashdall had rendered exceptional service to the cause.[45] Their support for George Tyrrell's theology reflected their own metaphysical convictions; religion was always subordinated to and perhaps confused with philosophy by the philosophers themselves. At the time of Mignot's visit, the idealists still habitually neglected history (save for the history of Greece and Rome), a position later regretted, but one which made them, in Webb's words, "underestimate the extent to which the distinctive doctrines and characteristic piety of the Christian religion . . . depends [*sic*] on what is historical in Christianity, and as such set it apart from all other instances of that kind of system . . . we call by the general name religion."[46] Von Hügel was genuinely alarmed that J. A. Smith seemed unable to draw his thought toward anything resembling Christian orthodoxy, but Smith never gave up the old idealist notion that reality was "spiritual through and through," a sentimental, unsatisfactory way of affirming that reality was alive and personal.[47] C. S. Lewis, who knew Smith, and knew the trouble this kind of talk had caused, wrote to Dom Bede Griffiths in 1940: "One thing we want to do is to kill the word spiritual in the sense in which it is used by writers like Arnold and Croce."[48] Here Lewis was reiterating a judgment offered by Chesterton, who was certainly familiar with the "spiritual" philosophy of the Synthetic Society's philosopher members in 1909; Chesterton's

---

[44]Smith, "Philosophy," 229. See SPM 3:12, 18, 19; SPB, 2, 17.

[45]Vidler, *Catholic Modernists*, 173. Von Hügel indicated for the archbishop those who had rendered exceptional service, and those to whom a token of esteem should be sent. Von Hügel considered J. A. Smith deserving of one of the archbishop's publications.

[46]Webb, *Religious Experience*, 30.

[47]Smith, "Philosophy," 237; de la Bedoyère, von Hügel, 300; C. C. J. Webb, Review of *The Life of Baron von Hügel*, by Michael de la Bedoyère, *JTS* 3 (1952): 147.

[48]C. S. Lewis to Dom Bede Griffiths, 16 April 1940, *LCSL*, 182.

conclusion was seconded by Eliot.[49] But in 1901 the "spiritual" was the common property of religion, theology, and philosophy. Few sensed the danger this entailed for the disciplines. Indeed, the Spirit, the *Geist* of Hegel's philosophy of history, was a kind of familiar in the house of wisdom, casting over Darwinian materialism a mantle of poetic sensitivity. Mackmurdoo's fluid Art Nouveau line was the banner of cultural rebellion against all things fixed and final. We stand, wrote the author of the *Hibbert Journal* in 1899, "for three positive truths: that the goal of thought is One: that thought, striving to reach the goal, must forever move: that in the conflict of opinions, the movement is furthered by which the many approach the One."[50] Nor was the philosophical interest entirely abstract. The pursuit of the spirit led Arthur Balfour and Henry Sidgwick to lend their support in 1882 to the founding of the London Society for Psychical Research, an organization in whose service distinguished intellectuals sat in darkened rooms hoping to verify or disprove the existence of the "spiritual."[51] Between 1905 and 1918 Evelyn Underhill and Charles Williams, both thinkers of a decidedly orthodox bent by 1930, belonged to the occult Hermetic Society of the Golden Dawn, and in the 1920s Owen Barfield was captivated by the theosophy of Rudolf Steiner.[52]

Gripped by this rationalizing idealism, theologians produced a series of books that identified the progress of the soul with the progress of the alienated self toward its ground in the Absolute and equated the progress of the Kingdom with the evolutionary development of history. In their zeal for a rapprochement between faith and reason, theologians began to take seriously the very idealism that at Oxford had become fragile and self-critical. Further, by compounding a kind of rationalizing psychology with the poetic use of the words "evolution" and "spirit," they created, a generation late, an English counterpart to the German move-

---

[49]G. K. Chesterton, *Orthodoxy* (London: John Lane, 1909) 137, 245-46; T. S. Eliot, *Selected Essays* (London: Faber and Faber, 1951) 485.

[50]L. P. Jacks and G. Dawes Hicks, "Editorial," *HJ* 1 (1902): 4.

[51]Alan Gauld, *The Founders of Psychical Research* (New York: Schocken Books, 1968).

[52]Christopher J. R. Armstrong, *Evelyn Underhill (1875-194?): An Introduction to Her Life and Writings* (Grand Rapids MI: Eerdmans, 1975) 36-37; C. S. Lewis's Journal, 7 July 1923, *LCSL*, 89; Lewis, *Surprised by Joy*, 201-208.

ment whose central monument was Feuerbach's *Essence of Christianity*.[53] The work that alarmed church people most was R. J. Campbell's *The New Theology* (1907). Campbell's new theology was to be a spiritual socialism, a religion of science that—based upon the immanence of God in the world, a theme developed, though in very different ways, both by the orthodox *Lux Mundi* group and by Darwinians like Herbert Spencer—would teach a Gospel through which cosmic emotion could be constructively focused. The Trinity could be understood as the infinite, the finite, and the action of the finite within the infinite.[54] The new theology contained two powerful but seemingly unreconcilable themes: the quasipoetic interpretation of reality as an all-encompassing, ever-unfolding process; and an almost positivistic understanding of history. The new theologians tended to consider the world process divine, while simultaneously denying that any human being, even Jesus, had been divine in a sense implying such transcendent attributes as omniscience and omnipotence. The new theology was seen for what it was, and answered almost immediately by Chesterton, who wrote *Orthodoxy* (1909) in response,[55] but views partly compatible with Campbell's conclusions were typical of the group brought together by B. H. Streeter: Lily Dougall, C. W. Emmet, W. H. Moberly, and for many years, R. G. Collingwood, and Clement Webb.

R. J. Campbell's influence was popular, not scholarly, and his place in Modernism was vacated when, in 1916, he abjured his radical views and became an Anglican. The English equivalent to the condemnation

---

[53]In 1836 David Friedrich Strauss published his *Life of Jesus*, denying the supernatural elements in the biblical accounts, and foreshadowing his last, and perhaps most influential, work, *The Old Faith and the New* (1872), in which Strauss applied his principles to the entire body of dogma. The other work on which the German "new theology" was founded was Ludwig Feuerbach's *The Essence of Christianity* (1841), which affected German theologians in the 1840s much as Campbell's work would unsettle Anglicans in 1907. The Magdalen metaphysicals perpetuated the Oxford custom of ignoring German scholarship apart from Kant and summaries of Hegel. Webb did not learn to read German well until late in life, Lewis never did (*LCSL*, 157).

[54]R. J. Campbell, *The New Theology* (London: Chapman and Hall, 1907). See also Langford, *In Search of Foundations*, 33-38.

[55]The quality of Chesterton's argument so far exceeds the significance of the debate that it is easy to forget that Campbell's book was in part the occasion of Chesterton's writing. See *Orthodoxy*, 24, 235, 249.

of Catholic Modernism by Pius X in 1906 did not come until 1911, when E. S. Talbot, a friend of Gore and one of the *Lux Mundi* authors, censured Magdalen's dean of divinity, James Matthew Thompson. Thompson, one of the founders of Streeter's theological group, had reduced to logical form the presupposition shared, but seldom enunciated, by some of that circle. Thompson wrote in 1911 that the miracles of the New Testament were mostly to be explained as manifestations of religious psychology.[56] Thompson, who had begun his ministry in the Church of England in 1909 with High Church sympathies, was following the Loisy line. He did not, for instance, think that rejection of the miraculous meant rejection of theism, and in this early period of his career appealed to the Church to supply for faith the authority that reason could not.

By pursuing the critical argument to its conclusion, Thompson raised a storm of protest. Talbot suspended his license, and J. R. Illingworth wrote *The Gospel Miracles* to counter Thompson's *Miracles in the New Testament*, arguing that the attempt to eliminate the miraculous "in the supposed interest of a more rational Christianity" would "substitute an ideal for an eventful religion, a theory of the wise and prudent for the revelation to babes."[57] Thompson was defended by Hastings Rashdall and by Lilley, but even Streeter urged against Thompson's wish to make a legal stand, and others of the Streeter connection, moved partly by caution, partly by principle, distanced themselves from Thompson's position. Clement Webb wrote that he could not associate himself with an overt attack on the truth of Scripture.[58]

After the Thompson affair, Oxford Modernism became guarded and subtle, but views partly compatible with *The New Theology* were typical of the Streeter group, whose members worked to reconcile Scripture,

---

[56]J. M. Thompson, *Miracles in the New Testament* (London: Edward Arnold, 1911). Thompson defended the hypothesis that the original events underlying the Gospel accounts "need not be regarded as miraculous" (18).

[57]J. R. Illingworth, *The Gospel Miracles* (London: Macmillan, 1915) 185. *Divine Transcendence and Its Reflection in Religious Authority* (London: Macmillan, 1911) was probably also written to refute Campbell and Thompson, since it was a defense of the authority of reason, the Bible, and the Church against the "psychological bias" (21).

[58]See Hastings Rashdall to Thompson, 11 July 1911; Streeter to Thompson, 31 July 1911; A. E. J. Rawlinson to Thompson, 1911; C. C. J. Webb to Thompson, 16 May 1911 [MS.Eng.lett.d.181].

science, and philosophy along rationalizing lines. The most important result of their efforts was *Foundations*, a work of doubtful, but only doubtful, orthodoxy, containing articles by Streeter, A. E. J. Rawlinson, R. Brook, R. G. Parsons, William Temple, and W. H. Moberly, the last a defense of the philosophic adequacy of the Absolute as a basis for Christian theism.[59] Other productions of the Streeter group included *Immortality: An Essay in Discovery, Co-ordinating Scientific, Psychical, and Biblical Research* (1917) and *The Spirit: The Relation of God and Man, Considered from the Standpoint of Recent Philosophy and Science* (1919). Though these representatives of the drive to reconcile theology and philosophy had various merits, they all combined to some degree a Platonic-idealistic parody of natural theology, representing the capture of theology by an idealism that could talk too easily of "spirit" and "the spiritual," with a naive, positivistic understanding of history.

When Edward VII died in 1910 the strange era of transition, during which idealism had held the ground by habit and default, was drawing to a close at Oxford. Philosophers knew the lines of advance laid down in their undergraduate days had been played out and promising younger men like Prichard and Joseph were striking out in new directions. Bosanquet was no longer an influence in Oxford, though he would continue to make important contributions to scholarly debate through books like *The Value and Destiny of the Individual* (1913) and *The Meeting of Extremes in Contemporary Philosophy* (1921). Bradley was a recluse. John Alexander Smith was struggling to develop the radical ideas he had discovered in Benedetto Croce. The orthodox in the Church of England and English Catholics had taken alarm. The reaction had been inaugurated by Pius X, who had condemned the thought of George Tyrrell and other Catholic Modernists in the summer of 1907.[60] Most of the philos-

---

[59]B. H. Streeter, ed., *Foundations: A Statement of Christian Belief in Terms of Modern Thought* (London: Macmillan, 1912).

[60]Before 1907 Gore's theological interests were directed primarily toward the interpretation of the Incarnation along lines laid down in *Lux Mundi*, and in the reform and renewal of Anglican institutions. After his answer to Campbell in *The New Theology and the Old Religion* (London: John Murray, 1907), Gore's thought developed consistently toward the works collected in *The Reconstruction of Belief*, a volume that provided a standard for Anglican orthodoxy during the years between the wars. Gore's *The Philosophy of the Good Life* (London: John Murray, 1930) was also decidedly classic in emphasis.

ophers who had entertained von Hügel and Mignot at Oxford in 1904 remained supporters of Tyrrell, but the tide began to turn. Von Hügel made no move toward rebellion. Illingworth was frankly frightened by what he read, and Charles Gore's career as an apologist for orthodoxy dates from the questionings aroused by the new theology.[61] By 1905 Gore, whose modest acceptance of critical methods in the 1880s had bitterly disappointed conservatives like Henry Parry Liddon, and Illingworth, whose essays in Gore's *Lux Mundi* had given immanence respectability as a theological category, were leaders of a reaction Modernists like Rashdall and Lilley considered a veritable persecution.[62]

Viewed retrospectively, English philosophy was beset by two difficulties: the collapse into empiricism, and the failure of philosophy and theology to solve the problem of the relation between the disciplines. That failure was represented by the tendency of the idealists to subsume theology into philosophy, and of Oxford philosophers generally, despite their knowledge of ancient history, to ignore the historical and to underestimate the relevance of history as a kind of knowledge. The second of these tendencies was represented by Moberly's chapter in *Foundations*, written about 1911, in which he defended the adequacy of the timeless, in some respects impersonal Absolute of Bosanquet and Bradley, with Webb and T. H. Green cited in support of the argument. The first was represented by Bertrand Russell's Herbert Spencer Lecture, given at Oxford on 14 November 1914 and titled "Scientific Method in Philosophy."[63] Russell argued that the unity philosophy had traditionally sought was an illusion fathered by presumption upon ignorance, and suggested that philosophy adopt the pluralistic, empirical approach of the natural sciences. Russell's position entailed the view that history either was ir-

---

[61]Illingworth to M. C. L., March, April 1907, October 1908, in Agnes L. Illingworth, ed., *The Life of John Richardson Illingworth* (London: Macmillan, 1917) 194, 223, 246.

[62]A. L. Lilley to Alfred Firmin Loisy, 4 April 1908, quoted in Vidler, *Catholic Modernists*, 129; Hastings Rashdall to A. L. Lilley, 18 June 1905, in Vidler, 182. When Rashdall became dean of Carlisle in 1917, A. L. Lilley wrote (19 December), "Already I hear members of the bench rejoicing that there is someone to stand up to Gore" [MS.Eng.lett.345].

[63]Bertrand Russell, "Scientific Method in Philosophy," *Oxford Lectures on Philosophy, 1910-1923* (Oxford: University Press, 1924) 4, 7.

relevant or was scheduled soon to be reformed in accord with principles derived from physics; Moberly held the belief that history was "spiritual." The missing bridge was obviously history as Croce, Smith, and Collingwood would later describe it, a discipline rooted on one hand in evidence, on the other in imagination and insight.

In 1910 there was as yet, among historians and philosophers of history, no common body of theory, and idealists tended ruthlessly to collapse the events of time into the timeless Absolute, while the realists were naturally attracted to the positivism of David Fredrich Strauss and Albert Schweitzer. Hegel's philosophy of history was a grand theodicy, not a philosophy of the doing of history. Though Bradley had made a beginning in his *Presuppositions of Critical History* (1874), and despite the enthusiastic researches of the antiquaries, in England the writing of history proceeded in the absence of any coherent study of historiography. Western civilization from Aristotle to Descartes was largely ignored.

The Oxford philosopher who, more than any other, demonstrated during a career of five decades the importance of history, including the history of medieval thought, for philosophy, and the necessity for careful reading of the text and careful research was Clement C. J. Webb. Webb also tried persistently to rehabilitate religious experience as a source for philosophy, to clarify the relation between philosophy and theology that in 1910 seemed hopelessly confused, and to defend the proposition that belief in a God was a metaphysical possibility. Of course, he was not alone in any of these efforts; there were other historians and other philosophers. But as a philosopher-historian whose work displayed the possibilities of the Greats curriculum, Webb would be a kind of model, focusing and refining the best of the idealism of his teachers, contributing to the establishing at Oxford of history as a discipline, and developing for fifty years a scholarly style that combined erudition, moral depth, humility, and candor.

·CHAPTER II·

Clement C. J. Webb and the Historical Element

A strong sense of the continuity of history was early aroused in me by Freeman's Sketches of European History *and encouraged by Stanley's* Westminster Abbey, *and has been fostered by . . . a life almost entirely spent . . . in . . . societies which bring home this continuity to the affections and imaginations of their members.*

Clement C. J. Webb,
"Outline of a Philosophy of Religion," 1924

The societies in which Clement Webb passed his life were the re-medievalized church that his father, Benjamin Webb of ecclesiological fame, had helped create, and three Oxford Colleges—Christ Church, Magdalen, and Oriel—all graced with distinguished pasts.[1] The books Webb remembered in his maturity as having formed his imagination were the *Historical Memorials of Westminster Abbey*, a pious architectural history written in 1868 by Arthur Penrhyn Stanley and a school history of Europe published in 1872 by Edward Augustus Free-

[1]On Benjamin Webb, see C. C. J. Webb, *DNB* 60, 95-96.

man, fellow of Trinity and later Regius Professor of History.[2] Soon after Webb married in 1905 he took his bride, Eleanor Theodora Joseph, another child of the rectory, to Holywell Ford.

Webb was a member of the first generation of English scholars to whom the Middle Ages were, thanks largely to their own labors, accessible, and for whom the study of things medieval was not hopelessly distorted by a politically or theologically prejudiced historiography. Beginning in the sixteenth century, interest in medieval civilization had gradually dried up in England, and knowledge of medieval literature and philosophy had faded from the life of the universities. The causes were complex. Even had there been no ecclesiastical revolution, the animus of great men like Thomas More (who as chancellor scolded university conservatives for teaching Latin instead of Greek) against Scholasticism would probably have prevailed. When, in the next generation, the Renaissance distaste for the recent Latin past was reinforced by a theological historiography that cast medieval corruption as the enemy of primitive purity and by political rhetoric that made things Catholic treasonous, the fate of medieval literature and medieval philosophy in the universities was sealed.

Two hundred years later the romantic movement began to overcome the narrow chronological confines into which the Enlightenment had pushed historical scholarship, but buildings, manuscripts, poetry, and mysticism still held priority over philosophy and theology in scholarly imagination. Anglo-Saxon literature, valued since Matthew Parker had interested himself in the collection and translation of the manuscripts in the sixteenth century, was studied with fresh interest by George Hickes, Humphrey Wanley, and Edmond Gibson during the early eighteenth century, and in 1750 Richard Rawlinson endowed the Anglo-Saxon pro-

---

[2]Arthur Penrhyn Stanley (1815-1881) was dean of Westminster, and a writer on architecture, history, and travel, as well as theology. See R. E. Prothero, *DNB* 54, 44-48. Edward Augustus Freeman (1832-1892) was a fellow of Trinity College, Oxford, then (1884) of Oriel upon his election to the Regius professorship of history. The historical work that influenced Webb was the *Historical Course for Schools*, in which the *General Sketch of European History* (London: Macmillan, 1874) was the first volume. Freeman was a Tractarian, ecclesiologically inclined, and passionately anti-Turkish on the Eastern question. See *Times*, 17 March 1892; Bryce, *Studies in Contemporary Biography*, 262-92; W. R. W. Stephens, *The Life and Letters of Edward A. Freeman* (London: Macmillan, 1895).

fessorship at Oxford.[3] *Beowulf*, discovered in 1705, was edited and published in translation in 1833.

Medieval influences were evident in architecture before 1800. The first architectural result was a sentimental Gothic—seen in country houses like Horace Walpole's Strawberry Hill and James Wyatt's Fonthill Abbey—built without much theoretical basis and calculated to delight and charm.[4] The influence of Scott, who beginning in the 1820s brought the medieval past to life in English imagination, is inestimable. The interest in medieval architecture and in the past as popularized by Scott began gradually to arouse a serious interest in the early Middle Ages.

Naturally, theologians did not begin with Scholasticism or the thirteenth century, but with the primitive literature of the second and third centuries. By 1830 antiquity meant, at least to men of John Henry Newman's stamp, an ever-expanding portion of history that stretched forward from the apostolic age through the second century; it included first the second century, then the great fourth-century councils and St. Augustine. Newman's *Theology of the Seven Epistles of St. Ignatius* (1836) and his *Arians of the Fourth Century* (1839) inaugurated an enormous literary production.

As it became clear that there was no neat division between pure antiquity and the corruption of Scholasticism, the English Church began to claim its full medieval heritage. Newman was among the first to realize that the defense of any Anglicanism that based its claims upon antiquity required the reappropriation of the entire medieval past. "In order to kindle a love of the National Church and yet inculcate a Catholic tone," he wrote, "nothing else is necessary but to take our Church in the Middle Ages."[5] The appropriation of the Middle Ages by Newman and

---

[3]For the history of the study of Anglo-Saxon in the university, see D. J. Palmer, *The Rise of English Studies* (London: Oxford University Press, 1965) 71-76. On the eighteenth-century background, especially the professorships in history established by George I, see C. H. Firth, "Modern History in Oxford, 1724-1841," *English Historical Review* 32 (1917): 1-21.

[4]Agnes Addison Gilchrist, *Romanticism and the Gothic Revival* (New York: Richard R. Smith, 1938).

[5]Newman to J. W. Bowden, 4 April 1841, John Henry Newman, *Letters and Correspondence of John Henry Newman*, ed. Anne Mozley (London: Longmans, Green, 1903) 1:187.

other Tractarians inaugurated a new historiography developed on the assumption that the church of Thomas à Becket was British, not Roman. Historians like Edward Churton began to write a new history, describing an ancient English Christianity, always independent or Roman only unwillingly, which had preserved the medieval heritage without assenting to papal usurpations.[6] By 1839, when Clement Webb's father began to labor in earnest for the ecclesiological cause, loyal sons of the Establishment had made the church of Aquinas and Bonaventure their own, although knowledge of medieval sources in England was still eclectic and hardly conducive to systematic study of the thought of the period. Benjamin Webb and John Mason Neale knew the relatively obscure William Durandus, author of *The Symbolism of Churches*, better than St. Thomas, but in principle the medieval period was accessible.[7]

Newman, with that insight typical of his genius, had realized by 1850 that the interest in history displayed by theologians was not merely apologetic, and no mere antiquarian recovery of information, but heralded a revolution.

> The science of criticism, the disinterment of antiquities, the unrolling of manuscripts, the interpretation of inscriptions, have thrown us into a new world of thought: characters and events come forth transfigured in the process; romance, prejudice, local tradition, party bias are no longer accepted as guarantees of truth; the order and mutual relation of events are readjusted; the springs and scope of actions are reversed.[8]

Modern, critical history had been born.

This mid-Victorian recovery of the past, limited in its beginnings by a historiography that continued to depict medieval theology and philosophy as products of the Dark Ages was, especially before 1850, encouraged as much by the architectural movement as by Tractarian apologetics. The theoretically serious, sometimes pretentious, side of the architectural revival owed its first successes to Augustus Welby Northmore Pugin, a convert to Catholicism. By 1836 he had begun, in graphically dramatic works like *Contrasts*, to popularize his idea that so-

---

[6]Edward Churton, *The Early English Church* (London: I. Burns, 1840).

[7]James F. White, *The Cambridge Movement: The Ecclesiologists and the Gothic Revival* (Cambridge: University Press, 1932) 69.

[8]*Lectures on Certain Difficulties Felt by Anglicans in Submitting to the Catholic Church* (London: Burns and Lambert, 1850) 129.

ciety—its landscape already wounded by the early industrial revolution, its towns disgraced by an inauthentic classicism—could be healed only if the great age of Christendom were recovered. For Pugin, the architecture of the Middle Ages was both cause and witness to the triumph of Catholicism that must inevitably occur in England. Newman came in the long run to distrust Pugin as too enthusiastic and his theories as antiquarian; but for a brief time in the 1840s the architect exercised great influence over John Mason Neale and Benjamin Webb,[9] who together organized the Camden Society at Cambridge and began to publish the *Ecclesiologist*. The theoretical sponsor of the ecclesiological revival was the medieval theologian William Durandus, whose treatise Webb and Neale translated because they found in it warrant for their belief that right faith and piety were imaged and encouraged by medieval architecture.[10] Guided by the architectural movement, ecclesiology, and the literary popularizations of the medieval past, Englishmen began zealously to refurbish and recreate the Gothic they had neglected for 300 years.

The powerful influence of the architectural movement on the revival of medieval learning was ambiguously benign in the disciplines of philosophy and theology. The greatest Victorian medievalizer was John Ruskin, who loved Gothic but disliked Catholicism and ignored Scholasticism.[11] In Ruskin, Englishmen found a model for their own attitudes. But the revival of Gothic was also a social protest, a graphic rejection of the industrial revolution and the classicism Pugin's *Contrasts* had so effectively associated with it.[12] There was also about the architectural movement, as well as early Tractarianism, a good deal of nation-

---

[9]James Patrick, "Newman, Pugin, and Gothic," *Victorian Studies* 24 (1981): 185-208; White, *Cambridge Movement*, 197-203.

[10]White, *Cambridge Movement*, 48-79; Guliemus Durantis, *The Symbolism of Churches and Church Ornaments*, trans. John Mason Neale and Benjamin Webb (Leeds: T. W. Green, 1843).

[11]See R. H. Wilenski, *John Ruskin: An Introduction to Further Study of His Life and Work* (New York: Frederick A. Stokes, 1934) 329-56 and John D. Rosenburg, *The Darkening Glass: A Portrait of Ruskin's Genius* (New York: Columbia University Press, 1961) 55-93.

[12]William Morris thought the Gothic Revival was "really connected with the general progress of the world, with those aspirations toward freedom, from which in truth no sincere art can ever be dissociated" ["The Gothic Revival I," *The Unpublished Lectures of William Morris*, ed. Eugene D. Lemire (Detroit: Wayne State University Press, 1969) 55].

alism, an insistence on English Gothic for English Christianity. Despite inevitable complications, the architectural movement did its work well, staking out in English imaginations a place for the thirteenth century and a positive image of medieval English life, making English cities "a forest of towers and steeples, all Gothic."[13]

By 1850 Scott, and interest in medieval architecture and in Christian antiquity, provided background for the scholarly study of English history and medieval literature. In 1865 Frederick James Furnivall (1825-1910) founded the English Text Society, with Ruskin and Tennyson as subscribers, and three years later began the Chaucer Society. Walter William Skeat (1835-1912) brought the new interest in the literature of the Middle Ages to the universities, beginning in 1866 his great translation of *Piers Plowman*, which was followed in 1871-1887 by the Anglo-Saxon Gospels and in 1881-1890 by Aelfric's *Lives of the Saints*. In 1870 a Regius professorship of history was established at Oxford, a chair held successively by two distinguished scholars: William Stubbs, who resigned in 1884 on his election tó Chichester; and Freeman, who held the professorship until his death in 1892.

Wherever one touched the Middle Ages, the dust of medieval religion rose, and with it English discomfort with any historiography that seemed to question the merits of the sixteenth-century events that had severed Britain culturally from Mediterranean Europe. J. A. Froude (1818-1894), who disliked the Middle Ages as heartily as his brother Richard Hurrell admired them, devoted a lifetime to a defense of the anti-Catholic historiography that had become a commonplace of English scholarship. From his monumental *History of England* (1856-1870) to *The Council of Trent* (1896), Froude pursued his studies of the Middle Ages polemically, arguing persistently the rightness of the acts and attitudes that had formed Renaissance civilization in England. Froude's brief tenure as Freeman's successor (1892-1894) marked the end of the passionately partisan and rationalist interpretation of English history at Oxford.[14]

---

[13]H. S. Goodhart-Rendel, *English Architecture Since the Regency: An Interpretation* (London: Constable, 1953) 89.

[14]See Basil Wiley, "J. A. Froude," *More Nineteenth Century Studies: A Group of Honest Doubters* (London: Chatto and Windus, 1956) 106-36.

That the chair Freeman and Froude held existed at all was a testimony to the success of a double revolution, one establishing modern history, the other English, as disciplines worthy of study in the universities. At Oxford the School of Law and Modern History had been founded in 1850, and the two separated in 1872. The Merton Professorship of Language and Literature (which J. R. R. Tolkien would inherit in 1946) was founded in 1885, with A. S. Napier as the first professor, but it was December 1893 before the Final Honour School of English was approved by Congregation. The movements in architecture, history, literature, and theology reinforced one another. Freeman's first book was a *History of Architecture* (1849),[15] and as medieval texts became better known, interest in the history of the language and in Old English flourished. Iceland became an important destination for scholarly tourists, among them William Gershom Collingwood and William Morris.[16] Old English and Old Norse were important intellectual strands in the Northernness C. S. Lewis discovered in Wagner and William Morris, and loved.[17]

Philosophy and theology were the last medieval disciplines to make some serious claim on English scholarship. By 1870 medievalism was fashionable in art and architecture, in literature, and even (within limits) in piety. The Anglo-Catholic successors of the Tractarians, brought up on the Tractarian doctrine of the Real Presence, were deeply interested in the devotional literature of Scholasticism. Edward Bouverie Pusey, on whom the mantle had fallen when Newman went to Rome in 1845, had published Anselm's meditations and prayers (1856), and *Cur Deus Homo* two years later; and in 1871 John Mason Neale published St. Thomas's *De Venerabili Sacramento Altaris*.[18] Interest in St. Augustine, which had

---

[15]Edward A. Freeman, *A History of Architecture* (London: J. Masters, 1849). Freeman continued to write on architecture throughout his life, and is among the founders of scholarly architectural history in England.

[16]W. G. Collingwood's journey is documented in W. G. Collingwood and Jon Stefánsson, *A Pilgrimage to the Saga-Steads of Iceland* (Ulverston: W. Holmes, 1899). Morris's visit to Iceland in 1871 marked his subsequent writing.

[17]Lewis, *Surprised by Joy*, 72-76; Lewis Journals, 8 February 1927, *LCSL*, 110; J. R. R. Tolkien to Michael Tolkien, 9 June 1941, *LJRRT*, 55-56.

[18]*Meditations and Prayers to the Holy Trinity and Our Lord Jesus Christ*, trans. E. B. Pusey (Oxford: J. H. Parker, 1856); *Cur Deus Homo* (Oxford: J. H. and J. Parker, 1853); *The Venerable Sacrament of the Altar: A Theological and Devotional Treatise*, trans. J. M. Neale (London: J. T. Hayes, 1871). The work is probably not by St. Thomas.

never failed completely in England, was renewed with the publication in 1838 of the *Confessions*, and subsequently much of Augustine was reissued in English in series like the *Library of the Fathers of the Holy Catholic Church* and the *Library of Spiritual Writers for English Catholics*.[19] Yet university philosophers and divines were slow to believe that the age characterized even in scholarly imagination by the persecution of Galileo and Bruno had any serious contribution to make.

The scholarly recovery of medieval philosophy, tenuous in its beginnings, is perhaps to be traced to 1830, when Renn Dickson Hampden argued in his Bampton Lectures that the rationalism of medieval philosophy had infected and destroyed theology, and that the Bible was in any event superior to the Church in authority.[20] Newman immediately objected, and an inevitable quarrel ensued, but the controversy had at least the merit of bringing Scholasticism, understood as a system making definite intellectual claims, to the attention of Oxford philosophers and divines.[21] At about the same time the Tractarians, who could read Athanasius and Cyril with comparative ease, determined that translations, usually selected with an eye to the support they offered the Tractarian cause, were in order. In 1838 the volumes of the *Library of the Fathers* began to appear, but interest was still focused on the period that seemed primitive. The doctrine of authority espoused by Newman and his friends—resting as it did upon the acceptance of antiquity as the arbiter of truth—had, however, a logic that could not easily be controlled. In Newman's own life that logic was worked out in the *Essay on the Development of Christian Doctrine*, a project through which Newman reappropriated the entire intellectual and ecclesiastical past of Latin Christendom.

Something of the same logic continued to work within Anglicanism after Newman's departure in 1845. Fueled by the new historical under-

---

[19]The Library of Spiritual Writers for English Catholics was a project of Rivington; The Library of the Fathers of the Holy Catholic Church a project of J. H. Parker, Oxford's High Church bookseller. There were others. Some got no further than the first volume.

[20]Renn Dickson Hampden, *The Scholastic Philosophy Considered in Its Relation to Christian Theology* (Oxford, 1833).

[21]John Henry Newman to R. D. Hampden, 28 November 1834, *Letters and Diaries of John Henry Newman* (Oxford: Clarendon Press, 1978) 4:377; cf. 201, n. 1.

standing, scholars assumed responsibility for providing a comprehensive and sympathetic account of the past. In 1856 Frederick Denison Maurice published his *Medieval Philosophy*, in part a response to the narrow Protestant reading of the Middle Ages that imputed to the schoolmen logic chopping and atheistic rationalism. Maurice laid out in broad outline the great intellectual achievement of the ninth to fourteenth centuries. Even earlier (1844), Samuel Roffey Maitland had published his *The Dark Ages; A series of Essays intended to Illustrate the State of Religion and Literature in the Ninth, Tenth, Eleventh, and Twelfth Centuries.* Though by 1890 Maitland's book would require a preface disclaiming enthusiasm for the doubtful social results his favorable presentation of the Dark Ages might have encouraged—the revival of monasticism among them—*The Dark Ages* and Maurice's *Medieval Philosophy* presaged the slow but steady increase of knowledge of Scholasticism and of medieval history among the clergy who were moderately or deeply influenced by the Tractarian legacy. When Charles Gore, John Richardson Illingworth, and the others who would write *Lux Mundi* were at Oxford in the 1870s, there was already a clear appreciation among Anglo-Catholics of the great medieval doctors; and by the time *Lux Mundi* was published in 1889, the authors commanded an impressive knowledge of the patristic and medieval past. Illingworth, in his essay "The Incarnation and Development," cited not only Thomas but Irenaeus, Augustine, Hugh of St. Victor, John Scotus Erigena, and Bonaventure.[22] The means by which these interests had become current in clerical circles are obscure. Pusey House and Keble College, foundations made at Oxford on the death of the two great Tractarians who had stayed, were certainly sources.[23] In the 1880s Thomas and Duns Scotus were admired by the Keble men who formed the nucleus from which the *Lux Mundi* group would grow.[24] Anglo-Catholics generally were responsive to things Roman, and in 1878 Leo XIII had published *Aeterni Patris*, commending

[22]J. R. Illingworth, "The Incarnation and Development," in Charles Gore, ed., *Lux Mundi* (London: John Murray, 1889) 184, 185, 187, 192.

[23]Knox, *Spiritual Aeneid*, 65; V. S. S. Coles, "Twenty-Five Years in Oxford," in J. F. Briscoe, ed., *V. S. S. Coles: Letters, Papers, Addresses, Hymns and Verses with Memoir* (London: A. R. Mowbray, 1930) 197-220; Arthur Templeton Lyttleton, *Modern Poets of Faith, Doubt, and Paganism and Other Essays* (London, 1904) 1-41.

[24]J. R. Illingworth to Wilfrid Richmond, 1875, Agnes L. Illingworth, ed., *Life*, 35.

the study of the great Fathers and Scholastics. English translations of St. Thomas's most important works appeared in the 1890s, and by 1910 Ronald Knox and others of the Anglo-Catholic intellectual connection routinely consulted Aquinas.[25]

The defense of the medieval intellectual tradition by Anglo-Catholics, rather than encouraging the study of medieval philosophy and theology in the university, probably inhibited it. F. H. Bradley named his dog Pusey in order to dramatize his estimate of the medievalizing religion sponsored by Pusey House and Keble College. Most Oxford philosophers in the years before 1914 tended to regard a fervid interest in medieval philosophy with suspicion. They supported George Tyrrell and defended his *Medievalism*—in fact a polemic against the scholastic system—in the face of the encouragement Neo-Scholasticism had received from Leo XIII and Cardinal Mercier on the Continent.[26] English modernists like A. L. Lilley considered Father Tyrrell, who died in 1909, a martyr to the intellectualizing dogmatism they associated with the revival of Scholasticism.[27] In 1910 firsthand knowledge of medieval thought was rare among the philosophers. J. A. Smith, whose study of Aristotle had led him to St. Thomas, perhaps before 1900, was an exception, but Webb, an authority on other medieval authors, probably did not begin to read Aquinas systematically until about 1923.[28] The first theological study of Thomism written by an Oxford scholar did not appear until 1930, when Martin D'Arcy's *Thomas Aquinas* was published.[29] Bede Griffiths wrote that about 1931 St. Thomas was "scarcely

---

[25]Knox, *Spiritual Aeneid*, 174.

[26]J. Lewis May, *Father Tyrrell and the Modernist Movement* (London: Burns, Oates and Washbourne, 1932). The condemnation of 1907 naturally carried no weight with Webb, who continued to arrange for the publication of Loisy's views in England. See von Hügel to Webb, 27 November 1908, 22 November 1909, Michael de la Bedoyère, *The Life of Baron von Hügel* (London: J. M. Dent, 1951) 222-23, 226. See below.

[27]Vidler, *Catholic Modernists*, 126-33; A. L. Lilley, Obituary of Father George Tyrrell, *Commonwealth*, 7 July 1909.

[28]J. A. Smith, "Art and the Beautiful in the Philosophy of St. Thomas," SPM, 1:8; WJB, 12 February 1924 [MS.Eng.misc.d.1115] 7, 18, 20 March 1925 [MS.Eng.misc.d.1117].

[29]Martin D'Arcy, *Thomas Aquinas* (London: Ernest Benn, 1930).

known in Oxford. His philosophy was not studied in any of the schools, and he had no place in the curriculum."[30]

That medieval thought as such had much impact among the growing number of tutors who had no partisan interest in the Middle Ages was in large measure the work of Reginald Lane Poole (1857-1939). James Bass Mullinger, who published *The Schools of Charles the Great* in 1877, had begun his work earlier.[31] The study of historical theology at Oxford would be encouraged by Frank Edward Brightman (1856-1932), a Pusey House librarian who had come to Magdalen in 1903, assuming the editorship of the *Journal of Theological Studies* the next year. Brightman's erudition in patristic studies, especially oriental liturgies, was immense; however, his theological interests were too technical to influence deeply the texts and tutorials of the Greats curriculum.[32] Poole in 1873 resigned his post in the manuscript section of the British Museum to devote himself to medieval studies. It was his *Illustrations of the History of Medieval Thought in the Departments of Theology and Ecclesiastical Politics*, first published in 1884, that made the thought of the Middle Ages accessible.[33]

When Poole's *Illustrations* was published, Clement Webb had already been at Christ Church for two years.[34] Benjamin Webb's youngest child, he was born when his father was already rector of St. Andrew's, Wells Street, and had grown up amid a welter of things medieval: liturgy, architecture, and piety. Clement Webb's career proceeded smoothly from Westminster School to Christ Church, and after his first in Greats in 1888, to the Magdalen fellowship he would hold until 1922. The influences on Webb at Oxford were of course Plato, Aristotle, and Kant. In Kant's *Foundations of the Metaphysics of Morals*, Webb, like Col-

---

[30]Bede Griffiths, *The Golden String* (New York: P. J. Kennedy and Sons, 1954) 57.

[31]*Times*, 22 November 1917.

[32]On Brightman, see S. L. Ollard, *DNB* 1931-1940, 103; "Frank Edward Brightman; 1856-1932," *JTS* 33 (1932): 336-39.

[33]Clement C. J. Webb, "Reginald Lane Poole," *PBA* 25 (1939): 311-20; G. N. Clark, "Reginald Lane Poole," *DNB* (1931-1940) 714-15; *English Historical Review* 55 (1940): 1-7. Poole became a fellow of Magdalen in 1898.

[34]G. N. Clark, "Clement Charles Julian Webb (1865-1954), *DNB* 1951-1960, 714-15; Webb, "Benjamin Webb," *DNB* 20, 1007-08.

lingwood after him, found his philosophical vocation.[35] Cook Wilson and J. A. Steward were his tutors, and Charles Gore, then principal of Pusey House, was an influential ideal. At Oxford the foundations were laid for a long career of productive labor, first in medieval history, then in a discipline "peculiarly his own, interpreting the facts of religious experience."[36] Webb was never ordained; rather, he became, like Smith and Joachim, a member of the second generation of Oxford dons who taught as laymen. Webb's failure to seek ordination argued no lack of zeal for Christianity. While at Christ Church he had, contrary to the pattern in households given to Tractarian doctrine and ecclesiology, experienced a conversion that left him, as he wrote, profoundly convinced "of the reality of God, and of the duty of open-mindedness and intellectual honesty."[37]

Clement Webb's first published work was a review of *Lux Mundi*,[38] and his early reviews and articles clearly owed something to both the Tractarian interest in the Middle Ages and to Poole. Webb tutored in philosophy, and like many of his contemporaries was interested in language, but the *differentia* in Webb's scholarly career was his interest in medieval and modern history; in the history of philosophy and theology and in the historical element in religion. Webb's method was usually historical: even in systematic essays—*Problems in the Relations of God and Man*, for example—he was likely to pass over easily into studies of the development of ideas. His bibliography during the 1890s was that of a promising student of medieval intellectual history. Webb's first scholarly article, a study of John Scotus Erigena, appeared in 1892, and the next year he published his first study of John of Salisbury.[39] In 1896 Webb wrote on Anselm's ontological argument, reintroducing to English scholarship the Anselmian texts that would later occupy Collingwood,[40]

---

[35]Webb, "Biographical," 336.

[36]Webb, *Religious Experience*, 19.

[37]Webb, "Biographical," 337-38.

[38]Clement C. J. Webb, Review of *Lux Mundi*, ed. Charles Gore, *Oxford Magazine* (12 February 1890): suppl., 3-4.

[39]Clement C. J. Webb, "John of Salisbury," *PAS* 2:2 (1894): 91-107.

[40]Clement C. J. Webb, "Anselm's Ontological Argument for the Existence of God," *PAS* 3 (1895): 25-43.

and the next year Webb published a discussion of newly discovered fragments of the fifth-century neo-Platonist Macrobius.[41] In 1903 he completed his translation of Anselm's prayers and spiritual letters, a task Pusey had begun in 1868.[42] During the next four decades there would be thirty reviews of books on medieval topics, a short article in the Festschrift for Poole, and finally his magisterial translation of the major works of John of Salisbury—a project encouraged by Poole, who had begun the task himself in 1881.[43]

About 1900, the focus of Webb's writing began to widen and to change, his dedication to history giving way to a broader interest in the philosophic analysis of religious experience, and necessarily to the relation between philosophy and theology. Two influences favored this shift in Webb's interests. Perhaps the single most important factor was his friendship with Baron von Hügel, whom Webb had met in 1896,[44] a relationship of lasting importance to both men. By 1904 von Hügel considered Webb the greatest friend of the modernists at Oxford; it was to Webb that von Hügel applied when there was an article to be placed or some cause to be defended.[45] Another influence important in Webb's life around 1900 was the tension generated by the unraveling of idealism and the effect of this failure on Webb and other Oxford philosophers. Webb had close friends, among them P. V. M. Beneke, Cuthbert Turner, Charles Shebbeare, and H. A. Wilson. The philosopher Webb most admired was Cook Wilson, to whom he dedicated *God and Personality* (1918), but his most important philosophical friendships after 1920 were with Horace Joseph, R. G. Collingwood, and J. A. Smith. Webb was

---

[41]"Some Fragments of Macrobius' *Saturnalia*," *Classics Review* 11 (1897): 441.

[42]Clement C. J. Webb, *The Devotions of St. Anselm* (London: Methuen, 1903).

[43]Reginald L. Poole, *The Early Correspondence of John of Salisbury*, *PBA* 25 (1939); rpt. London: Humphrey Milford, 1924; *Joannis Saresberiensis Historia Pontificalis quae supersunt*, trans. R. L. Poole (1927); Clement C. J. Webb, *John of Salisbury* (London: Methuen, 1932).

[44]Michael de la Bedoyère, *The Life of Baron von Hügel*, 90; *Clement C. J. Webb*, Review of *Von Hügel and Tyrrell: The Story of a Friendship*, by M. D. Petre, *JTS* 39 (1938): 215.

[45]Von Hügel to Webb, 27 November 1908, 22 November 1909, Bedoyère, *Von Hügel*, 222-23, 226.

himself no realist. In philosophy he was what the Greats curriculum of the 1880s had tended to make its students: loosely an idealist; deeply committed to the perennial questions; simultaneously sympathetic toward realism because of its obvious merits and suspicious of it because it seemed, as a system of thought, to move convincingly only in a world of objects.

By 1900 general agreement prevailed that F. H. Bradley was the greatest of the idealists, and that his *Appearance and Reality* was the supreme idealist manifesto; dissatisfaction with his absolutism was also widespread. The most serious difficulty concerned the status of personality. Bradley seemed to neglect Green's spiritual principle, and to render individual existence metaphysically illusory, and by 1900 the new psychology seemed, on wholly different grounds, to agree that the babel of ideas and intentions that characterized human individuality had no relation to reality.[46] Among the personal idealists the defense of real, self-identical existence became a primary project; "personality," Wilfrid Richmond wrote of the *Lux Mundi* authors, "became magical for us as symbolizing the philosophy of the future."[47] In 1887 Pringle-Pattison published *Hegelianism and Personality*, the first attack on Absolutism; then in 1894 John Richardson Illingworth delivered the Bampton Lectures on the topic *Personality Human and Divine*, perhaps the most eloquent Victorian defense of the primacy of personality.[48]

Prompted by the Oxford debate on personality and by the interest in religious experience that his friendship with von Hügel encouraged, Webb published in 1900 his long article, "The Idea of Personality as Applied to God." For the next twenty years the idea of personality would be interwoven with his historical and systematic interests. Eventually his thought on this topic found mature expression in *God and Personality* (1918) and *Divine Personality and Human Life* (1920). Closely related to

---

[46]Clement C. J. Webb, "Psychology and Religion," *JTS* 4 (1902-1903): 46-68; *God and Personality*, 241-44; Lewis, *Surprised by Joy*, 203-204; Collingwood, *Essay on Metaphysics*, 102-42.

[47]Wilfrid Richmond to Agnes L. Illingworth, Illingworth, ed., *John Richardson Illingworth*, 33.

[48]John Richardson Illingworth, *Personality Human and Divine* (London: Macmillan, 1894).

the systematic consideration of personality, and evident in most of Webb's books, was his interest in the relation between religious experience and formulations about such experience, or between religious experience and thought. Questions concerning the relation between grace and nature, and between theology and philosophy—questions no doubt generated by Webb's knowledge of the history of theology—were unavoidable.

His method was a tribute to the principle of the Greats curriculum, which required that philosophy and history be used to illuminate one another. One result of this background was the tendency of philosophers like Webb to resist the separation of logic from psychology, or of reason from history.[49] In one sense this was Kantian: the forms of intelligibility could not be separated from the thinking subject. It issued in a principle, first systematized apologetically by Illingworth,[50] from which Webb never prescinded. The believer in God, possessed of the object of his belief, had reasons that the unbeliever could know dimly or not at all. And yet these reasons were not merely feelings of dependence or reasons of the heart, but intelligible truths, objective in the sense that they were real; not mere figments or illusions, but known only within the hermeneutic of the intellectual act of believing. Knowledge was never impersonal, and therefore never unhistorical. This was the Kantian root and Green's spiritual principle. It was essential to Webb's lifelong defense of the proposition, challenged by liberal theologians and realists alike, that knowledge of God was a kind of real knowledge.[51]

Two works that exemplified Webb's approach, and which were summary of his career, were given as lectures beginning in 1911. In that year Webb had been appointed Wilde Lecturer in Natural and Comparative Religion, and during the next two academic years he delivered the lectures published as *Studies in the History of Natural Theology*. Nothing matched the scope of these studies in previous English scholarship. Natural theology, Webb wrote, was the reasoned account of religious expe-

---

[49]Webb, *Problems in the Relations of God and Man* (London: James Nisbet, 1911; rpt. 1918) 55-63.

[50]John Richardson Illingworth, *Reason and Revelation: An Essay in Christian Apology* (London: Macmillan, 1902) 42-43, 64.

[51]Webb, *Problems*, 55-63.

rience and of our experience of the world, taking as its sources both human experience of the self and human sciences.[52] Webb then offered the reader an exegesis of historical thought on these subjects that included Plato, Thomas, Anselm, Raymond of Sebonde, Pomponazzi, and Lord Herbert of Cherbury. Caird had written on Anselm in 1899, and Poole had discussed Abelard as a teacher in 1895, but no one had attempted to deal synoptically with the entire succession of philosophers whose thought about God formed the background for twentieth-century natural theology. Webb's *History of Philosophy*, published in 1913, accomplished on a larger scale the work of the *Studies*. The great succession was Plato, Aristotle, Plotinus, Augustine, Abelard, Anselm, Thomas, Descartes, Locke, Kant, Hegel, Green, Lotze, Spencer, and William James. The result was a tour de force demonstrating the continuity and power of the entire tradition and displaying Western thought about God as a continuous reflection that even in its skeptical moments had proved formative and fruitful.

While Webb was completing his *Studies in the History of Natural Theology*, he was also hard at work on the eight lectures, given in Hilary Term of 1911, which became *Problems in the Relations of Man and God*. Here Webb dealt with three topics: reason and revelation, nature and grace, man and God. The temper of his treatment was classic, even traditional. Reason and revelation were correlative. Kant's denial of the necessity of grace, though intelligible in the light of his ethical interest and defense of freedom, had been mistaken. The Trinity, Webb wrote, was the model for personal life and the ground of reality.[53] If Webb erred in his description of the relation between grace and nature, theology and philosophy, it was by identifying too closely the realms of revelation and reason. Nonetheless, he wrote amidst the debris of a century of eccentric and intemperate denials that any relation existed: the Ritschlians insisted that knowledge of God was gained by faith, not reason; the idealists argued that religion, to the degree that it existed, was philosophy misunderstood; the realists and new psychologists together held that re-

---

[52] Clement C. J. Webb, *Studies in the History of Natural Theology* (Oxford: Clarendon Press, 1915) 49-52.

[53] Webb, *Problems*, 231-36, 271-75.

ligion was in no sense knowledge. Against that background Webb's achievement was remarkable.

God and Personality, Webb's Gifford Lectures of 1918 and 1919, was his leading attempt to discuss the personality of God according to categories relevant to the central tradition of Christian theology, and to do so in the context of the metaphysics of the still-dominant idealism of the immediate prewar period. The question, Webb wrote, was really, "Is God the Absolute?" or "What is the Relation of Philosophy to Religion?"[54] Philosophers, he answered, are known by their search for unity, while other men proceed from their experience of reality: "Aesthetic experience reveals in nature a spirituality which apart from that experience cannot be shown to be there, so does the religious experience reveal in the ultimate Reality something which apart from religious experience is not there discoverable. This may properly be called personality, for it is revealed in and through an experience of personal intercourse."[55] It was almost axiomatic for Webb that knower and known enjoyed a complex relation that did indeed yield truth. However, truth could not be abstracted from the epistemological nexus and analyzed in purely objective terms—if indeed, (which Webb would have denied) such objective analysis were possible in the case of personal intersubjectivity.[56]

In *God and Personality* Webb also discussed the tension between the human desire for happiness and the requirement of Kantian ethics that duty be done disinterestedly. What Webb discovered in reality was the unity of the good and the beautiful with the reasonable, which meant that human personality was justified in hoping that goodness and happiness had some relation. Having worked his way through the philosophies of Lotze, Bradley, Bosanquet, Croce, and Bergson, Webb concluded at last that the highest philosophic idea in religion was Plato's form of the good, the perfect unity of reason and goodness,[57] with goodness understood as both moral and aesthetic.

---

[54]Webb, *God and Personality*, 213.

[55]Ibid., 240.

[56]Webb, *Problems*, 28-41.

[57]Webb, *God and Personality*, 236-40.

In 1930 Webb retired from his professorship, and entered upon a period of lecturing and writing undertaken apart from professorial duties. Of his later works, the most important was *The Historical Element in Religion*, in which Webb clarified his thought on the relationship between Christianity and history. Throughout his scholarly career, Webb stood between those, like Schweitzer, who argued that Christianity as traditionally received could not be true because the events essential to its account of reality had never taken place; and those who held with Durkheim that the truth of Christianity was a group supposition or even illusion, utterly independent of history.[58] Historical doubt, Webb wrote, was neither to be crushed by authority nor treated as though the practice of religion should be postponed until objective certainty is gained. The question of whether an event occurs is not irrelevant; for if it were shown that some great event in the Gospel cycle had never taken place, believers would be required to change their minds. On the other hand, knowledge of God and of truths revealed is knowledge from within, a personal knowledge unimpugned because it lacks obviousness or even objective probability.[59] By the historical element in religion, Webb meant the continuity within religious communities of personal experience, and hence of living memory, a position that related neatly to his insistence that no significant knowledge is impersonal.

Webb's interest during the 1930s in the philosophy of history reflected the influence of acquaintances, especially the work of Collingwood. The revival of historical studies had been closely related to the philosophical consideration of history since 1910. Webb believed, with good reason, that Hegel had given history a standing in philosophy, through his doctrine that the true significance of things and of reality as a whole could not be understood apart from the way in which they had come to be.[60] Hegel's historicism tended on one hand to break down into

---

[58]Webb, *The Historical Element in Religion* (London: George Allen and Unwin, 1934) 14.

[59]Clement C. J. Webb, *The Historical Element in Religion*, 75-115. For Webb's treatment of the idea, promoted especially by Durkheim, that religion is a group illusion, see *Group Theories of Religion and the Individual* (London: George Allen and Unwin, 1916) 155-63.

[60]Webb, *The Historical Element in Religion*, 59-63.

an Absolutism that denied the existence of the historical on behalf of the Absolute, and on the other to underwrite the kind of historical positivism that D. F. Strauss and F. C. Baur had used to criticize the Gospels and the history of the early church.[61] F. H. Bradley's *Presuppositions of Critical History*, a work to which Collingwood later appealed, had been written in 1874 to show that the positivist criteria failed, that history was the history of mind, the criterion of history the historian. But the influence of Bradley's book at the turn of the century was negligible. Before 1910 *Mind* published no study of historical thinking; the *Proceedings of the Aristotelian Society* for the years before 1920 include only two, both innocent of Bradley's argument, and neither close to the course that Collingwood would undertake.[62]

A more immediate inspiration for this reawakening in England of interest in the philosophy of history was the Italian idealist Benedetto Croce. The means through which Croce's thought gained influence at Oxford was John Alexander Smith of Magdalen, who had professed himself Croce's disciple in 1909.[63] Hegelian historicism was not new to England, but Croce's thought, and hence Smith's, was in some important respects revolutionary. Croce rejected Hegel's distinction between the real and the ideal in favor of principles borrowed from Vico and Kant that made all knowing historical and presented history as the content of consciousness.[64] In his inaugural of 1910, J. A. Smith defended the Crocean axiom: "All genuine knowledge is historical, is knowledge of his-

---

[61]R. G. Collingwood, *The Idea of History*, ed. T. M. Knox (Oxford: Clarendon, 1946) 127-33.

[62]The only article published in *PAS* before 1914 that recognized a debt to Bradley's *Presuppositions of Critical History* was Hastings Rashdall, "Causality and the Principles of Historical Evidence," *PAS* 6 (1905-1906): 1-34. See also David Morrison, "The Treatment of History by Philosophers," *PAS* (1913-1914): 291-321. Although there were several articles about time, *Mind* published nothing on history between 1898 and 1914. Collingwood thought the entire realist corpus contained only one reference to history (*Autobiography*, 84).

[63]Smith, "Philosophy," 229; Mure, "Croce and Oxford," 330.

[64]Croce criticized Hegel for leaving intact the dualism implicit in the philosophy of Kant, and devoted himself to describing a philosophic system in which reality simply is the historical and the historical is simply thought. This both Croce and Smith called Absolute Idealism, but it is not to be confused with the philosophy of F. H. Bradley, in which history is finally appearance.

tory"; and in 1915 he announced the corollary that "the only genuine and important history is contemporary history," by which Smith did not mean the topical, but the significant content of historical consciousness.[65] Within months this insight appeared in Collingwood's *Religion and Philosophy*, where Collingwood, following Croce and Smith, concluded that "historical fact is the only thing that exists and includes the whole universe."[66] The immediacy of the historical and the historical character of all knowledge became a kind of philosophic commonplace among the circle for which Smith provided inspiration. In Eliot's *Wasteland*, history is now and England. When the newly converted Magdalen don C. S. Lewis sat down to write *The Pilgrim's Regress* in 1932, history was the allegorical figure who provided the final, synthetic explanation that enabled the hero to return at last to Mother Kirk.

The recovery of history in England had been twofold. On the level of praxis, historical research had become important in every discipline, but especially in theology, philosophy, and literature. Patient research had become the model for scholarship, and the results were evident in the *English Historical Review*, in the *Journal of Theological Studies*, and in *Medium Aevum*, founded in 1932 by C. T. Onions. There were countless studies of political and ecclesiastical history, books and articles stretching in distinguished succession from Freeman's *General Sketch* to the *Cambridge History of England*; but for philosophy the most important scholarly result was the recovery of medieval thought inaugurated by Poole's *Illustrations* and developed by Webb and his contemporaries. Finally, there was the related development in the philosophy of history. Capping the theoretical development begun by Bradley in 1874 was *Human Nature and Human History*, the essay that became the heart of *The Idea of History*. All thinking was historical thinking, and the philosophical consideration of the writing of history and of the kind of knowledge gained was the most pressing task of metaphysicians.[67]

---

[65]Smith, *Knowing and Acting*, 18; "The Contribution of Greece and Rome," Francis Sydney Marvin, ed., *The Unity of Western Civilization* (London: Humphrey Milford, 1915) 69.

[66]R. G. Collingwood, *Religion and Philosophy* (London: Macmillan, 1916) 51.

[67]Collingwood, *Idea of History*, 205-31; *Religion and Philosophy*, 50-53; *Essay on Metaphysics*, 49-57.

C. C. J. Webb's career was roughly coterminous with the historical revolution that swept English letters. When he began to write in earnest in the 1890s, modern history was a discipline newly established in the university, and the Middle Ages were inaccessible to scholarship. It was Webb who presented Anselm and John of Salisbury to the early twentieth century as witnesses no less important for Western thought than Hobbes or Mill. Both Webb and his biographer were strangely diffident: Webb called himself an amateur, and L. W. Grensted wrote that Webb's historical studies were "rather a hobby than a part of his main taste in life."[68] But the hobby was prodigiously fertile. Webb's special gift to scholarship was an ability to see the fecundity of medieval thought, and hence of the Western intellectual tradition viewed in its entirety. Once Webb's pioneering studies broke ground, scholarly interest in the medieval philosophers became commonplace. Collingwood brought Anselm into the mainstream of English scholarship, and beginning with the generation of Collingwood and Lewis, St. Thomas, Dionysius the Areopagite, and John Scotus Erigena became familiar texts.

Webb the historian was never completely at home with Webb the idealist philosopher. Convinced that history was a significant kind of knowledge, he was still unsure that in this world, mind could have access to public truths of a final and comprehensive nature. Deeply religious, Webb was persuaded that reason must be free, that there was, as he wrote in his birthday address in 1944, no objective voice of authority in Pope, Church, or Bible.[69] This proposition, born of his idealism, was staunchly defended, from his early interest in Tyrrell to his scathing criticism in the 1940s of the works of Eric Mascall, whose theological certainty Webb found repugnant.[70] In theology Webb was a believing rationalist, falling in the ecclesiastical spectrum of the 1920s between Bosanquet, whose rejection of the historical claims of Christianity Webb found unacceptable, and Gore, whose near identification of Christendom with the Church Webb could not wholeheartedly share.[71]

---

[68]Webb, *Religious Experience*, 20.

[69]Ibid., 43.

[70]Clement C. J. Webb, "The Revolt Against Liberalism in Theology: A Study, in This Respect, of E. L. Mascall's *Christ, the Christian, and the Church*," *JTS* 48 (1947): 49-56; Review of *He Who Is*, by Eric Mascall, *JTS* 44 (1943): 110-15.

[71]Webb, "Bernard Bosanquet's Philosophy of Religion"; *Group Theories*, 193-94.

Webb had begun as a modernist sympathizer, but Modernism was itself a complex affair. Webb sympathized with the modernists' defense of critical historical method, and with their doubts that truth could be represented with finality by any historical institution, though as an idealist he did not share the almost positivistic understanding of real knowledge that typified Modernism.[72]

Webb's denial of the finality of any one truth, viewed objectively, was not a cause of despair or an occasion for his skepticism regarding ethical questions, but was in fact a testimony to his grand reliance upon the witness of both history and experience. Because he knew history, he knew that, viewed historically, the way is broad, while viewed in the light of personal knowledge and duty, it may be narrow indeed. Over a period of four decades the modernist element never triumphed. On his eightieth birthday Webb wrote that "neither the exercise of philosophical criticism upon Christian dogma nor the acknowledgement of the essential connection between Christian religious experience and that of those who do not 'profess and call themselves Christians' should divert from an adequate recognition of the uniqueness in fact of certain characteristics of Christianity which hinder it from taking its place alongside other religions and impose upon it a missionary vocation it cannot disavow."[73]

During his forty years as tutor and professor, Clement Webb touched hundreds of undergraduates and many of his colleagues. The sponsors of the volume published on his eightieth birthday formed a catalog of former students and fellow dons whose admiration Webb had won, including archbishops, distinguished intellectuals, and public servants.

Webb had broad acquaintance with philosophers and no detractors among them. The younger philosopher for whom Webb most consistently expressed respect was Collingwood. Their friendship had begun in the 1920s, when both had been among the philosophers Eliot liked to publish or review.[74] When Webb reviewed Collingwood's first book in 1917, he predicted that Collingwood would be a philosopher with whom the world would have to reckon, and Webb's prophecy was fulfilled by

---

[72]Webb, *Religious Experience*, 45.

[73]Ibid., 37.

[74]Eliot had reviewed Webb's *Group Theories of Religion* in the *International Journal of Ethicism* 27:1 (October 1916): 115-17.

Collingwood's books and by his election in 1935 to the Waynflete professorship.[75] Webb praised Collingwood's *Essay on Philosophical Method* in 1936 and his *Human Nature and Human History* in 1939. When Collingwood died in 1943, Webb wrote that he had been "one of the most brilliant thinkers of his generation."[76] Of course, the already venerable Webb did not need the younger philosopher's praise, but Collingwood called Webb's Gifford Lectures "learned and masterly."[77]

For C. S. Lewis, Clement Webb was a model of the Christian scholar. Webb was one of Lewis's five great Magdalen men, and the kind of debt Lewis owed is suggested by his reference in *Perelandra* to C. J., who had provided an etymology for *oyarsa*, the light-filled rulers of the planets.[78] The childless Professor and Mrs. Dimble who kept a Christian salon across the river from the college in *That Hideous Strength* are surely drawn from Clement and Eleanor Webb, whose hospitality at Holywell Ford was recalled by guests from undergraduates to von Hügel.[79]

Any summary of a scholarly life as diverse, full, and influential as Webb's will fail to do justice to the original, but two themes were seldom absent from his writing: the witness of history, both formal and personal; and the witness of reason to the intelligibility and truth of Christianity. If one of these interests had greater importance than the other, it was because one was novel. History had been used by the Victorians more to weaken than to commend belief in God. In Webb's hands, philosophers from Plato to Green were made witnesses to the reality of the apparently universal encounter with God. The shaping of Webb's mind

---

[75]Webb, Review of *Religion and Philosophy*, 281-82; Review of F. N. Powicke, *History, Freedom, and Religion, English Historical Review* 54 (1939): 520. Webb called Collingwood's *Essay on Philosophical Method* "one of the most remarkable and original among the philosophical books recently published in England" in "Nature and Grace," *JTS* 37 (1936): 113.

[76]Webb, Review of *The Idea of Nature*, 86; Review of *The Idea of History*, by R. G. Collingwood, *JTS* 46 (1945): 25.

[77]R. G. Collingwood, Review of *The Philosophy of the Good Life*, by Charles Gore, *Criterion* 10 (1930-1931): 560-62.

[78]Lewis, *Surprised by Joy*, 216; *Out of the Silent Planet* (New York: Macmillan, 1943) 152; Green and Hooper, *C. S. Lewis*, 162.

[79]C. S. Lewis, *That Hideous Strength* (New York: Macmillan, 1960) 28-33; Langstaff, *Oxford 1914*, 200; de la Bedoyère, *von Hügel*, 300.

had begun in a Tractarian and ecclesiological household. He had imbibed at Christ Church the best of the tradition of Green; indeed, without that experience his voluminous writing would have rung hollow. He had then been caught up in Oxford's new interest in history, and finally these influences had come together in a unique philosophical vocation.

When Webb spoke of those who had influenced him, he seldom failed to mention his first teachers, especially Cook Wilson and von Hügel.[80] Among his contemporaries there were three whose memory he especially treasured: H. W. B. Joseph, the gentle Harold Joachim, and John Alexander Smith.[81] With Smith, Webb had shared a philosophical conversation stretching over four decades, and his books have their share of acknowledgments to Smith. Though Smith could not write philosophy books, he could inspire them in others. Webb recalled him in 1944 as "that brilliant scholar, that master of discourse, the variety, originality, and suggestiveness of whose conversation will ever be treasured."[82]

Indeed, wherever one follows the threads of philosophic discourse at Oxford during the years 1900 to 1935, they lead—sometimes directly, sometimes circuitously—to John Alexander Smith, who during those years held a prestigious chair and served as lynchpin in a network of philosophical friendships based upon a love of language and of traditional metaphysical questions. Smith's dedication to paradox and good company, his Socratic pursuit of any and every question, and his fathomless patience and geniality made him seem hopelessly old-fashioned and benighted to the rising generation of Oxford positivists. Before their very eyes, camouflaged beneath his half-deliberate caricature of the great professor, he kept the idealist tradition alive.

---

[80]Webb, *Religious Experience*, 35-36; "Biographical," 339-40.

[81]Webb, *Religious Experience*, 36.

[82]Webb, *God and Personality*, 156n; *Religion and Theism*, 23n; *Studies in the History of Natural Theology*, 349; *Religious Experience*, 36.

•CHAPTER III•

John Alexander Smith and the Persistence of Metaphysics

He was not only a man of very great learning and of almost excessive ingenuity, but also by far the best teacher I have ever known. He had a wonderful gift for entering the minds of others. . . .

H. J. Paton,
"Fifty Years of Philosophy"

The Balliol tutor Paton knew in 1908 was an unforgettable teacher whom Lewis would revere twenty years later; whom Collingwood would still consider in 1939 one of Oxford's best philosophers; whom prudent men like Clement Webb would enjoy and respect, and brilliant contemporaries like H. H. Joachim would follow, some said almost uncritically.[1]

Smith's contemporaries and pupils were not, however, universally kind in their judgment of his attempt to erect a new idealism on the intellectual foundations provided by Kant and Croce. His Gifford lectures of 1930 were titled *The Heritage of Idealism*, but Smith, in Sir Malcolm Knox's words, "meandered on, at last broke down altogether, and nothing was published because there was nothing to publish."[2] Collingwood recalled in 1939 that Smith and Joachim had notoriously "failed to avert

---

[1]Joseph, "Harold Henry Joachim," 486-87.

[2]Malcolm Knox to the author, 23 January 1973.

the collapse of the school to which they belonged."[3] W. D. Ross believed that Smith's versatility "militated against the continuous efforts needed for the working out of a consistent system of thought, and his self-critical temper prevented him from writing much for publication." Further, Ross agreed with Bosanquet that Smith's enthusiasm for Croce had been unfortunate.[4] R. F. Harrod offered a darker view that was perhaps typical of Oxford's scientific establishment, recollecting J. A. Smith's conviction that philosophy could comprehend and criticize the sciences as a sign of "the insippiated parochialism and complacency" that had sapped England's strength between the wars.[5] Smith himself partly agreed, speaking in his farewell to his colleagues of a career in which "more might have been done," and of failures "owing to avoidable mistakes."[6] But beyond these admitted weaknesses, there was a quiet and considerable accomplishment. For forty-five years (especially after 1909, when he first took up a definite philosophical position of his own) Smith presided over a conversation that kept the metaphysical tradition he had inherited from Green and R. L. Nettleship alive, playing an important part in the intellectual formation of contemporaries like Hastings Rashdall, H. H. Joachim, and C. C. J. Webb, as well as younger philosophers like Collingwood, H. J. Paton, G. R. G. Mure, and Lewis.

John Alexander Smith, son of Andrew Smith, the clerk of County Ross, was born in 1863 at Dingwall in the Scottish Highlands. After Inverness Academy, Smith went on to Edinburgh, where he was Ferguson scholar in classics, and then, in 1884, to Balliol. The accent of County Ross never wore thin, and forty years after Smith left Edinburgh, Clement Webb noted that in the annual philosophy lecture to the British Academy, J. A. had defended idealism "in a strain of impassioned Scottish eloquence."[7]

---

[3]Collingwood, *Autobiography*, 18.

[4]Bosanquet to G. Dawes Hicks, 18 November 1912, in Muirhead, ed., *Bernard Bosanquet*, 145; Ross, "John Alexander Smith," 819.

[5]R. F. Harrod, *The Prof: A Personal Memoir of Lord Cherwell* (London: Macmillan, 1959) 21.

[6]J. A. Smith, Address to the Oxford Philosophical Society, 1936, SPM.

[7]Edinburgh *Scotsman*, 20 December 1939; WJB, 10 November 1924 [MS.Eng.misc.e.1167].

Smith's intellectual development was founded on a double interest in language and philosophy that the Greats curriculum naturally encouraged. He had an amazing insight regarding language and an inextinguishable enthusiasm for lexicography and etymology. During his undergraduate years he developed the facility that would make him by 1900 the foremost Aristotelian scholar at Oxford and a natural successor to Ingraham Bywater as president of the Oxford Aristotelian Society. From 1888 to 1891 Smith served as assistant to S. H. Butcher, professor of Greek at Edinburgh, but he then chose to return to Balliol as a tutor in philosophy.

The move back "to Oxford and philosophy" Smith described in 1924 as "little more than chance," and once there he dedicated himself chiefly to Aristotle—a study in which his duty as a philosopher could be discharged through his love for language—and to the dialectical exposition of the contending theories of knowledge current among the realists and idealists. Between 1891 and 1910 he gradually read the modern philosophers, though Hegel he "only dipped into and occasionally consulted," and though Green and Bradley, he wrote, "passed over my head." The only philosophers Smith found reliable during the years before his discovery of Croce were Kant, whose thought "seemed to afford a solid framework (but only a framework) of ethical theory," and John Grote (1813-1866), the Knightsbridge Professor of Moral Philosophy at Cambridge, who greatly influenced Smith, and in whose writings Smith found "not indeed a system, but fundamental principles illuminated by a wealth of detail."[8] Smith's affection for John Grote, who combined the idealist defense of traditional ethics with an interest in philology, and who was willing to argue the theories of Mill and John Venn on their own ground, might have provided a clue to the philosophy Smith would adopt as Wayneflete professor.

In 1900, however, there was no indication that Smith would become the postwar defender of idealism at Oxford. Since his attachment to idealism was personal, involving chiefly piety toward Nettleship and Edward Caird, Smith felt free to join Cook Wilson in experimenting with realism. As early as 1905 his conversion to the school of Wilson and

---

[8]Smith, "Philosophy," 228-29. On Grote, see Lauchlin D. Macdonald, *John Grote: A Critical Estimate of his Work* (The Hague: Martinus Nijhoff, 1966).

Prichard was rumored, and in 1908 Smith was still wrestling with the realist proposition that knowledge was merely objective, though as H. J. Paton remembered Smith's saying, "with ever increasin' difficulty."[9] Smith recalled in his intellectual autobiography that he had indeed "for a time defended a 'realistic' account," which "implied that what was known was and was what it is in utter independence of and priority to its being known by any knower." But, he added, "I do not regret the time I spent under its spell, for it was then I learned to know it for what it is." Yet the dalliance with realism had been unproductive: "We were (most of us) agreed in opposition to the 'subjective' or 'personal' forms of Idealism, . . . to the psychology . . . connected with it, and . . . to the Protean forms of the then vociferous Pragmatism." "Though I would have been prepared, as I still am, to look upon these as forms of un-philosophy," Smith added, "I had no philosophy of my own."[10] Lacking any firm philosophical convictions, he naturally published little, but as a teacher Smith was highly successful, and through his daily contacts with colleagues and weekly conferences with students, he gained a personal influence second only to Cook Wilson's. When the Waynflete Chair was vacated unexpectedly by Thomas Case in 1909, it was certain that Smith would be among the candidates.

From the point of view of an unprejudiced elector, the most promising scholar might have been Hastings Rashdall (whom Case himself probably favored), Clement Webb, or Harold Joachim. In 1907 Rashdall had published *The Theory of Good and Evil*, which, when added to his *Personal Idealism* (1902), and a monumental history of European universities published in 1895, made him the most prolific writer.[11] Rashdall was also a gifted teacher, but his unorthodox theological views,

---

[9]Paton, "Fifty Years of Philosophy," 341. Hoernlé wrote Bosanquet late in 1905 that J. A. Smith was suspected of having become a committed realist. Bosanquet replied that Hoernlé was surely mistaken. Probably he was not. See Muirhead, ed., *Bosanquet*, 104. Sir Malcolm Knox believed "J. A. Smith was one of the Oxford Realists until he went to Italy" (Knox to the author, 24 January 1973).

[10]Smith, "Philosophy," 230.

[11]When Rashdall left the university to become dean of Carlisle in 1917, Case wrote (3 November), "You differ from most of your contemporaries in being always an authority on subjects about which you write, and ought most certainly to have been promoted to a professorial chair in Oxford" [MS.Eng.lett.349 (59)].

unexceptionable in a lay tutor, clouded his candidacy.[12] By 1909 Clement Webb was an acknowledged authority on medieval theology, and had begun to produce the treatises that would make him Oxford's most important philosopher of religion. Even the diffident Joachim had written *The Nature of Truth* (1906), which Collingwood considered the finest book on metaphysics published by any of the idealists after Bradley's *Appearance and Reality*.[13]

Given this distinguished competition, J. A. Smith's election to the Waynflete professorship was not inevitable. Partly because his intellectual *habitus* made him acutely aware that any solution might conceal further contradictions, partly because he came from an Oxford tradition in which conversation was preferred to publication, Smith had by 1909 published almost nothing. "Books," he more than once remarked, "can't answer back."[14] His discourse was complicated by a love for philology that led him from logic to language and back again. When the cable telling of Case's resignation reached him in Naples, Smith launched a successful campaign, with the encouragement of his friends, for the Waynflete professorship. His most obvious asset was his towering reputation as a teacher, to which former students like William Temple and G. L. Stevenson (later C. S. Lewis's tutor in history) and university powers like J. L. Strachan-Davidson, master of Balliol, testified. In March 1910 Smith included in the testimonials submitted to the Waynflete electors a partial list of topics on which he had given public lectures in the university: "The *Republic* of Plato, the *Ethics* and *De Anima* of Aristotle, the *Novum Organum* of Bacon, the Logic of Aristotle, the Metaphysical System of Aristotle; the Pre-Socratics, the Psychology of the Stoics and Epicureans, the Ancient Skeptics; the Concepts and Methods of Modern Science; the Theory of Knowledge from Descartes to Kant (including Locke, Berkeley, Hume, Spinoza, and Leibnitz), the Philos-

---

[12]Brand Blanshard recalled that Rashdall did not believe God to be omnipotent (Schilpp, 28), and in 1911 Rashdall was the only member of The Group who took J. M. Thompson's part without qualification.

[13]Collingwood, *Autobiography*, 18.

[14]Smith to Rashdall, December 1922, in Matheson, *Hastings Rashdall*, 221. Smith probably had in mind Plato's reflection that those who go to written texts with a question will find one unvarying answer.

ophy of Religion from Kant to Hegel, the Proofs of the Existence of God; Logic." "I have," he added, "of late years directed my studies and public teaching specially to Metaphysics."[15]

Nor was Smith without impressive claims to scholarly distinction. He was editor of the Oxford Aristotle, and president of the Oxford Aristotelian Society. As a pupil of R. L. Nettleship and a friend of Edward Caird, Smith also held a place in the succession of Green. A master of academic politics, well connected socially, J. A. was among the most popular figures in Oxford, numbering among his close acquaintances Rashdall, Webb, A. L. Smith, A. J. Carlyle, and F. S. Marvin.[16] On the death of Strachan-Davidson in 1914, J. A. was considered for the mastership of Balliol, but A. L. Smith, whom the electors thought better known in London, was preferred.[17]

Respected, a gifted teacher, his scholarship almost universally admired, Smith lacked only one thing: a coherent and well-worked-out philosophical position that touched contemporary thought. This deficiency was fortuitously erased by Smith's discovering in Naples, as he returned to England to take up the duties of his chair, the writings of the Italian idealist Benedetto Croce. What Smith found in Croce was a philosophic method rooted in language and in history, an appealing alternative to the English tradition of Hume and Mill, whose roots ran ultimately back to the thought of the seventeenth-century Italian Giambattista Vico. Smith read "around and behind Croce, so as at least to place him in his proper setting and perspective." Croce, Smith wrote, "made clear to me where lay or ran the main currents of modern, that is

---

[15]*Letter of Application to the Electors to the Waynflete Chair of Moral and Metaphysical Philosophy from J. A. Smith, M.A., Balliol College, Oxford, with Testimonials in Favor of his Candidature*, SPM. Typical was Strachan-Davidson's comment that Smith "always learns while he teaches, and what he learned is vivified by a spark of originality which I venture to think is not far from genius."

[16]On J. A.'s friendship with A. L. Smith, see *Arthur Lionel Smith, Master of Balliol (1866-1924): A Biography and Some Reminiscences by His Wife* (London: John Murray, 1928) 136, 152. Carlyle's letters are in the Bodleian. Francis Sydney Marvin (1863-1943) devoted his life to education by organizing summer schools, in which J. A. Smith sometimes participated, and serving as inspector of schools for various English districts. Apart from education, his interests were mainly historical, and he edited several collections of historical and historiographical essays. Marvin's letters are in the Bodleian.

[17]Langstaff, *Oxford 1914*, 256.

living, philosophy, gave me good conscience in throwing over masses of antiquated lumber, and steadied my mind upon large, fertile and vital principles."

Smith was aware that the objectivity of the realists made human nature and human history mere artifacts, and aware as well of the tendency of the subjective idealists to banish the solid world of common experience. He discovered in Croce and thus began to teach, with all the force of his conversation and personality, the principle that "the Real is a (or the) History, and every genuine part of it is historical."[18] It followed that all thinking is historical thinking. The position Smith developed answered, at least in theory, the realist critique of personal, or subjective, idealism, by making the presuppositions of thought public, and in that sense objective. At the same time it located knowledge in the moral and personal context, apart from which the followers of Green and Caird considered it sterile.

To many of Smith's colleagues, his enthusiasm for the Italians represented a kind of backsliding into a discredited idealism, distinguishable from the idealism of Green and Nettleship only by its questionable paradoxes. The Waynflete electors, who had voted before Smith's newfound interest in the Italians could have been known at Oxford, had believed they were electing a polymathic, thoroughly competent academic, an expert on Aristotle with realist leanings. The sense of betrayal men like Thomas Case (in the face of whose determined opposition Smith might never have been given the chair), Cook Wilson, and Bosanquet felt does much to explain Smith's isolation from his own contemporaries, few of whom were by 1910 still zealous for the school of Green. Bernard Bosanquet thought Smith's new allegiance a pity, and after 1917

[18]Smith, "Philosophy," 236. G. R. G. Mure called Smith "the only quite wholehearted Crocean among Oxford thinkers" ["Benedetto Croce and Oxford," *Philosophical Quarterly* 4 (1954): 330]. Brand Blanshard recalled hearing Smith say that "he had acquired a strong interest in Croce from hearing talk about him in England; that when he went to Rome he caught flu, and had to spend that day in the hotel room; that he used his time to read an Italian grammar; and that he was reading Croce by the end of the week" (Blanshard to the author, 31 May 1984). The cause of Croce's popularity in England about 1909 was probably his presence and impressive performance at the International Congress of Philosophy in Heidelberg in 1908.

was unwilling to claim the title idealist in even a qualified sense.[19] But Bosanquet was in London and Bradley was inaccessible, while Smith, now a committed Crocean, was available to the undergraduates and to the vast network of formal and informal societies—ready to talk philosophy with any don or student whom he considered serious. In 1913 Josiah Royce thought of inviting Smith to Harvard, but to no avail. "J. A. Smith is really great," Royce wrote to Ralph Barton Perry, "but as inaccessible for our purposes as an archangel, and as dialectical as Mephistopheles,—although otherwise a beautiful personality."[20]

Between 1910 and the end of the war in 1918, Smith labored to clarify and establish his philosophical position. Before the university began to empty itself in 1914, he had probably met a young Pembroke tutor who would, at least to some degree, adopt him as a model. Robin Collingwood was the son of William Gershom Collingwood, a painter who had been John Ruskin's steadfast companion at Brantwood during the long twilight of the old man's genius, then carved out a substantial reputation as Ruskin's biographer, and as an archaeologist. The youngest of four children and the only son, Robin Collingwood was educated by his father in a household that was full of painting, books, and music, but less generously provided with middle-class means. In 1908, after a stormy, half-successful career at Rugby, during which he learned mostly from books of his own choosing, Collingwood was admitted to his father's college, University. There his tutor was Carritt, "another prominent member of the realist school," who duly sent Collingwood to the lectures of Cook Wilson and H. A. Prichard.[21]

Collingwood remained vaguely committed to the realist epistemology until 1917. In his first years as a tutor, he concentrated not on the

---

[19]Bosanquet to Dawes Hicks, 18 November 1912, Muirhead, ed., *Bosanquet*, 145; Bernard Bosanquet, "Realism and Metaphysics," *Philosophical Review* 26 (1917): 6: "For myself I reject the term idealism. . . ."

[20]Josiah Royce to Ralph Barton Perry, John Clendenning, ed., *The Letters of Josiah Royce* (Chicago: University of Chicago Press, 1970) 591. Royce was intent on recruiting an English idealist for Harvard. Smith, he quickly realized, would never leave Oxford, but R. F. Alfred Hoernlé did go to Harvard in 1914.

[21]On R. G. Collingwood's education, see William M. Johnston, *The Formative Years of R. G. Collingwood* (The Hague: Martinus Nijhoff, 1967); Peter Jones, "Collingwood's Debt to his Father," *Mind* 78 (1969): 437-39; Collingwood, *Autobiography*, 22.

doctrine of knowledge as such, but on developing a method of reading and questioning the text—"Let us see if this is what Kant really said"—and had become something of an expert on Aristotle as well, having by 1913 translated three books of the *De Anima*. By 1912 Collingwood had also become interested in the newly popular Italian idealists, and was at work on a translation of Benedetto Croce's *Philosophy of Giambattista Vico*.[22] Aristotle, Vico, and the Italian idealists would remain interests of Collingwood throughout his life, but it is hard to find in his early manuscripts much evidence that history and philosophy of history were important intellectual concerns. Collingwood wrote in 1939 that no single philosopher or argument, but rather history itself, had first made him aware that the realism of his undergraduate days would fail: "If I had thought it possible to forewarn the 'realists' . . . I should have said, 'You must pay more attention to history. Your positive doctrines about knowledge are incompatible with what happens . . . in historical research, and your critical methods are misused on doctrines which in historical fact were never held by those to whom you ascribe them.' "[23] His reflections on the Albert Memorial in 1915 or 1916 and his study of the archaeology of Roman Britain had already proved fruitful.

Collingwood wrote in the *Autobiography* that he had worked out "the idea of the living past together with a good many [ideas] connected with it" by about 1920.[24] In this Collingwood had undoubtedly been helped not only by Croce, but by Smith, whose inaugural of 1910 had built toward the point that "All genuine knowledge is historical—is knowledge of history." The living past was, of course, the past constructed by historical imagination. The earliest testimonies to the currency of this idea in Oxford are to be found in "The Value of History," an essay Smith read, perhaps around 1900, before an informal society and in a typed manuscript, obviously intended for publication, entitled "The Theory of History," included among the Smith papers, but not his work. In "The Value of History," Smith insisted that the past "is present to us only by

---

[22]*The Philosophy of Giambattista Vico* (London: Macmillan, 1913). Collingwood had written Douglas Ainslie about this translation in 1912, and the second edition of Ainslie's translation of Croce's *Aesthetic* was corrected by Collingwood.

[23]Collingwood, *Autobiography*, 28.

[24]Ibid., 97, 98.

an activity of mind. We recreate it and bring it before ourselves."[25] "The Theory of History," which exists only because Smith kept it, was written probably about 1915 by an author who cites Smith, Croce, Vico, and Gentile as authorities.[26] Its argument is a defense of Croce's principle that "you cannot write history without a philosophy, and, second, that philosophy does not stand outside history." The philosopher does not dwell on an innumerable series of "facts" or "incidents," but recreates the past in imagination.[27]

The principles assumed by "The Theory of History" and "The Value of History" were 1) the inseparable, hermeneutic relation between philosophy and history; 2) the conviction that the past exists only in the present, as it is reconstructed by imagination; and 3) the concomitant belief that the present alone is real. These ideas, absent or incompletely developed in Collingwood's *Religion and Philosophy*,[28] which he finished about 1914, are themes of his metaphysics after 1920. Indeed, Collingwood is the most obvious candidate for author of "The Theory of History." While proof of this claim must await more careful study, denial of his authorship would require discovering another Oxford philosopher whose writings Smith would have preserved, who would have cited Smith, Croce, and Gentile favorably, and who would have concluded his essay with this sentence: "We must say what we believe, we must write history as we see it: it is only a stupid interruption of our task if we are always to assure one another that these are only our personal opinions."

Given his interests: Aristotle, Croce, history, philosophy, and religion, it is hard to doubt that Collingwood knew Smith during his undergraduate years, or that Smith's enthusiasms had to some degree inspired Collingwood even before the war. The first evidence of their ac-

---

[25]SPM, 1:1.

[26]SPM, 2:4 (132). "The Theory of History" was written when Bosanquet's *The Value and Destiny of the Individual* (1913) was recent (121); before the German emperor was deposed in 1918 (54); when Asquith was prime minister, that is, between 1908 and 1916 (85); after the war had begun in 1914 (50); and after the author had developed an interest in the career of the wartime prime minister of Belgium, M. de Broqueville (52), all of which suggests a date about 1915 or 1916. The Greek calligraphy (62, 99), the only handwriting on the paper, is probably Collingwood's.

[27]"The Theory of History," 1, 10, 12.

[28]Collingwood, *Religion and Philosophy*, 49-52.

quaintance is in 1916, when Smith praised Collingwood's translation of Croce's *Vico* in the *Hibbert Journal*.[29] By then Collingwood—his flirtation with the realism of Carritt and Prichard declining—was in London. With his father and his sister Barbara, he worked at the Admiralty. There Collingwood met Evelyn Underhill, an acquaintance from which his later essay on mysticism would grow,[30] pursued his meditations on Scott's doubtful monument, and published his first book. *Religion and Philosophy* (1916) was an ambitious effort to prove, in the face of the new psychology, that thought about religion was a kind of knowledge, not mere feeling, and that the Christian religion might be considered critically as the solution to certain metaphysical problems.[31] Clement Webb reviewed the book for the *Oxford Magazine*, and Eliot examined it for the *International Journal of Ethics*. Both reacted favorably, though *Mind*, inaugurating a tradition of withholding approval from Collingwood's efforts that would last his lifetime, believed the defense of religion Collingwood offered was too intellectual.[32] The translation of Croce and *Religion and Philosophy* secured Collingwood's reputation as a promising academic.

The war over, Collingwood wrote, "I came back to Oxford an opponent of the 'realists.' I had not learned the uselessness of reading papers and holding discussions on philosophical subjects; so . . . I read a paper to my colleagues, trying to convince them that Cook Wilson's central positive doctrine, 'knowing makes no difference to what is known,' was meaningless."[33] In the early 1920s Collingwood still occasionally spoke of himself as an idealist. Indeed, with J. A. Smith, H. Wildon Carr, Paton, and G. R. C. Mure, he gave substance to the new idealism

---

[29]Smith, Review of *The Problem of Art and History*, 505.

[30]Margaret Cropper, *Life of Evelyn Underhill* (New York: Harper and Brothers, 1958) 58-59. Underhill recalled Robin Collingwood and his sister Barbara (later Barbara Gnospelius) as young artistic intellectuals. See also Underhill and Collingwood, "Can the New Idealism Dispense with Mysticism?"

[31]Collingwood, *Religion and Philosophy*, v, xiii.

[32]George Galloway, Review of *Religion and Philosophy* by R. G. Collingwood, *Mind* 28 (1919): 365-77. Galloway wrote: "The writer exaggerates the intellectual side of religion," and "seriously understates the importance of feeling" (365). See C. Lewy, "*Mind* under G. E. Moore," *Mind* 85 (1976): 42-43.

[33]Collingwood, *Autobiography*, 44.

that flourished briefly in Oxford at the close of the war, and of which Collingwood's *Speculum Mentis* (1924) is perhaps the chief monument. The Oxford philosophers who identified themselves as idealists, or who were at least clearly not of Wilson's following, still had written little, and did not, in 1918, consider themselves part of any movement. Collingwood's *Truth and Contradiction* was rejected by a publisher in 1917. In it he had argued that the propositions into which the realists reduced the arguments of their opponents might have little or nothing to do with the questions their opponents wished to answer.[34]

It was, Collingwood remembered, an era of *epigoni*. Smith mused in 1916 that during the last fifty years "no stars of the first magnitude" had appeared in the philosophical firmament.[35] In the 1920s, few graduates sought careers in philosophy; "Collingwood and I," Paton noted, "were the only representatives of our generation—a slender bridge between predecessors at least ten years older and successors at least ten years younger."[36] If during this period of eclipse idealism had a center at Oxford, it was within the Deipnosophic, a society over which Smith usually presided, and which was apparently an alternative to the Oxford Philosophical Society as Schiller had founded it. Webb and Collingwood attended the Deipnosophic faithfully, as did Ross, Carritt, Prichard, and a few others. Collingwood read his paper on realism, his first attack on it, to the Oxford Philosophical Society in November 1920, and later wrote de Ruggerio, "No one seemed much interested, but afterwards a small and rather exclusive body of philosophers which meets every week under J. A. Smith's presidency asked me to join them, they being all men much older than myself and evidently intending to do me an honor." Collingwood complained, as he would throughout his career, that teas and papers did little good, but he nevertheless attended, often in Webb's company.[37]

Collingwood and Paton were indeed the young philosophers whose careers bridged the chasm separating the Edwardian university and the

---

[34]Ibid., 18.

[35]Ibid., 18; J. A. Smith, "Philosophy and Theism," *Quarterly Review* 225 (1916): 291.

[36]Paton, "Fifty Years," 345.

[37]Collingwood to de Ruggiero, 20 March 1921, *HAS*, 23.

chastened, self-doubting Oxford of 1918. Among the men who came back from France in 1918, there was one aspirant to philosophy in whom his tutors saw special promise. Carritt, who had examined him when he first applied to University in 1916, recalled in 1922 that Clive Staples Lewis had been an astonishingly well-read candidate.[38] Lewis had soon left Oxford for service in France, but he returned to University College in January 1919, took a first in Classical Moderations in 1920, and began Greats. Like Collingwood, his philosophy tutor was Carritt, who found in Lewis a willing pupil. Lewis was very much "against government" in 1919, and since idealism still seemed to dominate, Carritt's realism appealed.[39] Mark Studdock, the young academic who serves as the hero of Lewis's *That Hideous Strength*, is perhaps Lewis's commentary on his own aspirations during the immediate postwar period. Studdock was an unhappy, fashionably skeptical, decently ambitious scholar who salved his violations of his conscience with the advice, "It's better to be on the inside."[40] In 1924 Lewis had explained to his father his willingness to take an academic post he did not really want: "Well, its poorly paid and temporary, . . . but its better to be inside than out."[41]

Realism was a likely philosophy for a promising scholar, but by 1922, having taken his first in Greats, neither labor nor ambition had yet won Lewis an appointment. In July he gave up a holiday to devote himself to the writing of a paper he hoped would win a fellowship at Magdalen; besides, it was good "to be on the spot," to be seen.[42] But in November President Warren of Magdalen returned the "Hegemony of Moral Value" to Lewis, noting, "I am afraid you cannot have done yourself full justice."[43] Then the aspiring philosopher buckled down to complete the English school, English being a "rising subject" that would add a string to his academic bow.[44]

---

[38]LJ, 8:163 [23 June 1922].

[39]Lewis, *Surprised by Joy*, 209.

[40]Lewis, *That Hideous Strength*, 17.

[41]C. S. Lewis to Albert Lewis, May 1924, *LCSL*, 93.

[42]Ibid., July 1922, *LCSL*, 79.

[43]Herbert Warren to C. S. Lewis, 4 November 1922, SPM, 3:3.

[44]C. S. Lewis to Albert Lewis, 18 May 1922, *LCSL*, 75.

In the early 1920s the future looked as bleak to Smith as it did to the struggling Lewis. The Harvard realist W. P. Montague had come to Oxford in the summer of 1920, and Montague's presence had made J. A. Smith acutely aware that the realism he combated so vigorously was hydra-headed, sporting an American branch capable of producing works like *The New Realism* (1912). Smith read the book, then wrote Professor Montague a seven-page letter denying that the idealism he espoused was subjective within Montague's meaning, and attacking the realist cliché that the act of knowing left knower and known unchanged.[45]

Apart from the disturbing vitality of realism at home and abroad, Smith was struck by his apparent inability to transmit his metaphysical ideals. He probably knew something of Lewis, for as Magdalen's most distinguished philosopher, Smith would certainly have reviewed the candidates for the post Lewis had sought in 1922. But Lewis was then comfortably, if loosely, in the camp of the realists, sufficiently sympathetic to Carritt's realism to have been appointed Carritt's substitute when Carritt accepted an invitation to lecture at the University of Michigan in the fall of 1924.[46] Perhaps Collingwood afforded Smith some comfort, for they were certainly friends by 1920, but beside Collingwood there was only Paton. Apart from Joachim and Webb, Smith was isolated among his contemporaries. By 1920 his unfashionable defense of Croce had cost him the sympathy of Bosanquet, who disapproved of Smith's enthusiasm for Croce as soon as he had heard of it, and was willing to disagree in print with Smith's assessment of Croce's importance. He announced that he was "shocked to find" in the Italian philosopher's work "what seems an overstraining of the undeniable truths—the conversion of familiar platitudes into untenable paradoxes."[47]

The mind of the Waynflete professor was laid bare in a letter he wrote to Hastings Rashdall on 29 December 1922:

> I . . . find it so difficult to get in touch with my juniors in the subfaculty that I am not sure of my diagnosis. . . . Certainly (with Joachim

---

[45]J. A. Smith to W. P. Montague, 4 October 1920, SPM. See also William P. Montague, "The Story of American Realism," *Philosophy* 12 (1937): 140-61.

[46]C. S. Lewis to Albert Lewis, May or June 1924, *LCSL*, 93.

[47]Bernard Bosanquet, Review of *The Philosophy of Giovanni Gentile* (Aristotelian Society, 1919) by J. A. Smith, *Mind* 29 (1920): 369.

in my company) I feel a growing isolation. In spite of all personal obligations I seem to myself still to be bourne along the old Idealistic stream, but as I have said in diminishing company. It is odd how strong the old Cook Wilson tradition is. . . . I find myself constantly but fruitlessly suspecting that my failure somehow connects with his taking mathematics as the type of what knowledge is at its best, while my own tendency is to look for it in what has been accomplished in philosophy itself when that "proves" itself in the interpretation of the higher levels of experience. . . . In brief, what appears to me the most urgent *philosophandum* is the substance of history as it has been slowly fashioned and transmitted in religious, moral, political &c experiences, explicated in doctrine, and embodied in operative institutions. I am less and less disposed to look for this matter or reflection in the works of professional philosophers and regret nothing more than that I have so late discovered the academic narrowness of the basis on which my thinking rests. I cannot see any clear signs among our juniors that the necessity of such widening is recognized (forgive the growls!), rather a tendency to a sort of provincialism, or even parochialism, in speculation. You have done your part in preserving the memory of the older wider vistas and larger issues.[48]

Smith's letter was the complaint of a philosopher who believed metaphysics as he knew it was endangered, and who saw little future for himself or his school. But just as Smith's disappointment seemed justified, his intellectual friendship with philosophers of the younger generation seemed to bear fruit. In 1924 Smith's *The Nature of Art* appeared, and in the next year came Collingwood's *Outlines of a Philosophy of Art*. Discernible in each was the same traditional and idealistic metaphysical context and a pronounced loyalty to Croce.[49] Smith's earliest extant letter to Collingwood dates from 1925, and is a lengthy critique of "The Nature and Aims of a Philosophy of History," which Collingwood had read for the Aristotelian Society on 16 March 1925.[50] The next year Collingwood

---

[48]J. A. Smith to Hastings Rashdall, 29 December 1922, [MS.Eng.lett.362 (66)].

[49]J. A. Smith, *The Nature of Art: An Open Letter to the Professor of Poetry in the University of Oxford* (Oxford: Clarendon Press, 1924); R. G. Collingwood, *Outlines of a Philosophy of Art* (London: Oxford University Press, 1925). *Speculum Mentis or the Map of Knowledge* covers much of the same ground. Collingwood's interest in Croce was increasingly evident. See *CUM* 310; R. G. Collingwood, "Croce's Philosophy of History," *HJ* 19 (1920-1921): 263-78.

[50]SPM. Smith's manuscript is titled "History and Philosophy of History (suggested by Collingwood's paper Arist. Soc.)," and dated 6 March 1925. These notes were intended for Collingwood.

complimented Smith by asking him to provide a preface for an English translation of Croce's *Autobiography*. Between 1927, when Croce's *Autobiography* was published, and 1932, the deepening friendship between Smith and Collingwood is unattested by any document; but three letters from Collingwood to Smith, with Smith's responses, written in 1932 and 1933, display their alliance in its maturity.

The first is Collingwood's response to a summary of H. A. Prichard's "Duty and Ignorance of Fact." Collingwood had left the lecture early, and Smith, realizing the significance of Prichard's essay, had forwarded a synopsis. Collingwood replied to Smith at length, concluding:

> These are rough notes hastily written down, and only sent because of my belief you will understand what I mean better than I have been able to say it. That it will be worth your while to read them I can hardly hope: but if you and I are to be fellow conspirators against the minute philosophers we ought, I suppose, to indulge in a certain amount of conspiratorial correspondence.[51]

The minute philosophers (a reference to Pope's *Dunciad*) would appear as a chapter title in Collingwood's *An Autobiography*.[52] Prichard's essay was in its way as important as G. E. Moore's "Refutation of Idealism" (1903), for in it Prichard argued that obligation was not an idea or a thought, but a fact—a circumstance irrelevant to the will or knowledge of a moral agent. This was, as Webb put it, Prichard's "curious and arid moral doctrine of duties which need not be good actions," which denied "any meaning to 'the good.' "[53] It was this doctrine Collingwood had in mind when he wrote of the decay of the teaching of moral philosophy at Oxford in the *Autobiography*.[54]

Another long exchange followed in November, but the most telling testimony to the friendship between Smith and Collingwood was Col-

---

[51]R. G. Collingwood to J. A. Smith, 27 June 1932, SPM 1:22. Prichard's "Duty and Ignorance of Fact" was the Annual Philosophical Lecture of the Henriette Hertz Trust of the British Academy. It was published in *PBA* and reprinted in W. D. Ross, ed., *Moral Obligation: Essays and Lectures by H. A. Prichard* (Oxford: Clarendon Press, 1949) 18-39.

[52]Collingwood, *Autobiography*, 15. See also Cicero, *de Divinatione*, 1:62.

[53]WJB, 6 March 1930 [MS.Eng.misc.d.1122].

[54]Collingwood, *Autobiography*, 47-49.

lingwood's letter of December 1933. Collingwood had sent J. A. a copy of his *Essay on Philosophical Method* (1933), and Smith had responded with a lengthy criticism. To this Collingwood replied:

> First I must thank you, and most heartily, not for your expressions of interest and good will towards my speculations,—I knew I could count on that—but for the care and candor with which you stated your doubts concerning their foundations. That is a real service, and one of whose value I am deeply sensible.

What follows is a long defense of the possibility that any philosophical method might exist against the ever-Socratic J. A., who doubted that any predetermined method was possible. Collingwood concluded:

> It is perhaps mean to quote a man against himself, but you once said that metaphysics is the best possible knowledge of the best possible object. . . .
>
> But I have written too much already for your forebearance. Thank you for giving me the opportunity: in writing to you I write to myself and seem to come nearer to what I have learnt from yourself to regard as the goal of philosophy—the knowledge of my own ignorance.[55]

The following year, 1935, Collingwood was elected J. A. Smith's successor in the Waynflete Chair. The only testimonial Collingwood presented the electors was from Samuel Alexander. This choice circumvented overt reliance on the recommendations of the politically unpopular idealists and appealed to Collingwood's fierce sense of his own independence as well as to his genuine admiration for Alexander; but J. A. had urged the appointment, and had probably campaigned as earnestly as he had when Joachim was considered for the Wykeham professorship in 1919.[56] In his inaugural Collingwood duly acknowledged "the predecessor whose wisdom and friendship have enriched me these many past years."[57] Collingwood read "On the so-called Idea of Causation" for the Aristotelian Society on 24 January 1938,[58] and Smith wrote

[55]Collingwood to Smith, 16 December 1933, SPM, 3:20.

[56]Tomlin, "The Philosophy of R. G. Collingwood," 117.

[57]R. G. Collingwood, *The Historical Imagination: An Inaugural Delivered at Oxford 28 October 1935* (Oxford: Clarendon Press, 1935) 3.

[58]*PAS* 38 (1937-1938): 85-112.

in response, Καλῶς, καλῶς . . . substantially right, sound, and wise. I am grateful to you for having done so much of my thinking for me."[59] The kind of influence J. A. had exerted is suggested by Collingwood's note in *An Essay on Philosophical Method.* Noting that the Platonic dialogues were intended not as studies in the history of thought but as "models for the conduct of philosophical discussion," Collingwood wrote, "I am not sure whether or not I had the first suggestion of this idea many years ago, from the conversation of Professor J. A. Smith."[60] Part of the careful tone of respect evident in Collingwood's letters and references to Smith was born of Collingwood's desire for a chair and his knowledge that J. A.'s support was important to that quest.[61] But one asks prefaces of those for whom one has deep respect and sympathies of long duration, and the correspondence of the years 1929 to 1939 cannot in substance be considered anything other than the memorial of a friendly and sincere philosophical alliance.

The other young philosopher Smith certainly influenced in the 1920s was C. S. Lewis. How the letter from Herbert Warren, president of Magdalen, informing Lewis that he had not won the fellowship he sought in 1922 made its way into the J. A. Smith papers is a puzzle. Perhaps it was passed on to Smith through P. V. M. Beneke, Lewis's tutor and Smith's close friend. That Smith kept for seventeen years a letter explaining in the most solemn language Lewis's unsuitability for a college post is certainly a testimonial to Smith's early interest in Lewis. C. S. Lewis was finally made a fellow of Magdalen in 1925 with the understanding that he would "help out in philosophy" as well as tutor in literature.[62] When he came to Magdalen, Lewis in fact left the chance of a career in philosophy behind. He had, he wrote his father, brought back from the philosophic heights something of value; but, he added, "I escape with joy from the one definite drawback of philosophy—its solitude. . . . No one sympathizes with your adventures because no one understands them."[63]

---

[59]J. A. Smith to R. G. Collingwood, 30 January 1938, CPB.

[60]Collingwood, *Essay on Philosophical Method*, 14, n. 2.

[61]Collingwood had asked Croce to recommend him for the White's professorship of moral philosophy in Corpus Christi in 1928. The post went to H. A. Prichard. See Rubinoff, "Philosophy and History," 53.

[62]C. S. Lewis to Albert Lewis, 26 May 1925, *LCSL*, 103.

[63]Lewis to Albert Lewis, June 1925; Lewis, *Selected Essays*, viii.

After Lewis's election, Smith, perennially vice-president of Magdalen, welcomed Lewis; they shared anecdotes and walks around the garden, the great professor's attentions warming the heart of the still-ambitious younger scholar.[64]

C. S. Lewis wrote of his undergraduate years, "I had been defending it (realism) ever since I began reading philosophy," but by 1922 he had concluded that this rising philosophy demanded conclusions in ethics, logic, and aesthetics that he found "unbelievable, . . . in a quite literal sense." Therefore, he had become an exponent of the atheistic, "stoical monism" that characterized his New Look.[65] Barfield had been the immediate cause of Lewis's abandonment of the realist epistemology, but after 1925 Lewis found at the breakfast table another philosophical guide, and it was Smith, with Beneke, C. T. Onions, C. C. J. Webb, and F. E. Brightman who provided for Lewis an ideal of the learned life. Gradually Lewis passed from idealism to pantheism to theism. On the first stages of that journey he would have found Smith a genial guide, willing to talk philosophy far into the night.[66] By 1929, when Adam Fox came to Magdalen, Smith, Lewis, and P. V. M. Beneke were breakfast companions, and Fox remembered that though Lewis, "a philosopher as well as a man of letters," had "a great respect for Beneke, he had real reverence for J. A."[67] Perhaps it is not too much to suggest that J. A., "an old Scotsman who had devoted a long life to clearing up his own mind and other peoples'," who espoused a careful philosophic agnosticism, and "had no great opinion of the Church" was the model for the Socratic, unbelieving MacPhee who appears in *That Hideous Strength* as the goodwilled but wrongheaded and skeptical defender of reason. The patient toleration of MacPhee in the eschatological community of St. Anne's mirrored the Christian Lewis's charitable exasperation with Smith. J. A. could, for example, see quite clearly that the world longed for a resolution of the tension between transcendent reality and the finitude of our experience—"some solution which will harmonize the

---

[64]C. S. Lewis Journal, 6 June 1926, 3 February 1927, *LCSL*, 109, 110.

[65]Lewis, *Surprised by Joy*, 208-209.

[66]C. S. Lewis to Arthur Greeves, 1 June 1930, Hooper, ed., *They Stand Together*, 355-56.

[67]Fox, "At the Breakfast Table," 92, 93.

claims of the one and the other without derogation from either"—but could not entertain the idea that God had done this by becoming man. He remained dogmatically convinced that there could in matters religious be no final answers.[68]

The young philosophers whom Smith influenced formed no self-conscious movement. The relationships between Lewis and Collingwood were formal and ephemeral. After 1935, when Collingwood's appointment to the Waynflete Chair made him a member of Magdalen, Lewis and Collingwood routinely had opportunities for conversation; but in 1936 J. A. Smith left the college for Norham Gardens, so the catalyst was wanting. They did quote one another's works favorably,[69] but there was no philosophical community in which the ideas Smith's and Joachim's pupils shared could be given voice, and by then only Collingwood was still a practicing philosopher.

The question of influence is invariably dangerous and seldom answered decisively. It is more dangerous if it is conceived on the presupposition that ideas belonging to one thinker are appropriated by another. Since neither Smith, Webb, Lewis, nor Collingwood believed ideas to be property, and since each considered the discovery of truth by successive generations of thinkers to be the work of philosophy, none was much concerned with originality. Collingwood's sparing use of footnotes was perhaps a testimony to this conviction, not necessarily a desire to obscure the debts he owed to the philosophical conversations of Oxford.[70] Lewis and Collingwood both participated in those conversations during the 1920s and 1930s. Both were heirs of the renewed interest in medieval history and literature that great Magdalen scholars like Smith, Webb, and Frank Edward Brightman had done so much to recover, and which by 1920 in England intersected with the growing interest in scholasti-

---

[68] J. A. Smith, "Morals and Religion," *HJ* (1921): 624.

[69] Collingwood, *New Leviathan*, 57; C. S. Lewis, "Psycho-Analysis and Literary Criticism," *Selected Literary Essays*, 298; C. S. Lewis to I. O. Evans, 26 September 1945, *LCSL*, 207.

[70] This may be the meaning of his remarks to Croce on 20 April 1938 that his omitting of notes placed him in a long line of English philosophers (Rubinoff, "Philosophy and History," 55). The convention of documenting with footnotes inevitably suggests that present ideas are the result of past thought, which Collingwood would have denied.

cism that Maurice De Wulf and Etienne Gilson had initiated among Continental Catholics.[71]

Perhaps Lewis's first intellectual turning point was his rejection of chronological snobbery, the tendency of his undergraduate contemporaries to patronize the past, especially the Middle Ages, and to give medievalism the sense it had taken as the title to Tyrrell's polemic.[72] In 1921 Lewis had visited the Carlyles at Hollywell, and came away not only charmed with the long, uneven rooms and beamed ceilings, but bemused that Oxford had only recently taken down the plaster that the eighteenth century had used to substitute "elegance and civility for Gothic rudeness."[73] Lewis's *The Allegory of Love*, published in 1934, owed, as Lewis noted in the preface, much to J. A. Smith. Moreover, *The Discarded Image*, published in 1954, was a reprise of the medieval themes that had shaped Lewis's own thought and informed his lectures for three decades. Collingwood, who had written in the preface to *Speculum Mentis* (1924) that he claimed only to represent the great romantic tradition, was perhaps the first British philosopher since the Reformation who wrote as though Anselm and Aquinas were as important as Descartes.[74] Their belief in the integrity and fecundity of the philosophic past, an inheritance from Smith, and also from Clement Webb, at least echoed the principles and method Smith and Webb had represented at Oxford.

---

[71]Maurice de Wulf (1867-1947), a pupil of Cardinal Mercier and professor at Louvain, published his *Histoire de la philosophie médiévale* in 1900; *Scholasticism Old and New; An Introduction to Scholastic Philosophy, Medieval and Modern* was published in Dublin in 1907. *Medieval Philosophy Illustrated from the System of Thomas Aquinas* was published in 1926. Etienne Gilson (1884-1978) was professor of the Sorbonne (1921-1932) and the College de France (1932), founder in 1932 of the Institute of Medieval Studies in Toronto. Gilson began to publish about 1922, when his *Thomisme* appeared, and in 1931-1932 delivered the Gifford Lectures, *The Spirit of Medieval Philosophy*. A third philosopher, especially important in England, was Jacques Maritain (1882-1973), whose *Art et scholastique* (1920; trans., 1927) influenced Eliot and other poets, among them Allen Tate.

[72]Tyrrell's *Medievalism* (London: Longmans, 1908) was subtitled *A Reply to Cardinal Mercier*, and was an attack upon a pastoral Mercier had issued on 20 May 1908 defending *Pascendi* and Scholasticism.

[73]C. S. Lewis to Warren Lewis, 10 May 1921, *LCSL*, 59.

[74]Collingwood, *Philosophical Method*, 125-35.

That method was a development of an interest in the philosophy of history that Smith and Collingwood found in Croce and Gentile, and its effect was the exposition and defense of a nonpositivistic theory of historical knowledge. By 1919 J. A. Smith had concluded that the most pressing work of philosophy was "that the mind should frame and hold some theory of its activity as the interpreter of its own history," and further, that the "critical presuppositions of history" should be determined and systematized. Four years later, in his contribution to the Muirhead *Contemporary British Philosophy* series, Smith restated much that he had said earlier, and went on to develop the doctrine that the framing of suppositions is the primary work of philosophy.[75] This notion next appears in Collingwood's *Speculum Mentis* in the same year, and was developed further by him in his essays on history and the philosophy of history, finally making its way into his posthumous *Idea of History*. In the fifth, eighth, and ninth of his Gifford Lectures of December 1929-January 1930, Smith traced the development of the Platonic and Aristotelian hypothesis into the modern supposal, on which, he claimed, both science and history were founded.[76] The assumption that philosophy precedes the disciplines of science and history in discovering and testing presuppositions or suppositions is the intellectual heart of Collingwood's *Essay on Philosophical Method* (1933) and his *Essay on Metaphysics* (1940). It is difficult to imagine Lewis's introduction to *The Discarded Image*, or his lectures on medieval literature—especially the chapter "Reservations," in which he explains his use of supposal in the history of science—having been written without reference to Smith or Collingwood.

A third common conviction of the Magdalen group that can be traced to Smith was the belief that language is the body of thought, hence of history and, indeed, life. Smith had begun as a philologist, and W. D. Ross thought Smith had always regretted giving up the study of lan-

---

[75]John Alexander Smith, "The Philosophy of Giovanni Gentile," *PAS* 20 (1919-1920): 66; "Philosophy," 241. Cf. Collingwood, *Speculum Mentis*, 180-88; *Metaphysics*, 21-48, 66.

[76]Printed synopses of "The Heritage of Idealism" are in SPM, 2:27. Summaries were published in the Glasgow *Herald* in December 1929 and January 1930, the report of the eighth lecture appearing on 8 January 1930.

guage for philosophy.[77] In fact, as his bibliography shows, Smith never abandoned philology; his nephew remembered J. A. listening in the 1930s to recordings of his latest linguistic find on the phonograph, a tortoise-shell ear trumpet in each ear so that nothing of the voiced body of the language would be lost.[78]

In his philosophy this love of language took the form of a persistent defense of the Crocean theory that words are intended to express, not simply to communicate. This theory presupposed the falsity of the current positivist idea that language had distinguishable, indeed separate, functional and emotional components, a point of view ably defended at Oxford by I. A. Richards.[79] Smith's aesthetic, essentially Croce's, was first published in his long letter to the professor of poetry in 1924 as *The Nature of Art*. This essay, greeted by the *Times* literary critic as a sign of the vitality of Oxford philosophy, was a defense of the Crocean principles that art is one; a knowing, not a doing; an active seeing rather than passivity; the expression of the perfectly individual rather than the universal; a language; and a work of imagination, with imagination understood as something other than irrational dreaming.[80] These were positions Collingwood would express eloquently in his *Principles of Art* in 1938, and upon which Lewis would rely in *The Abolition of Man* in 1943, though Lewis considered himself a neo-Aristotelian, not a disciple of Croce. Smith returned to the argument in 1930, when he wrote against the proposal that some universal, artificial language might be invented, a proposal developed from a "misconception of the very nature of language."

> This misconception is that language is . . . the creature of Man's practical will, as it has for its end the betterment either of his commodity

---

[77]Mure, "Croce and Oxford," 330; Ross, "John Alexander Smith," 819-20; Smith, "Address to the Oxford Philosophical Society."

[78]Ian Ross-Smith to the author, 16 August 1981.

[79]On Richards (1893-1979), see *Times*, 23 November 1979; I. A. Richards, *Complementarities: Uncollected Essays*, ed. John Paul Russo (Cambridge MA: Harvard University Press, 1976) i-xxiv; M. C. Bradbrook, "I. A. Richards at Cambridge," *I. A. Richards: Essays in His Honor*, ed. Reuben Brower, Helen Vendler, and John Hollander (New York: Oxford University Press, 1973) 61-72.

[80]Arthur B. Walkley, *Still More Prejudice* (London: William Heinemann, 1925) 49-53; Smith, *The Nature of Art*, 16-19, 20, 22, 24, 27-29.

> of living or his own and his fellows' character and conduct. . . . It leads at once to a misleading emphasis on the aspect of it as a means of communication, and that a communication restricted to practical collaboration. That leads further to speaking and thinking of it as "artificial," a complex of artifices or collection of conventions, or to assimilating it to a mechanism or box of tools, and so, down a buttered slide, to condemning it because parts of it are useless or superfluous or overcomplicated or what not.

In fact, language is neither practical nor logical, but is "an aesthetic fact and function." Language exists so that man might "express himself, might project before his inward view what moved or stirred him, . . . and might furnish him with objects to delight in; this is still the chief service it performs for us."[81]

The gulf that separated the Magdalen group from the positivists on the point of language was perhaps best expressed in the last chapter of Collingwood's *An Essay on Philosophical Method*. The chapter was entitled "Philosophy as a Branch of Literature," and its purpose was to argue that philosophy was not a symbolism but a language, the use of which required the philosopher to "go to school with the poets in order to learn the use of language."[82] Collingwood's philosophy always had a literary quality that threatened to make it poetry. *Speculum Mentis* is full of Browning, Shakespeare, Pope, and Virgil. Quoting poetry does not make writing into literature, but in *Speculum Mentis* (to take only one example) the text itself, apart from the quotations, had rhetorical qualities that render it poetic. Collingwood realized the nature and power of words, and worked throughout his life at the pole furthest from the philosophic school that sought to transform philosophy into mathematics.

Smith came finally to believe not only that philosophy is a kind of literature, but that the content of philosophy was essentially literary. At the sixth International Congress of Philosophy at Harvard in 1926, Smith had argued before the philosophical world that taking literature as the highest intellectual achievement of man "delivers us from the 'beggarly elements' of popular psychologies, with their random collec-

---

[81] J. A. Smith, "Artificial Languages," Society for Pure English, Tract No. 34 (Oxford: Clarendon Press, 1930) 471.

[82] Collingwood, *Philosophical Method*, 214.

tion of trivial anecdotes, and the pseudo-scientific tabulation of results got by the circulation of questionnaires among the unobservant, the unimaginative, the uneducated, and the inarticulate." It was literature that preserved "man's painfully acquired knowledge of his own mind."[83] Lewis dealt with his own conviction that the life of imagination could not be separated from reason by allowing what had originally been metaphysical in his thought to pass into poetry. Lewis said in a letter to his father that he was glad to take up his position in literature at Magdalen because though he might have the mind for philosophy, he had neither the brain nor the nerves.[84]

Philosophy, as he had experienced it in the 1920s, had already become the lonely realm of the expert. As an undergraduate Lewis had missed the notion that J. A. Smith had taken over from Green and propagandized endlessly, that philosophy existed for the sake of the ordinary person who wished to think clearly about his life and its duties; though in an uncanny way Lewis had resisted the tendency of the poets of the 1920s to construct a private and inevitably surreal language. Lewis was not a great poetic talent, but a historian of literature and ideas, a moralist, an apologist, and a critic, reaching always for the style and for those images that would touch and convert. His own thought, as *Pilgrim's Regress* and *The Abolition of Man* show, remained heavily metaphysical; but the kind of philosophy that really interested him, obvious enough to a follower of Green, Bywater, or Caird, was radically unfashionable. Extrapolated as a systematic metaphysic, it was the ancient wisdom that the linguistic and analytic schools found amateurish and platitudinous; but clothed in the positive and Morrislike images Lewis loved, it was free to touch ordinary life.

Though examples of the specific positions Smith, Lewis, and Collingwood held *contra mundum* could be multiplied, it was finally the profound belief in the possibility of metaphysics and in the relevance of thinking for acting that distinguished the pupils of the idealists from their peers. In May 1920 J. A. Smith wrote a paper entitled "The Study of Ancient Philosophy," a defense of the requirement that Greats students gain a thorough knowledge of certain classical texts.

---

[83]Smith, "Nature of Mind," 133.

[84]C. S. Lewis to Albert Lewis, 1925 [LJ, 8:299].

> The aim of teaching philosophy in the course of Litt. Hum. is then to awaken, stimulate, and maintain interest in the self and its world, to stir and if possible in some degree to satisfy curiosity about that—to awaken and arouse the need of such knowledge. And its efficacy lies just there. It is to rouse up to self consciousness or self knowledge, or at least to the sense of a need for such self consciousness and such knowledge, and with that to make us aware of the dignity and duty of man.[85]

Collingwood had understood Smith's point quite clearly. The older idealists, he wrote, "when introducing their pupils to the study of moral and political theory would say to them whether in words or not—'Take this subject seriously, because whether you understand it or not will make a difference to your whole lives.' The 'realist,' on the contrary, said to his pupils, 'If it interests you to study this, do so; but don't think it will be of any use to you.' " They had convinced their pupils that philosophy was a "silly and trifling game," and given them "a lifelong contempt for the subject and lifelong grudge against the men who wasted their time. . . ." The school of Green had, on the other hand, taught them that philosophy was not the preserve for professional philosophers, but everyone's business.[86] It had, as Smith had written, made undergraduates aware of the dignity and duty of man.

Their metaphysics made Collingwood and Lewis signs of contradiction. Collingwood bore the burden of loneliness that his interest in perennial questions brought upon him with a labored patience, working persistently to gain a hearing for his philosophy on its own merits through his books and essays. Lewis was never given a professorship at Oxford, and finally Cambridge invented a chair for him. But whatever loneliness they experienced—and Collingwood, who had chosen to persist in philosophy, undoubtedly suffered most—was compensated by their ability to speak beyond the tight community of Oxford. Collingwood, who from first to last despised the notion of professionalism, tried to write for the ordinary artist, philosopher, or teacher of religion.[87] Lewis, who had left philosophy partly because he could not imagine the

---

[85]SPB, 4:8.

[86]Collingwood, *Autobiography*, 48.

[87]Collingwood, *Speculum Mentis*, 18-19.

philosophy he knew touching life, addressed his apologetic to the ordinary person who thought there might be something in Christianity. Knowledge was intended to be sought and valued both in itself and as a means of action. The tradition ran to Plato, Aristotle, Jowett, and Green.

The belief of these metaphysical survivors that philosophy was not unrelated to action had classic roots and entailed a respect for the history of philosophy, and therefore for the past. Lewis, while he blazed a path of apologetic success unparalleled in modern times, repeatedly warned his readers that he wrote from a world of classical and medieval thought to which they might lack imaginative access. In his Cambridge inaugural, he depicted himself as a survival from some literary prehistory, an example useful for challenging the presuppositions of modernity, but hardly a creature of the age.[88] Collingwood remarked in the preface to *Speculum Mentis* that he wished to restate that *philosophia quaedam perennis*. Their metaphors ought not be allowed to obscure their essentially progressive assumption that their predecessors had, for the most part, made important contributions to the great human questions that they proposed to reconsider yet again.

Both Lewis and Collingwood considered Christianity a corollary of clear thinking, and hence of truth. Lewis believed his life had been shaped by his intellectual progress from realism to idealism, from idealism to pantheism, from pantheism to theism, and from theism to Christianity.[89] Beginning in 1916, when *Religion and Philosophy* was published, Collingwood wrote consistently as though thinking about theological questions was not only possible but necessary for philosophers who wished to think in the Western tradition. Throughout his Oxford years he contributed to The Group, and in the end he considered Christianity the presupposition fundamental to historical, and hence to philosophic thinking. Lewis's Christianity became increasingly apparent, some might have said intrusive, during the 1930s. Collingwood was known as a believer and, like Webb at Old Marston, served on the parish council. Both Collingwood and Lewis occupied Newman's pulpit in the

---

[88]C. S. Lewis, "De Descriptione Temporum," *Selected Literary Essays*, 8-14.

[89]Lewis, *Pilgrim's Regress*, 5.

university church on at least one occasion.[90] Neither learned his Christianity from J. A. Smith, but Smith did encourage them, and anyone else who would listen, to trust the tradition that had since Plato encouraged thought about the gods.

When J. A. Smith died on 19 December 1939, the Edinburgh *Scotsman* titled the obituary "Famous Scot, Professor Who Impressed Oxford," noting that John Alexander Smith had been "enormously interested in everything and everybody," and that his real work had been "to act as a stimulus to younger dons, and to mould the thought of students who came under his influence." The funeral was in Magdalen chapel. Lewis and Webb were among those representing the college. J. M. Thompson and A. L. Lilley, old allies in the modernist wars, were present. Harold Joachim had died the August preceding, but his widow and daughter came, as did W. D. Ross, H. J. Paton, Mrs. A. J. Carlyle, and other professors and heads of colleges. The *Times* did not name Collingwood among the mourners, but he later told G. R. G. Mure that with Joachim and Smith gone, there were no more good philosophers at Oxford.[91] Lewis collected his J. A. Smithana for the Magdalen Library;[92] Webb would recall Smith as a brilliant scholar,[93] and Benedetto Croce, still alive, who had been Smith's guest at Magdalen, recalled his host as "un esprit très clair."[94]

Smith's achievement as a philosopher had been flawed. Though he had written more than most of his critics knew, he had never written a book. Few who considered themselves his disciples held important positions in professional philosophy. He had inherited the leadership of the idealist school when it still had at least an autumnal vigor; when he retired in 1936 idealism had, as a body of thought that serious philosophers routinely took into account, ceased to exist. The chair he had passed on

---

[90]Collingwood preached "Rule Making and Rule Breaking" at St. Mary's on 5 May 1935 (CPB); Lewis, "The Weight of Glory," on 8 June 1941.

[91]G. R. G. Mure to the author, 23 January 1973; Collingwood, *Autobiography*, 18.

[92]SPM; *Times*, 22 December 1939.

[93]Webb, *Religious Experience*, 36.

[94]Mure, "Benedetto Croce," 327.

to Collingwood would fall to Gilbert Ryle, an exponent of the analytic school, two years after Smith's death.

So the contribution had not been to books, but to a tradition that lived in the work of Collingwood, Lewis, Mure, Paton, and a host of contemporaries. It would be enough to claim that J. A. had abetted the writing of *Speculum Mentis* and *Pilgrim's Regress*. In his unpublished Gifford Lectures of 1930, Smith claimed that the idealism he spoke for represented the central tradition of philosophy from Descartes to Caird.[95] The idea of a metaphysical tradition has not been popular for half a century, but if anything is certain in philosophy, it is the pattern in which a critical testing of the past that seems tantamount to its rejection is succeeded by rediscovery.

John Alexander Smith had made the great questions live when philosophy was gripped by that failure of courage called realism.

---

[95]John Alexander Smith, *The Heritage of Idealism (Philosophy as a Way of Supposing)* [Prospectus of Smith's Gifford Lectures, 1929-1930] SPM, 2:27.

•CHAPTER IV•

R. G. Collingwood as a Philosopher of the Christian Religion

The idea of a general philosophy of religion is barren and empty. . . . The idea of a philosophy of the Christian religion is concrete and fruitful.

"The Philosophy of the Christian Religion," 1920[1]

There was, as he wrote in his *Autobiography*, always one Collingwood content to live as a professional thinker, aloof from the practical affairs of life; there was one who knew the falsity of this attempt to divide the theoretical from the practical but ignored it; and there was yet another anxious for engagement in the world, ready to address the local antiquarian society, find Arthur's roundtable, or take on Spanish fascism.[2] "All thought," proclaimed the opening sentence of *Speculum Mentis*, "exists for the sake of action." Just as life could not be divided into practical and theoretical halves, thought itself could not be compartmentalized. Thinking, whether metaphysical, economic, or political, always involved the axiom that "the parts of the whole exist in mutual support,

---

[1]CPB. The essay was submitted to *Theology*, but never published.

[2]Collingwood, *Autobiography*, 150-51; 160-62. His archaeological work was roundly criticized. See I. A. Richmond, "Appreciation of R. G. Collingwood as an Archaeologist," *PBA* 19 (1943): 479-80. McCallum remembered Collingwood as "always the man for some subject off the beaten University track whether it was yachting, fairy stories, or *graffiti*." "Robin George Collingwood, 1889-1943," *PBA* 19 (1943): 465-66.

and the aspects of an objective reality become more comprehensible when seen in their interrelations."[3]

Collingwood wrote as he lived, treating all knowledge as his province, to the irritation of a scholarly Oxford in which specialization was increasingly the warrant of professional competence. His forays into politics and archaeology embarrassed his friends. His writings included major works on religion (*Religion and Philosophy*, 1916), the taxonomy of knowledge (*Speculum Mentis*, 1924), metaphysics (*Essay on Philosophical Method*, 1933; *Essay on Metaphysics*, 1940), art (*The Principles of Art*, 1938), politics (*The New Leviathan*, 1942), the philosophy of nature (*The Idea of Nature*, 1945), and the philosophy of history (*The Idea of History*, 1946), as well as translations and distinguished series of occasional essays on topics ranging from Ruskin's philosophy to Roman Britain. Collingwood's thought has been fruitful. *The Idea of History* is arguably the most important twentieth-century work in the philosophy of history; Collingwood's philosophy of art has been developed by Suzanne Langer,[4] aspects of his metaphysics by Errol E. Harris,[5] Alan Donagan, Louis O. Mink, and Lionell Rubinoff,[6] his political philosophy by Willmoore Kendall.

Yet Collingwood remains enigmatic, both personally and as a philosopher, as solitary as Smith was companionable, as devoted to his father as Lewis was detached from his, as acerbic as Webb was patiently urbane. Although he expressed his regard for Croce and Samuel Alex-

---

[3]Collingwood, *Speculum Mentis*, 47. This was a metaphysical analog to Ruskin's vew that his own interests had been like the buttresses of a cathedral, seemingly in opposition but in fact reinforcing one another.

[4]Susanne K. Langer, *Feeling and Form* (New York: Charles Scribner's Sons, 1953) 280-89.

[5]Errol E. Harris published an article defending Collingwood's interpretation of the ontological argument in 1936 ["Mr. Ryle and the Ontological Argument," *Mind* 45 (1936): 478-80] and works about Collingwood often thereafter. See *Hypothesis and Perception: The Roots of Scientific Method* (London: George Allen and Unwin, 1970).

[6]Donagan's *The Later Philosophy of R. G. Collingwood* (Oxford: Clarendon Press, 1962) was the first book-length study of Collingwood's philosophy. Louis O. Mink, *Mind, History, and Dialectic: The Philosophy of R. G. Collingwood* (Bloomington: University of Indiana Press, 1969).

ander, respect did not lead to friendship. Apart from J. A., T. M. Knox,[7] Clement Webb, R. B. McCallum,[8] and G. R. G. Mure, Collingwood had few important intellectual friendships at Oxford; none evident from his manuscripts, none claimed by his biographers. The loneliness Lewis had declined when he left philosophy in 1922 had befallen Collingwood—not so much because, as Lewis had feared, no one could understand a philosopher's work but because Collingwood's contemporaries for the most part disagreed with his approach to philosophy. Realism, he wrote de Ruggiero in 1927, prevails, and "those who disagree with it are either abused or merely neglected."[9]

For his own part, Collingwood began early to display an ill-concealed contempt for the professionalism that directed his colleagues away from fundamental metaphysical questions, and toward a new role as experts.[10] He had paraded his own omnicompetence in history, philosophy, archaeology, and draughtsmanship, his lifelong ability to paint and to compose. And he had insisted, in an Oxford newly agreed that religion was a private, not an intellectual matter, that thinking about religion, indeed the Christian religion, was essential to civilization. In his own life Collingwood refused to separate thought and action, professing Christianity by speaking on religious or quasireligious topics, and identifying himself from 1916 to at least 1930 with the apologetic projects of the Streeter group. It would be difficult to name another lay Oxford philosopher of the 1920s and 1930s whose interest in Christianity and philosophical defense of the Christian religion were more stubborn or

---

[7]T. M. Knox (1900-1979) had been tutored by Collingwood at Pembroke. From 1931 to 1936 Knox was at Jesus College, then (1934) at Queen's. He was subsequently professor at St. Andrew's.

[8]R. B. McCallum (1898-1979) was a fellow of Pembroke, where he was tutor in history and author of several books on politics. McCallum, who admired and befriended Collingwood, provided Collingwood's obituaries in *Oxford Magazine* and *PBA*. McCallum was also a sometime participant in the Inklings, and friend of J. R. R. Tolkien. He was master of Pembroke from 1955 until 1967.

[9]Collingwood to De Ruggiero, 4 October 1927, quoted in *HAS*, 22. The studied neglect of Collingwood by his contemporaries was noticed by 1930. See E. W. F. Tomlin, Review of *The Principles of Art*, by R. G. Collingwood, *Criterion* 18 (1938-1939): 118.

[10]Knox, "Collingwood's Philosophical Work," 69.

persistent. Collingwood's claims for Christianity are, if anything, more precise than Webb's.

The attempt to analyze the place of the Christian religion in Collingwood's thought has yielded a variety of interpretations. T. M. Knox, Collingwood's pupil and literary executor, understood that all his life Collingwood had been "deeply interested in religion," but suggested that his thought had developed from an early liberalism characterized by admiration for Schweitzer's *Quest of the Historical Jesus*—a work that found moral significance in Jesus' life after proving in the best positivist manner the failure of his prophecies—toward "the more positive and even dogmatic attitude" of the *Essay on Metaphysics*. Knox believed that Collingwood's historical skepticism had finally led him into a reliance on religious affirmation bordering on credulity.[11] Mink also saw a development, though a different kind, suggesting that between 1916 and 1933 Collingwood's thought on the relation between religion and philosophy shifted

> from an emphasis on similarities to an emphasis on differences. The fields allocated to science and history hardly changed, but philosophy is increasingly distinguished from religion, whose function becomes more and more existential as it becomes less cognitive.

Collingwood, Mink concluded, "had virtually nothing to say about religion after 1928." Like Knox, Donagan understood the importance of religion for Collingwood, and wrote in 1966 that Collingwood's intent in his later treatment of religion was the most difficult of the disputed questions posed by Collingwood's mature philosophy: "It is as though Collingwood divined in Christianity something which compelled his veneration, while eluding his attempts to define it."[12] But in a later, more

---

[11]McCallum ("Collingwood," 465) says that Collingwood was "extremely interested in the philosophy of religion and in the fundamental problems of Christian truth." Knox (*DNB* 1941-1950, 170) says Schweitzer had been an early influence. This is confirmed by Collingwood's "Lecture on the Philosophy of St. Paul" prepared for Somerville College in 1918 (CPB), in which he wrote of Jesus' belief in the imminent end of the world, an interpretation popularized by Schweitzer: "Well, the belief was a mistake. Jesus' teaching was none the worse."

[12]Mink, *Mind, History, and Dialectic*, 243; Donagan, *Later Philosophy of R. G. Collingwood*, 307.

informal essay Donagan considered Collingwood's treatment of the great themes of creation, fall, and atonement superficial, "less blasphemous than laughable." Donagan suggests that at bottom Collingwood could not accept Christianity; and that his "lifelong attempt to expound Christian faith in terms of a metaphysics on principle of which was its own autonomy, was ultimately inconsistent."[13] Theologians who have considered Collingwood's writings have not been much kinder, pronouncing his approach relativistic despite its provocative character (Casserley) or insufficiently personal and unable to account for those events that simply befall passive mankind (Bultmann).[14] Austin Farrer, who was inclined to admire Collingwood the man, still found his philosophy relativistic, and characterized his *Essay on Metaphysics* as a "most paradoxical" call "to rally round the Athanasian Creed and save scientific civilization."[15]

To this tendency to pronounce Collingwood's philosophy of religion inconsistent, unsuccessful, or paradoxical there have been exceptions. T. S. Eliot saw clearly that Collingwood intended his *Religion and Philosophy* (1916) to be taken as a serious effort to solve the problem that liberals since Schleiermacher had posed by denying intellectual content and metaphysical relevance to theology, and C. C. J. Webb concurred.[16] E. W. F. Tomlin, Collingwood's pupil in the 1920s, wrote sympathetically of Collingwood's early defense of the idea that religion is "essentially a form of knowledge," not, as Otto or William James held, mere emotion or desire.[17] In recent scholarship Rubinoff has taken seriously the pos-

---

[13]Alan Donagan, "Collingwood and Philosophical Method," in Michael Krauss, ed., *Collected Essays on the Philosophy of R. G. Collingwood* (Oxford: Clarendon Press, 1972) 19.

[14]Rudolf Bultmann, *History and Eschatology* (Edinburgh: The University Press, 1957) 132-47; J. V. Langemeade Casserley, *The Christian in Philosophy* (New York: Charles Scribner's Sons, 1951) 200-203.

[15]Austin Farrer, *The Glass of Vision* (Westminster: Dacre Press, 1948) 101.

[16]T. S. Eliot, Review of *Religion and Philosophy* by R. G. Collingwood, *International Journal of Ethics* 27:4 (July 1917): 543; Webb, Review of *Religion and Philosophy*.

[17]E. W. F. Tomlin, *R. G. Collingwood* (London: Longmans, 1957) 17. Tomlin contrasts Collingwood's view with that expressed by Whitehead's oft-quoted phrase that religion is "what a man does with his solitude."

sibility that religion might be an important key to Collingwood's thought.[18]

In fact the Christian religion was for Collingwood an indispensable intellectual hermeneutic and the *Essay on Metaphysics*, in which Christian dogma appears as the intellectual presupposition of Western civilization, is the culmination of a consistent development begun in *Religion and Philosophy*, not an anomaly. Of course religion is not the single key to Collingwood's thought. History was the method, and any of the forms—religion, art, philosophy, or science—will tend in Collingwood's writings to function from time to time as the single hermeneutic illuminating all the others. Collingwood wrote in his *Autobiography* that his lifework had been the investigation of the relation between history and philosophy, but philosophy should probably be taken in this text as a synecdoche for all knowledge. Among the forms of knowledge, religion is not the one Collingwood handles most easily or self-confidently nor is it the most obviously pervasive, but religion—specifically the Christian religion—is the most fundamental.

The critics deserve their due. Collingwood's thought on religion and on the Christian religion is not consistent in every respect. His treatment is historical and critical; he writes as a philosopher determined to discover the philosophic truth of Christianity insofar as philosophy can know it. There is in his writings an implicit rationalism, a tendency to identify the content of faith with the content of reason and to assume that just as the redemption of men is a reasonable solution to a philosophical problem, the presuppositions of metaphysics are somehow revealed. Reason is then, to quote a title Collingwood had used in 1927, faith cultivating itself.[19] Faith is the presupposition; reason presupposes and tests. Aquinas asked in the opening article of his most famous book whether there were truths necessary to the fulfillment of human destiny that, while reasonable in themselves, might be unavailable to reason

---

[18]In 1968 Rubinoff published many of Collingwood's essays on religion in *Faith and Reason: Essays in the Philosophy of Religion* (Chicago: Quadrangle Books, 1968). His preface is the first essay that suggested the fundamental place of religion in Collingwood's philosophy. See also "Philosophy and History," 14.

[19]R. G. Collingwood, "Reason Is Faith Cultivating Itself," *HJ* 26 (1927-1928): 3-14.

apart from faith.[20] Collingwood shared with Aquinas the belief that such truths did exist. St. Thomas called them simply the science of the blessed, and that is the body of truth that, as Anselm had insisted, we believe in order that we might have understanding.

I

The greatest influence on R. G. Collingwood was his father, W. G. Collingwood, whom he consistently remembered as his first and best teacher;[21] and in the background was always John Ruskin, and that revolutionary dedication to the unity of art and thought and civilization that Ruskin had hammered home for half a century. Friendship between the Collingwoods and Ruskin reached back to 1856, when Robin Collingwood's grandfather William (1819-1903), already embarked on a successful career as a watercolorist, had won Ruskin's notice with a painting of the Matterhorn. William Collingwood's life was characterized by his dedication to art and his impassioned allegiance to his evangelical religion, rich in those noble, archaic loyalties that seemed generation after generation to mark the family. William Collingwood's art would finally

---

[20]Though Thomas would have insisted that there existed a sphere of experience and reality accessible to reason unaided by faith (or in Collingwood's language, accessible without revealed or given presuppositions), he would certainly have agreed with Collingwood that the content of faith is entirely reasonable, though often known to us as mysteries revealed. Further, the content of reason includes ultimately the propositions of faith, though in this life human intellect may grasp this reasonableness of faith only in part.

[21]On Collingwood's relationship with his father, see T. M. Knox, Review of *The Formative Years of R. G. Collingwood*, by William M. Johnston, *Philosophical Quarterly* 19 (1969):165. R. G. Collingwood wrote the obituaries for his father that appeared in the London *Times* on 3 July 1932, and in *Transactions of the Cumberland and Westmoreland Antiquarian and Archaeological Society*, n.s. 33 (1933): 310-11. William Gershom Collingwood married Edith Mary Isaac, daughter of Thomas Isaac, in 1883. The Collingwoods were originally Northumbrian; the Isaacs were an East Anglian family. W. G. Collingwood's father William (1819-1903) married Marie Elizabeth Imhoff, daughter of a notary of Arbon, Switzerland, whom he met in England when she was the guest of his relatives in 1851. It was William Collingwood's marriage that took him to the Alps, where he painted the mountains Ruskin loved. William Collingwood's father was Samuel Collingwood, architect and contractor, his mother Frances Collingwood, daughter of Samuel Collingwood, printer to the University of Oxford.

The children of W. G. and Edith Isaac Collingwood, besides their son Robin, were Susan, who married Dr. Ernest Altounyan of Aleppo; Ursula, wife of the Reverend Canon R. B. Luard-Selby; and Barbara, wife of Major Oscar T. Gnosspelius.

make him a fellow of the Royal Watercolor Society; zeal for religion would make him first contemplate the foreign missions, then devote himself to preaching and pamphleteering for the Plymouth Brethren. William Collingwood's acquaintance with Ruskin never became friendship, but Ruskin bought his pictures, made William's son his inseparable companion, and, if tradition may be trusted, kept one of the elder Collingwood's evangelical tracts on his study table in old age.[22]

When Robin Collingwood's father, William Gershom (1851-1932) went to University College in 1872, Thomas Hill Green was at the height of his influence, Bernard Bosanquet had just been appointed to a fellowship at University and Ruskin was Slade Professor of Art. The philosophical movement inaugurated by Green became a dominant influence, and under its inspiration W. G. Collingwood produced the Lothian prize essay, "The Institution and Purposes of Knighthood." Bernard Bosanquet, to whom he later ascribed great influence, was his tutor, and at Oxford he became Ruskin's disciple and friend. W. G. Collingwood, who had a gift for drawing, began as a painter, but the contrast between his own moderate talent and the greater abilities of his father was painfully evident, and his painting gradually yielded to literary and historical interests. In 1882 he accompanied Ruskin to Europe, and soon after moved to a cottage on Windemere, not far from Ruskin's Brantwood. In 1891 W. G. Collingwood moved to Lanehead—a house near Coniston that R. G. Collingwood would inherit in 1932—in order to be nearer Ruskin. His biography of Ruskin and his books on Ruskin's teaching of art were successful. He became increasingly interested in the writing of history and in the archaeology of Cambria, especially the Norse settlements. Around these interests his son would build his university career.

Ruskin died in 1900, the year Robin Collingwood went to Rugby. The Ruskin the boy remembered was no longer the compelling reformer his father and grandfather had admired. Still, from the circle formed by Ruskin's thought, R. G. Collingwood learned that art could not be separated from life or from truth. To the degree that the religion of his grandfather, who lived until 1903, was an influence, he learned that religion was not irrelevant to art, life, or truth. The interrelationships be-

---

[22]I am indebted to Teresa Collingwood Smith for her personal knowledge of family incidents in the life of William Collingwood.

tween art, politics, philosophy, and religion characteristic of medieval Europe—at least the relations Ruskin and his followers discovered in their efforts to find an alternative to the aspects of a newly urbanized, industrialized, and secular society they disliked—were presupposed at Ruskin's Brantwood and at Lanehead.

From both his father and his grandfather, Robin Collingwood would have learned the great Victorian themes: an affection for the noble, a profound belief in the intelligibility and unity of experience, a conviction that thought should change life for the better. The influence of the evangelical religion of William Gershom Collingwood's own boyhood on his son is hard to document.[23] Whatever its character and intensity, it evoked no specific religious profession on Robin Collingwood's part until 1905 when he chose, at sixteen, to be baptized into the Church of England at Rugby. The next year, on 27 March 1906, Collingwood was confirmed, taking as his confirmation name George, thereby trading the soft and allusive Robin for the businesslike and fashionable R. G. That a boy who had been fascinated by Kant at seven, and who had taught himself to read Dante at Rugby, should have sought baptism is hardly surprising.[24] Collingwood was, like C. S. Lewis in another sense and Webb in yet another, an adult convert to Christianity.

In the Oxford Collingwood first knew in the autumn of 1908, the familiar theories of Ruskin, Green, and Jowett regarding the unity of thought still formed the Greats curriculum, which assumed the relevance of ancient history for modern England and of philosophy for history.[25] Edwardian idealists routinely assumed that philosophy was barely distinguishable from theology and moral philosophy. Collingwood once

---

[23]The nature of the evangelical religion William Collingwood professed, and presumably taught to his children, is indicated by the titles of the tracts he wrote: *The Bible Its Own Evidence* (Kendall, England: T. Wilson, 1895); *Sanctification as Set Forth in Scripture* (London: John F. Shaw, n.d.). The character of William Gershom Collingwood's religion is suggested by his comments on Ruskin's faith in *The Life of John Ruskin* (New York: Houghton Mifflin, 1892) 2: 512-14. George Mac Donald (1824-1905), an Evangelical and writer of fiction and fantasy, was often a guest at Brantwood. Mac Donald was especially admired by C. S. Lewis.

[24]Collingwood, *Autobiography*, 43.

[25]This is the burden of Collingwood's *Ruskin's Philosophy: An Address Delivered at the Ruskin Centenary Conference, Coniston, August 18, 1919* (Kendall, England: Titus Wilson and Son, 1922).

observed that "it would be hard to tell from his works which chair T. H. Green occupied,"[26] and in Collingwood's youth intellectuals like Charles Gore and J. R. Illingworth still produced works like *Reason and Revelation* (1908), in which philosophy was treated unself-consciously as an apologetic property. By philosophy the typical university-educated Englishman probably meant moral philosophy; metaphysics existed for the sake of action.

This emphasis upon unity of mind and experience was grounded in the conviction that logic and psychology were inseparable; that the truth of propositions enjoyed reality only as the content and function of some mind. It was, of course, judgments in which logic and psychology were interrelated, and by 1908, when Collingwood went up to University College, Cook Wilson's disciples were in revolt against this unity of empirical or logical "fact" and nonempirical "value." The realists considered knowledge, or the act of knowing, to be essentially objective, and sought persistently to rescue metaphysics and ethics from the implicitly personal, and hence implicitly psychological, moral and theological context in which both had been taught at Oxford. Truth was a fact or logical proposition, duty an obligation born of circumstance or context, religion and art emotions. This movement away from the synthetic Oxford philosophical tradition that stretched from Plato to Green and Edward Caird, toward the positivism that A. J. Ayer would champion in the 1930s, provided the background for Collingwood's career. At Oxford, influenced by the same urbane realist who would befriend C. S. Lewis, Collingwood, fed by the lectures of Prichard and Joseph, became something of an advocate of Cook Wilson's new philosophy. He excused what he later considered the realists' superficial refutations of Berkeley, Kant, and F. H. Bradley on the grounds that Wilson and his followers professed "philosophy, not history; that their business, strictly as philosophical critics, was to show whether a certain doctrine was sound or unsound."[27] As late as 1916, Collingwood was still tolerant of the idea he would spend much of his life repudiating: the realist doctrine that knowledge was objective,

---

[26]Collingwood, *The Philosophy of the Christian Religion*, *CBP*, 10.

[27]Collingwood, *Autobiography*, 23.

occurring apart from any personal and historical context, leaving both knower and known unchanged.[28]

The interests that would characterize Collingwood's thought before 1924 were in place by 1912. He was in correspondence with Douglas Ainslie, the first English translator of Croce, he was at work translating Aristotle's *De Anima*, and his interest in religion continued unabated. Testimony to what Collingwood later called his early interest in theology is a manuscript entitled, "The Devil in Literature: An Essay upon the Mythology of the Evil One Read before Eranos, 1908; a study of Hebrew sources, Dante, Loki myth," one of the juvenile studies in theology he mentioned in the *Autobiography*.[29] By 1912 Collingwood was at work on a book entitled *Religion and Philosophy*, and in 1913 he wrote for Lily Dougall's *Concerning Prayer* a chapter entitled "The Devil," obviously a development of the essay of 1908.[30]

Collingwood's association with the erudite Modernist group organized at Oxford by B. H. Streeter lasted into the 1930s. Collingwood shared their interest in the reasonableness of religion, and in an Oxford in which he belonged nowhere, probably valued his association with members of The Group.[31] But between the rationalizing spiritualism of Streeter, Brook, and A. E. J. Rawlinson, and Collingwood's very precise thought on religion, there were important differences as well as common ground. T. M. Knox insisted that by 1939 Collingwood had become decidedly dogmatic on the point of the necessity and comprehensiveness of presuppositions taken from Western theology.[32] If "The Theory of His-

---

[28]Ibid., 22.

[29]CPB; Collingwood, *Autobiography*, 43.

[30]Dougall, ed., "Concerning Prayer," 449-75; reprinted in Rubinoff, ed., *Faith and Reason*, 212-33.

[31]In *Faith and Reason: A Study in the Relation Between Religion and Science* (London: Ernest Benn, 1928), Collingwood enthusiastically recommended the works of Streeter and Needham as typical of the movement he wished to support. Joseph Needham, born in 1900, was editor in 1925 of *Science, Religion, and Reality*, to which Webb contributed an article. Needham wrote about both theology and science. See also R. G. Collingwood, "Science, Religion, and Civilization"—"The third in a series of lectures under that title delivered in Coventry Cathedral, Oct.-Dec. 1930, by Joseph Needham, B. H. Streeter, and R. G. C.," CPB.

[32]Collingwood, *Idea of History*, xvi.

tory" was indeed written by Collingwood, his reservations about Modernism date from before 1918. The author of that essay noted that the Modernists wished "to write history like men of the world and interpret it like the pope. Unhappily for themselves, they are disowned by both parties: the pope will have none of their history and historians (accustomed to paying attention to the real world) none of their religion."[33]

In "The Devil," his first published theological essay, Collingwood argued that the devil is God's counterfeit, not his antithesis, and suggested that mythic events, though arguably historical in the most obvious sense, derive their power not from the mere fact of their occurrence but from their character as "typical truth." The aspects of Collingwood's thought that would finally make him at best a lukewarm Modernist were evident in 1915. The essay breathes an unapologetic, reasonable faith, standing against the Modernist assumption that God can be accommodated to modernity, or psychology.

> True religion lies not in making God in our image, but in making ourselves in God's image, for God alone exists. . . . The type of all false religion is to believe what we will to believe, instead of what we have ascertained to be true; supposing that reality must be such as to satisfy our desires; and if not, let us go alter it.

The essay concludes with a quotation from T. H. Green on the point that man is incomplete, incapable of being a standard of anything, and with the reflection that although prayer "may not be the whole of religion, it is the touchstone of it."[34]

The author of "The Devil" was clearly not, in 1915 or 1916, a member of Wilson's realist school, and Collingwood's memory that he had indeed become, under Carritt's influence, a realist is itself perhaps misleading. Collingwood passed through at least three stages in his relation to the emerging positivism. From 1910 to 1915 or 1916 he was sympathetic to the philosophy of his tutor in the sense that he thought realism to be well motivated and to contain some truth. During these years he probably held the sanguine notion of the neophyte that he would be able to discern the best in both realism and idealism and to show that the

---

[33]"The Theory of History," 120.

[34]Collingwood, "The Devil," in Rubinoff, ed., *Faith and Reason*, 228, 232-33.

quarrels of his elders were merely verbal. By 1917 he was no longer sympathetic to realism, belonging by then clearly to the school that saw its roots in Aristotle and Plato and its future in the principles developed by Croce and Gentile. From 1918 to 1933 there was opposition to realism, but little bitterness. Then, after the publication of the *Essay on Philosophical Method* in 1933 and his controversy with Gilbert Ryle about the ontological argument in 1935, Collingwood became an outspoken and implacable foe of the realist-positivist school. The summary of this last phase was his attack in the *An Essay on Metaphysics* (1940) on A. J. Ayer. But the end was in the beginning and the author of "The Devil" was not, and without a massive reorganization of intellect and imagination could never have become, a realist.

When "The Devil" was written, Collingwood was at work on his first book-length manuscript. *Religion and Philosophy* was published in 1916, but Collingwood had written it "some years earlier," between 1912 and 1914, "in order to tidy up and put behind me a number of thoughts arising out of my juvenile studies in theology." The argument was philosophic rather than dogmatic, and in the preface Collingwood justified its publication on the grounds that in 1916 any young Englishman's expectation of long years of productivity was qualified by the war, and because the past year had seen "a considerable output of books treating religion from a philosophic or intellectual point of view."[35] Christianity was to be approached "as a philosophy," and its various doctrines regarded "as various aspects of a single idea which, according to the language in which it is expressed, may be called a metaphysic, an ethic, or a theology."[36] The influences at work as Collingwood wrote were perhaps represented by the men he thanked in the preface: E. F. Carritt, his tutor; F. A. Cockin (1888-1969), and S. G. Scott (1879-1941). Cockin, later a missionary, vicar of St. Mary's, Oxford, and bishop of Bristol, would invite Collingwood to preach at St. Mary's in 1935. Sebastian Gilbert Scott, son of the famous architect and already a distinguished physician, the Collingwoods had perhaps met in London in 1915.

It was in some ways an odd book for an aspiring philosopher in 1916, in the sense that Collingwood certainly knew the way philosophy was

---

[35]Collingwood, *Autobiography*, 43; *Religion and Philosophy*, v.

[36]Collingwood, *Religion and Philosophy*, xiii.

going at Oxford, and argued in a long note that he intended to contradict the best of neither realism nor idealism;[37] but by the very assumption that Christianity had intellectual content, the book might be taken as a throwback to Edward Caird, or even to Paley or Butler. For the new realism God was, as a leading American exponent wrote, "an exciting hypothesis" that one might or might not need, and H. A. Prichard's thesis that moral philosophy did indeed rest on a mistake was a popular success.[38] The Christian idea, which Collingwood called almost interchangeably religion and the Christian religion, was not a ritual designed to evoke or express emotions. His book had been written, Collingwood recalled in 1939, not against William James's *Varieties of Religious Experience* but against "every psychological theory of religion."[39] Nor was religion chiefly (as Ritschl and Schweitzer suggested) a matter of conduct. It was a single fundamental, though necessarily complex supposition to which both expressive ritual and right conduct were inextricably related. Philosophy and religion were the same thing, though their vocabularies differed. Religion was "on the intellectual side, . . . a theory of the world as a whole; . . . the religion of Homer is inconsistent with the philosophy of Auguste Comte but Comte's own religion and his philosophy are views of the same thing—the ultimate nature of the universe."[40]

As for morality, Collingwood wrote, it could not be separated from religion because thinking could not be separated from acting. John Alexander Smith had written in 1910 that "thought and action are simply left standing side by side in the psychological *Quicunque Vult*."[41] They remain, Collingwood wrote, "side by side and absolutely distinct, though each is necessary to the other." Yet there are not two elements in walking but only one, and finally there is "only one kind of activity; namely, that which is at the same time thought and will." In love, as the Johannine author knew, "the two elements are not connected merely ex-

---

[37]Ibid., n. 101.

[38]William P. Montague, "The Story of American Realism," 161.

[39]Collingwood, *Autobiography*, 93.

[40]Collingwood, *Religion and Philosophy*, 18.

[41]Smith, *Knowing and Acting*, 18.

ternally; knowledge is the way of obedience and obedience the approach to truth." Because religion is indispensable to action, "no legitimate interest is foreign to religious life."[42] Thus Collingwood abandoned the attempt to save religion by denying its relation to metaphysics and hence to truth.

It was also in *Religion and Philosophy* that Collingwood first undertook his lifelong defense of the proposition that all knowing is in some sense historical. By historical knowing Collingwood did not mean—and here he followed Croce, Smith, or both—that kind of historical reconstruction at which English theologians had become expert by 1910. This positivistic history was in Collingwood's judgment exactly analogous to a positivistic psychology that studied the human mind without studying what one is conscious of—an exercise yielding not knowledge but "barren and trifling abstraction." Such an approach "cannot answer ultimate questions; . . . it is left with the cold unreality of thought which is the thought of nothing, action with no purpose, and fact with no meaning." The historical Jesus, presumably Schweitzer's,

> can never solve the problem of Christianity because there never was a "historical Jesus" pure and simple. . . . By considering him as a mere fact in history, instead of also an idea in theology, we may be simplifying our task, but we are cutting ourselves off from true understanding. . . . To speak of studying the mind of Jesus from within may seem presumptuous; but no other method is of the slightest value.[43]

And so one of the fundamental theses popularized by the *Idea of History* after 1946 was born about 1912 or 1913, when Collingwood was at work translating Croce's *Vico* and writing his first book about religion. Neither positivism nor historicism was possible; history "cannot exist without philosophy. . . . History cannot proceed without philosophical presuppositions of a highly complex character."[44]

The discrete metaphysical and theological ideas that Collingwood discusses in the second and third sections of *Religion and Philosophy* add little to his methodology, or to his defense of the axiom that religion is a

---

[42]Collingwood, *Religion and Philosophy*, 32, 35-36.

[43]Ibid., 42-43.

[44]Ibid., 46-47.

kind of knowing, an intellectual activity, indeed the presupposition of all thought about the world. In the second part Collingwood offered a consideration of the classical proofs, defending them from the common charge that as fruits of the Middle Ages they were necessarily credulous or defective, that because they were medieval they must necessarily be the products of authority and faith, or that "a proof of some belief which is itself held on other grounds is illegitimate and insincere." Collingwood denied that to philosophize about God one must "first cease to believe in his existence." We are not, he wrote, dealing with abstract ideals, but with the ways and means of ordinary life and everyday thinking. Collingwood therefore felt free "to state as simply as possible certain beliefs concerning God and the world which are at least central to Christian theology, and then to examine certain alternatives to these, or objections alleged against them, which are familiar to modern readers."[45]

Collingwood's method stood Strauss on his head. D. F. Strauss had assumed that philosophy gave the lie to the propositions of Christian theology; Collingwood assumed the metaphysical fecundity of certain theological propositions, bringing to them for illumination the world of ordinary experience. By writing *Religion and Philosophy* Collingwood began to repair the shortcomings of the romantic tradition he self-consciously represented. Though Illingworth and Gore had insisted that religion had an irreducible intellectual content, the great popularizers Ruskin and Morris had never been able to come to terms with even a diluted supernaturalism. Collingwood's statement in the preface that he hoped to make some contribution to renewed interest among persons "not specially trained in technical philosophy or theology in the intellectual form of Christianity" should be taken seriously. He had not changed his mind in 1936, when he wrote that "in religion, the life of reflection is concentrated in its intensest form, and . . . the special problems of theoretical and practical life all take their special forms by segregation out of the body of religious consciousness."[46]

---

[45]Ibid., 51.

[46]Collingwood, *Idea of History*, 315.

II

"The war ended," Collingwood wrote, "I came back to Oxford an opponent of the 'realists.' "[47] He also returned a scholar well established for one so young, as author of one original work, one translation, and the long essay in *Concerning Prayer*. To these achievements was added his place as a pupil of the most famous archaeologist of Roman Britain, F. J. Haverfield (1860-1919), a relationship and enterprise upon which his growing interest in history would feed. The axiom around which his metaphysics would be developed, a restatement of the principle of the curriculum, was set down clearly in *Religion and Philosophy*, in which Collingwood had argued that "history cannot exist without philosophy" while "philosophy is impossible without history; for any theory must be a theory of facts." Since "the philosophical presuppositions of history are not something different from history itself," but "philosophical truths which the historian finds historically exemplified," it could be said that history and philosophy were the same thing.[48]

Religion was still a dominant concern after 1918, and Collingwood's continuing interest would be exemplified in essays like "Can the New Idealism Dispense with Mysticism?," his contribution to a symposium with Evelyn Underhill. There he reiterated his conclusion that philosophy could not live a life independent of either religion or religious experience: "It is the business of philosophy to criticize mysticism, not the business of mysticism to criticize philosophy. But, as the old verse has it, which is philosophy and which is mysticism, God bless us all, that's quite another thing." A paper on religious intolerance in which Collingwood argued that real religion must always consider its claims to truth exclusive belongs to this period, as does "The Philosophy of the Christian Religion," sent to *Theology* in 1920, but never published; "Lectures on the Philosophy of St. Paul," prepared for Sommerville College in 1918; "Money and Morals," 1919; and an essay titled "The Church" in which Collingwood defended its necessity and infallibility. Each of these essays was formed by Collingwood's conviction that the Christian idea

---

[47]Collingwood, *Autobiography*, 48.

[48]Collingwood, *Religion and Philosophy*, 51.

had content that was necessary to both thought and civilization. He also began his career as a lecturer by reading topics related to Christianity or to ethics. In 1915, and again from 1923 to 1925, he lectured on the philosophy of religion. In 1920 through 1923 he offered lectures on the ontological proof, and from 1921 to 1927, and again from 1929 to 1933 he presented annually a course on moral philosophy. It was 1926 before Collingwood offered his first lectures on the philosophy of history.[49]

By 1923 Collingwood felt competent to undertake a synthesis. The book was *Speculum Mentis* (1924), "mirror of the mind," and of it Collingwood wrote fifteen years later, "I . . . find it better than I remembered."[50] The problem Collingwood saw was the failure of the unity of mind that had characterized the Middle Ages. His solution was to be "in principle the Christian solution." *Speculum Mentis* was addressed to "the ordinary artists, the ordinary ministers of religion and students of philosophy," and in its preface, Collingwood, having admitted the occasional silliness of Coleridge, Ruskin, and Morris, claimed "no more than to be following and working out the great tradition founded over a century ago by the great men of the Romantic movement; purifying it." Appearing as one "anxious above all not to pose as repositories of a new revelation, . . . but to say once more, in words suited to our generation, something that everybody has always known."[51] The influences were obvious: Ruskin, Croce, Oxford idealism, the Christian religion.

Unlike *Religion and Philosophy*, which had the narrow goal of making some contribution to the philosophy of the Christian religion, *Speculum Mentis* was to restore integrity to a failing civilization—or at least to make a start—by constructing "a map of knowledge on which every legitimate form of human experience should be laid down, its boundaries determined, and its relations to its neighbors set forth."[52] Collingwood believed that in his earlier work the erroneous conclusion that religion, theology, and philosophy were identical had led "into a too intellectualistic or abstract attitude toward religion." In *Religion and Philosophy* he

---

[49]*HAS*, 433-34, compiled by van der Dussen from the *Oxford University Gazette*.

[50]Collingwood, *Autobiography*, 56 n.1.

[51]Collingwood, *Speculum Mentis*, 38.

[52]Ibid., 306.

had failed to see that "for religion symbol itself is always an end, never a mere means to the expressing of an abstract concept." I failed, he wrote, "to give an account of the uniqueness of Christ, or miracle, and of worship; I failed to discover any real ground for the concrete distinction not only between God and man, but between man and man."[53]

Speculum Mentis opens with a discussion of knowing as a process of question and answer, Collingwood's first treatment of the methodological key that he had borrowed from his tutors and developed through reflection on the Albert Memorial: If the architect had not intended to create ugliness, what had he intended? He next discusses art, treating it as a form of error, but error predicated on truth and containing both intuitive or imaginative and expressive or cognitive elements. Any work of imagination contained, so Collingwood believed, what Kant had called purposiveness without purpose, being "valuable, beautiful, just in so far as it is significant or expressive," yet standing silent before the questioner who asks what it signifies.[54] Religion then becomes a corrective for the silence of art, the means by which art may "assert what it imagines," and "believe in the reality of the figments of its own imagination." Religion "relatively to art" becomes "the discovery of reality." This reality belongs to history: it is nurtured and propagated by a society, in which it achieves "an explicit logical structure." "That which art cannot express except in its immediate intuitive shape, can by religion be stated in words in the form of a creed."[55]

The object of religion, Collingwood goes on to say, is itself understood as the experience of belief dialectically differentiated and bathed in the light of that holiness which teaches us that in religious experience we are "face to face with something other than ourselves and our imaginings, something infinitely real, the ground and source of our own being."[56] The form of that knowledge of God is faith, "the specific form of religious reason, . . . the knowledge of ultimate truth which, owing to its intuitive or imaginative form, cannot justify itself under criticism."

[53]Ibid., 108 n.1.

[54]Ibid., 89.

[55]Ibid., 111-17.

[56]Ibid., 120.

Other modes of knowledge, science and history, Collingwood admits, also "fail to justify themselves under criticism, . . . and yet are not forms of faith." For faith is "essentially intuitive and not assumptive." God "is the object of faith, not an hypothesis: Euclidean space is an hypothesis, not an object of faith."[57] In a profound sense the warrant for God's existence is our belief, but Collingwood sees quite clearly that in another sense the warrant for causality is belief, or something very like it, though that belief is assumptive not intuitive. There is a difference, an important difference, between an interpretation of experience that sees the God who may be imagined as thereby imaginary and the interpretation that sees imagination as the mirror of reality.

Two further problems were raised by Collingwood's discussion of religion and its object. The first was the attempt to explain the relation between hypothesis or supposal; that is, those assumptions that render historical and therefore scientific understanding possible; the second was faith, or that form of reason that affords knowledge of God. Collingwood discussed these at some length in *Faith and Reason: A Study in the Relations Between Religion and Science* (1928). There he argued that the problem had been occasioned, or certainly complicated, by confusion surrounding the meaning and history of the term *faith*. The Greeks had paid little attention to faith, devoting their efforts to knowing God or nature by means of the senses. This, certainly, had been the program of Aristotelian metaphysics. But Christianity, in league with neo-Platonic metaphysics, had proposed the possibility of an intuitive knowledge of all being, a knowledge that Christians called faith. Faith then came gradually to mean our knowledge of the infinite object, while finite being could still be known rationally.[58] Yet, quite obviously, the finite always leads us toward the infinite and presupposes it, while the infinite itself is known only through the finite. Anselm, for whom rational knowledge of the finite presupposed a knowledge of the infinite attained by faith, had, to Collingwood's mind, grasped the significance of this dilemma. Then Descartes had understood that Anselm's argument had a perfect analog in our experience of the self; and, again, Kant had wished to treat God, freedom, and immortality as Descartes had treated

[57]Ibid., 132.

[58]Collingwood, "Reason Is Faith Cultivating Itself," 1-18.

the self, as realities known in super-rational ways upon which rationality itself somehow depended.[59] Perhaps it would be correct to say that, for Collingwood, there was a sense in which every scientific or historical fact is known by faith with respect to its participation in those fundamental presuppositions that render it knowable at all, and known by reason insofar as that fact testifies in its finite relations and characteristics to the accuracy and intelligibility of those fundamental supposals or presuppositions. This scheme is, of course, complicated if we allow God to be more than that being whom all humans call God or if we allow faith to be an infused virtue. But this does not weaken Collingwood's insight on its own philosophical ground. In *Faith and Reason* the Crocean tendency of *Speculum Mentis* to see religion as possessed of content it could not explain clearly gave way again to the view of *Religion and Philosophy* that these two disciplines were identical, at least in the sense that both comprehended a general view of the world. Collingwood was actually working in the shadow of two ideas. One was the notion that religion was a kind of thought necessarily "intuitive" and implicitly inferior to philosophy; the other the position that religion clarified by reason contained all the intellectual content philosophy could know, but set in a context of faith or emotion. The movement from *Religion and Philosophy* (1916) to *Speculum Mentis* (1924) to *Faith and Reason* (1928) is the movement Knox was describing when he wrote that Collingwood had first identified religion and philosophy, then doubted their identity, then later reestablished it on a firmer basis.[60]

The other endemic problem of philosophy of religion Collingwood considered in *Speculum Mentis* and frequently thereafter was religious language and its limits. Art, he wrote,

> cannot be translated because it has no meaning except the whole meaning submerged, in the form of beauty, in the flood of imagery. Religion cannot translate itself not because it has no meaning . . . but because, although it had a meaning and knows that it has a meaning, it thinks that it has expressed this meaning already. And so it has but only metaphorically.[61]

---

[59]Collingwood, *Faith and Reason*, 13-19, 21.

[60]T. M. Knox, "Notes on Collingwood's Philosophical Work," *PBA* 18 (1943): 469.

[61]Collingwood, *Speculum Mentis*, 129-30.

The realm of metaphor includes analogy, the figurative language of Scripture, and perhaps the acts of liturgy. It then becomes the task of the philosopher and the theologian to elicit meaning from the metaphors proposed. The philosopher does this by rational criticism of the doctrines in themselves; the theologian works through rational criticism that, while carrying out the analytic work of theology by converting the implicit thought of religion into explicit thought, is nevertheless "committed to the defense of religion" and "willing to take religion's word for the point at which it finds his analysis intolerable."[62]

What the rational examination of religion reveals is an experience whose positive characteristics are "its freedom; its power of saving the soul; in a word its priceless gift of ultimate truth," and whose negative characteristics are

> that it lives by faith, and not by sight, that God is now not known only worshipped, "reached" but not grasped by the mind, that it cannot justify itself to reason or rise wholly above the level of superstition, and that therefore in the long run and in spite of all its best efforts it falls back into feeling, emotion—love, awe, and so forth—and therefore, like art, is an intermittent and unstable experience.[63]

Here Collingwood is expounding the epigraph of *Speculum Mentis*: "Now we see in a glass darkly" (1 Corinthians 13:12). But it is still religion that provides this partial knowledge, making possible the assertion of those elements of imaginative vision that constitute reality. The goal of religion is a universal church worshiping a universal God. And this must mean "the breaking down of the middle wall of partition between men and God."[64] The Christian religion is probably to be considered the ultimate form of religion because it is "difficult to see that religion . . . can ever achieve anything higher or more ultimate or absolutely satisfying than the twin conceptions of the Incarnation and the Atonement." Collingwood paraphrases Irenaeus: "God made himself man that he might make us God."

---

[62]Ibid., 149-50.

[63]Ibid., 133.

[64]Ibid., 139.

The great dogmas were, of course, ideas for Collingwood, and he could routinely appeal to the truth of Christian beliefs while forcing each toward a reasonable ground that threatened to reduce it to a sophisticated rationalization—not because he doubted the truth of these propositions but because it was the work of a theologian, and certainly of a philosopher of religion, to act as saboteur of the unexamined claims of revelation. This partly explains his interest in the Streeter group, whose members shared some of his understanding but who would have almost certainly taken his theological rationalism in the context of their own poetic Darwinism rather than on its own terms. It also explains his use in the *Essay on Philosophical Method* of theological principles as somewhat dry philosophical and historical presuppositions. The work of a philosopher of religion was different from the work of a preacher or teacher of the Christian religion. The philosopher of religion might argue that there were aspects of the Christian religion that were intellectually, and in Collingwood's sense, psychologically indispensable, without raising the question of faith.

Austin Farrer, who knew that Collingwood was a believer in God, was puzzled by *The Idea of History* because Collingwood seemed to assert that thought makes history, then to stress alternatively the similarities between human thought in all ages and the ability of thought to change the world. Farrer did agree that theism at least threw something else into the scales,[65] but the instability of that human thought which was supposed to constitute history made Collingwood's philosophy seem flawed. Yet if God establishes reality with his thought, which theologians might call his Word spoken as history, thought becomes something more than subjective. Collingwood nowhere suggests that the faculty that determines history belongs to nature. Perhaps Rudolf Bultmann was right when he remarked in his Gifford Lectures of 1955 that Collingwood's philosophy of history leaves the question of all knowledge—and all knowledge is historical—open to a future that can be known only if revelation delivers it.[66]

---

[65]Austin Farrer, "Thought as the Basis of History: Dr. Austin Farrer on R. G. Collingwood," *The Listener* 20 (March 1947): 425.

[66]Rudolf Bultmann, *History and Eschatology* (Edinburgh: University Press, 1957) 132-33.

III

In 1935 Collingwood was elected Waynflete Professor in succession to John Alexander Smith. Superficially, and viewed perhaps in the light of the subsequent popularity of *The Idea of History*, Collingwood seems during the 1930s to have passed from a concern for religion to an ever-deepening interest first in art and subsequently in history. This historiography obscures the complexity of his intellectual development during the 1930s, and especially the place of religion in it. He continued to read papers to The Group: "War in its Relation to Christian Ethics" and the "Historical Background of New Testament Thought" were read in 1930, and in December of that year "Science, Religion, and Culture" was delivered in Coventry Cathedral, the third paper in a series in which B. H. Streeter and Joseph Needham had preceded Collingwood. On 5 May 1935, Collingwood took Newman's pulpit at St. Mary the Virgin to preach "Rule-Making and Rule-Breaking."[67] Each of these evinced, though of course in different ways, Collingwood's conviction that religion was the fundamental human activity. Genuine happiness, he wrote, "can only be found by cultivating and trusting to something that is not science, but the very opposite of science: I mean the *religious* element in our nature," and if "to be civilized means to be happy, this inward flame of religion, even in an age dominated by science, must always be kept burning in the heart of the civilization."[68]

These occasional topics were indications of the more fundamental direction his thought had taken, reflected in his work in 1933 and 1934 on the manuscript that would become the heart of *The Idea of Nature*.[69] This short book is important because it is, apart from Collingwood's inaugural, his first formal and straightforward exposition of his belief that historical thinking is the form of thought upon which all other thinking, even science, depends. The argument of the essay was itself historical, consisting chiefly of a brilliant reinterpretation of the ideas of nature held

---

[67]CPB.

[68]"Science, Religion, and Civilization," 12, 16.

[69]R. G. Collingwood, *The Idea of Nature* (Oxford: Clarendon Press, 1945) prefatory note.

from the Ionians to Alexander and Whitehead.[70] For his philosophy of religion, the most important aspect of *The Idea of Nature* was Collingwood's claim that thought about nature is ultimately thought about God, a relationship that he discovers and criticizes in Plato, Aristotle, the Renaissance, Eddington, Jeans, Bergson, and Samuel Alexander. Collingwood found in Alexander's *Space, Time and Deity* a philosophy "in the grand manner," full of promise but impaired by "a strain of empiricism." Alexander fails to tell the reader why space and time should generate man: "Yet if the child is father to the man, surely the first duty of natural piety is to respect, and endeavor to satisfy, the childish tendency to ask questions beginning with *why.*" Collingwood continues: "In its extreme form the weakness appears in Alexander's exposition of the idea of God. . . . One's thoughts of God are no doubt childish; but such as they are, they begin by thinking that God created the heavens and the earth. Alexander, on the contrary, says that in the end the heavens and the earth will create God." Collingwood suggests that the logic of Alexander's system might be reconsidered, especially "the question whether categorical characteristics pervading nature as a whole do not imply something outside nature, something prior to space and time."[71]

The argument of *The Idea of Nature* proceeds smoothly toward Collingwood's conclusion that nature is dependent for its existence on something else, and natural science is a kind of reasonable activity that depends on some other kind of thinking. That other form of thought is history. The reader is left to tell himself that the something else upon which nature depends is God. The dogmatism and skepticism that Knox discovered in Collingwood's later writings were complementary aspects of his tendency to allow his historical method to yield certainty only on the basis of an imaginal act and the concomitant realization that the *regula* for those acts through which history was known and civilization formed was theological. Donagan rightly complains that Collingwood, who set out to show that metaphysics was independent, persistently failed: philosophy, being a historical discipline, was necessarily related closely to thought about God.[72]

---

[70]Parts 1 and 2 survey the literature, a pattern Collingwood used in his attempt to move from history to philosophy.

[71]Collingwood, *Idea of Nature*, 158, 164.

[72]Alan Donagan, "Collingwood and Philosophical Method," 1, 18.

Written in 1933 and 1939 and published in 1940, the *Essay on Metaphysics* was, save for *The New Leviathan*, the last work Collingwood saw through the press. Oddly, *The Idea of History*, which *The Idea of Nature* had presaged, though written for the most part by 1936, had remained unpublished. Retrospectively, the necessity for the *Essay* seems clear, for though metaphysics was, as Collingwood had argued since 1916, a kind of historical thinking, there was still not much in his writings that explained systematically the relation between metaphysics and history. In the *Essay*, metaphysics appears as the science of absolute presuppositions, and those presuppositions are also historical.

> Metaphysics has always been an historical science. . . . Thus it is not a "metaphysical doctrine" or a "metaphysical theory" of Spinoza that nature is the same as God. If you understand the metaphysical rubric when you read what he says about this you will see that what he is doing is to state an historical fact about the religious foundation of seventeenth-century natural science.[73]

Thus historical fact is for Collingwood an absolute presupposition, and absolute presuppositions take their places in a constellation of absolute presuppositions, each "consupposible with all the others." The relation between the various presuppositions and the constellations is not mathematical. They are related in what Collingwood calls "a *catalogue raisonné*, as in the seventh book of Aristotle's *Metaphysics* or in the *Quaestiones* of the medieval metaphysician.[74] Comprehending Collingwood probably depends upon the insight that in his thought suppositions, supposals, presuppositions, absolute presuppositions, and the question-answer dialectic all serve the same function, are in great measure similar, and are the hermeneutic of experience, and hence of historical knowledge. In the highest term, these presuppositions are theological.[75]

This idea of the work of philosophy was of course incompatible with the conclusions of the realists, and Collingwood devoted some pages to a discussion of what he considered the pathology of contemporary philosophy, criticizing in some detail positivism and, in particular, Ayer's

---

[73]Collingwood, *Essay on Metaphysics*, 68-69.

[74]Ibid., 68.

[75]Ibid., 213-27.

Language, Truth, and Logic. Ayer's mistake, Collingwood believed, lay in first confusing propositions, statements that can be verified by an appeal to facts, with those suppositions that are necessarily prior to all thought and with respect to which argument is futile, and then attacking the suppositions for failing to behave like propositions. Ayer had failed to pursue his own inquiry with proper seriousness, for he had failed to give any account of his opponents' errors. If the statements of metaphysicians were not propositions (in Ayer's sense), what were they?[76]

The first and most telling supposition through which Collingwood illustrates the argument of the *Essay* is reminiscent of *Faith and Reason*, for he chooses as his primary example the absolute presupposition that modern science derives from religion: "All modern scientific work rests on the absolute presupposition that nature is one and that science is one: that the different realms of nature are in part governed by one and the same code of absolutely identical laws, . . . and in part by special codes."[77] For Aristotle, Collingwood notes, nature, governed by laws such as those of the *Metaphysics*, simply was God. The Fathers corrected the Greek mistake of thinking that nature and hence God could be known by the senses (and in Collingwood's terms, described by propositions). Absolute presuppositions are not "derived from experience," but are catalytic agents that the mind must bring out of its own resources to the manipulation of what is called "experience." Of these absolute presuppositions the chief is—or so Collingwood believed—the complex postulate of a self-differentiating God, self-subsistent and capable of existing alongside a world that has its own derivative existence. This Collingwood called a kind of "Catholic Faith" that, as "preserved by the institutions of Christendom, was the key to the constellation of presuppositions constitutive of the civilization."[78] The chapter was entitled *Quicunque Vult*, an obvious reference to the function of religious assertions as prerequisite to other kinds of thought.[79] The very foundation of

---

[76]Ibid., 165.

[77]Ibid., 206.

[78]Ibid., 227. See also R. G. Collingwood, Review of *The Nature of Belief*, by M. C. D'Arcy, *Criterion* 11 (1931-1932): 336.

[79]The use of the term *Quicunque Vult* has a rich history: Smith, *Nature of Art*, 19; *Knowing and Acting*, 18; Collingwood, *Essay on Metaphysics*, 213. For Smith and Collingwood the first phrase of the Athanasian Creed was a code word referring to the presuppositions or supposals that made thought possible.

science and of history was a presupposition about God, and the guarantors of the Catholic faith, as Collingwood defined them, were the historical institutions of the Western world. In one sense this was a magnificent solipsism; but if intellect and imagination do, as Collingwood maintained, discover reality, the map of the mind will indeed be a map of the world.

By 1939, Collingwood had moved into that stage of his thought that Knox would describe as credulity. There was no more flirtation with Modernism. There were personal crises: his conclusion before 1938 that the government of Great Britain was implicitly sympathetic to the Fascists, a position that his friends mistakenly saw as a rejection of his lifelong conservatism; his deteriorating health; strains in his marriage. Having spent the academic year 1938-1939 at sea, where the *Essay on Metaphysics* had been written, he returned to Oxford in April, only to leave again in June for a six-week cruise of the Mediterranean with several of his students. Collingwood's thoughts about religion, valuable because unguarded, are displayed in his *First Mate's Log*, his published journal of that summer voyage.

The ship's company had come upon a monastery on Santorin, and the crew, befriended by the monks, had nevertheless felt uncomfortable and suspicious in the presence of a way of life that seemed useless and superstitious. Collingwood became the monks' defender, arguing that the crew should approach the monastery and its work in the framework provided by the monks's own presuppositions.

> In this way the traveler who began by thinking the men of Santorin ignorant, unenlightened, and superstitious, may possibly, unless he is very careful, find within his mind a court sitting wherein the men of Santorin rise up in judgment against his own world and the Protestantism, secularism, and utilitarianism of which it is so proud.

Collingwood, who had embarrassed his student crew by venerating the icons and crossing himself, took the occasion to reflect that the choice was always between utilitarianism and judgments based on the intrinsic worth of deeds and men. "If utility is the only goodness," he wrote, "if nothing is good except insofar as it is useful, there is no utility, and therefore no goodness." Collingwood found the abbot of Santorin an especially appealing character, somewhat reminiscent of an Oxford don, "yet he was not really like them, because he had a warmth and sweetness . . .

which they mostly lacked, and none of the bitter obsession with personal rivalries and unsolved problems which . . . disfigures even the best of them."[80]

The New Leviathan, written in 1941 and 1942, was Collingwood's last book. In it Collingwood consistently assumed the indispensability of the Christian doctrines of freedom, original sin, and the atonement, and recommended the Christian Fathers to those who would understand European history. Christendom was simply the world, the world whose absolute presuppositions were defended in the *Essay on Philosophical Method*, and whose existence the barbarians always attack.[81]

An even more specific witness to Collingwood's thought on the place of religion in civilization was his essay "Fascism and Nazism," written while *The New Leviathan* was in preparation. There Collingwood argues that a successful civilization is invariably inspired by its devotion to a religion that contains and propagates the important principles upon which the civilization is built. During the past three hundred years, religion had suffered

> a curious double fate. Whatever in it is capable of logical formulation as a system of first principles has been analyzed and codified and has come to function as the axioms upon which our science of nature and history, our practice of liberal economics and free or democratic politics—in short, all the things that make up our civilization—are built. But whatever is not capable of logical formulation, whatever is in the nature of religious emotion, passion, faith has been progressively exterminated, partly by ridicule and partly by force.

But the axioms when abstracted from their religious context prove powerless. Religion is

> the only known explosive in the economy of that delicate internal-combustion engine, the human mind. People that have reached the top of the hill by wise use of religious energy may then decide to do without it; they can still move, but they can only move downhill, and when they come to the bottom of the hill they stop.[82]

---

[80]Collingwood, *First Mate's Log*, 151-53.

[81]Collingwood, *New Leviathan*, 94, 121, 165, 194, 198; Knox, "Collingwood," 170.

[82]Collingwood, "Fascism and Nazism," 169.

Religion is the matrix in which thought, and hence history, is formed.

T. M. Knox, whose introduction to the *Idea of History* is central to the popular scholarly view of Collingwood's thought, believed that for Collingwood the *Essay on Metaphysics* represented a departure, on the whole ill considered, from the more carefully tempered thought of the *Essay on Philosophical Method*, and indeed from the best of Collingwood's earlier writing. Knox thought that Collingwood's understanding of religion and its character as fundamental or absolute presupposition had shifted. The Collingwood of the 1928 essay on *Faith and Reason*, like the author of the *Essay on Philosophical Method*, had indeed taught something like the necessity of a presupposition religious in nature, "a rational faith, universal in everyone and necessary to all thought," but in the late 1930s there was a philosophical skepticism "bound up with a new dogmatism"; our attitude toward our own absolute presuppositions (that is, toward our own religion) is to be one of "unquestioning acceptance." And Knox asks if, having considered realism a philosophy based on human stupidity, Collingwood may not have gone on "to erect his philosophy on the foundation of human credulity."[83]

What Collingwood was confronting was the fundamental relation between faith and reason. With the great philosopher-theologians of medieval Europe, Collingwood assumed that knowledge of the entire order of reality insofar as reality can be known does depend on presuppositions that cannot be derived from our immediate historical experience. In that sense we believe before, and in order that we might, understand. Collingwood always looks like a rationalist when he insists on rendering those presuppositions intelligible. He looks like a fideist—or, in Knox's words, a dogmatist—when he is insisting that the ultimate presuppositions are simply given. He is reasonably clear and consistent regarding the use of the terms theology, religion, and the Christian religion. Theology is religion driven as far toward its rational ground as reason can take it, faith cultivating itself philosophically. Religion is an experience, of which the Christian religion is a specification, but both have a certain content that is known by faith more completely and sometimes before it is known by reason. The Christian religion functions as the fundamental presupposition or constellation of presuppositions. There is no major

---

[83]Collingwood, *Idea of History*, xvi.

work of Collingwood that does not make religion the presupposition of metaphysics and history. In "The Principles of History" (1936) Collingwood had observed that our obligation to pay attention to scientific evidence had "roots in certain religious beliefs about nature and its creator God." He added that this seemed paradoxical "only because the facts have been obscured by propagandist literature, beginning with the illuminati movement of the eighteenth century." "Take away Christian theology," Collingwood wrote, "and the scientist has no longer any motive for doing what inductive thought gives him permission to do."[84] That the Christian religion provides the constellation of presuppositions central to science and civilization was the point of the 1928 essay *Faith and Reason*, though Knox is right when he says that Collingwood had not then elaborated any of the content necessary for the faith that reason discovers when cultivating itself. The principle can be traced to the first sentence of the introduction to *Religion and Philosophy*: "This book is the result of an attempt to treat the Christian creed not as a dogma, but as a critical solution of a philosophical problem." The idea had developed, but it had never changed. The attempt to make of Collingwood a liberal Christian on the Streeter model, anxious to show that a purged Christianity is rational, is doomed to failure. Some passages in *Speculum Mentis* can be adduced to support such a conclusion, but it inverts the pattern and substance of Collingwood's mature philosophy, in which religion is not the failure of reason but the only matrix in which thought can live, and the ground of every presupposition formative of civilization.

If this interpretation of Collingwood's thought is correct, he shares the tradition represented by Augustine, Anselm, and Thomas. Theologians looking for a philosophy on which to build always face difficulties, though a twentieth-century theologian might find in Collingwood fewer problems than Augustine discovered in Plato or Thomas in Aristotle. Apart from the problem posed by the rationalizing passages in *Speculum Mentis* and (perhaps) *Faith and Reason*, there is the difficulty posed by his use of superstition—is Christianity superstitious or not, and if not, why? There is also in *Speculum Mentis* the ghost of the old (and futile) use of "spirit" and "spiritual" with the latter sometimes taken as a synonym for "higher." To minds formed after Neo-Scholasticism began to

---

[84]Ibid., 255-56.

emphasize the difference between theology and philosophy, what is most obviously missing is something analogous to the traditional distinction between natural theology and theology properly so called; or, better, between theism and Christianity. In fact, Collingwood knows only one kind of theology, the theology that is Christianity, which "makes terms with rationalism." It partly protects religion from rationalism and from superstition, and it partly succumbs to the rationalizing impetus of science. The presuppositions of thought belong to history, and Christianity is both the summary Western presupposition and, in itself, the religion possessed of the unsurpassable ideas of the Incarnation and the Atonement. The distinction between the presuppositions belonging to theology and the absolute presuppositions of metaphysics is never clear, perhaps because it exists no more than the distinction in Justin Martyr between the logos as Christ and the logos as cosmic reason. If this is the case, the constructive interpretation of Collingwood's thought might most profitably begin by taking up Knox's hyperbole that in the end Collingwood had made metaphysics rest on credulity, and asking what that might mean.

If Collingwood did not mean that knowledge of the world depends upon some infused virtue or subjective excellence, he must, if Knox was right, have intended his readers to understand that knowledge of history, and hence all knowledge, is a function of truth given, not merely discovered.

•CHAPTER V•

Pilgrim's Regress: Reason, Orthodoxy, and England

On the intellectual side my own progress has been from realism to Philosophical Idealism; from Idealism to Pantheism; from Pantheism to Theism; and from Theism to Christianity. I still think this is a very natural road. . . .

C. S. Lewis,
Pilgrim's Regress, 1943

Smith had abandoned realism by 1909; Collingwood by 1918. Webb had never considered it more than a criticism, tendered seriously and in good faith, of the tradition of Plato and Green. But C. S. Lewis, who would furnish English readers with a tightly knit fabric of ideas derived from the philosophy he had learned in Greats and his extensive reading in theology and literature, was a realist throughout his undergraduate years. Elements of the "New Look," his monistic realism of the years 1920-1922, would persist even after he began the metaphysical pilgrimage that ended in his return to the Anglicanism he had abandoned as a schoolboy. The sign of his return was *Pilgrim's Regress*, written in Ireland at Bernagh, the house of his friend Arthur Greeves near Belfast, in August 1932.[1] It is of all Lewis's major works least studied, perhaps

[1]Lewis had sketched several attempts to tell the story of his conversion. The work was published by Dent in May 1933. In 1943 Lewis added to the third edition a preface and the running headlines. References are to the third edition.

because the texture of the allegory is so dense, so full of references to ideas embodied in the theological and philosophic ground he had traversed, that the popular reader founders. But this same density, coupled with the work's many references to Lewis's authorities and contemporaries, makes *Pilgrim's Regress* the best witness to the mind of the newly converted scholar.

Lewis had been converted, insofar as human means prevailed, by thinking, and the stages in his intellectual progress from realism to orthodoxy can be dated with some precision from his autobiography and his letters. It is a progress best understood in the context of the two themes that run like royal threads throughout Lewis's life and writing. The first persistently converting strain in Lewis's experience was "the longing that was joy."[2] The boy who had watched the green hills of Antrim in 1910 had become by 1932 John of Puritania, the protagonist of *Pilgrim's Regress*. The experience of joy, Lewis wrote, is one of intense longing, distinguished from other longings by two things. First, joy was "a hunger better than any other fullness," the mere wanting of it was delight. Second, there was "a peculiar mystery about the *object* of this desire." When it is evoked by the distant hills, the boy may think, "if only I were there." When it is evoked by a romantic poem, he may think he is wishing that "faerie lands forlorn" really existed. Yet it was, Lewis wrote, the sole merit of *Pilgrim's Regress* that its author knew that the object of this desire was not distant hillsides, and certainly not sex: "Every one of these supposed objects for the Desire is inadequate to it." And the end of the dialectic of desire, through which, one by one, those false objects were sought, found, and surpassed, was "clear knowledge that the human soul is made to enjoy some object that is never fully given—nay, cannot even be imagined as given—in our present mode of subjective and spatiotemporal experience."[3] Joy had remained an essential theme of Lewis's theology and experience. He would later write that it was the linking up of the ideas of joy as satisfied only in some supermundane object and idealism (which taught that it was more important that heaven really existed than that any of us achieved it) that formed the

---

[2]Lewis, *Pilgrim's Regress*; C. S. Lewis to Warren Lewis, 24 October 1931, *LCSL*, 144.

[3]Lewis, *Pilgrim's Regress*, 7-10.

crucial link between experience and thought through which he was converted.[4]

Lewis's estimate of the importance of joy was not unique. Ruskin was describing the same experience when he wrote of his youthful "perception of Sanctity in the whole of nature, from the slightest thing to the vastest; an instinctive awe mixed with delight; an indefinable thrill. . . ." Chesterton had recalled the wonder that invested everything with a light that cut objects out very clearly and made the world seem solid, creating a mood in which there was "something of an eternal morning."[5] In the preface to *Pilgrim's Regress*, Lewis almost identified Desire, another name for joy, with Romanticism; but in this use of Romanticism Lewis (like Chesterton and Ruskin) intended nothing belonging to the soft, fetid swamps that lay south of the road in Lewis's allegory. Indeed, it was characteristic of joy that it had about it an intelligibility, like Coleridge's primary imagination, directing those who sought it not toward the daemonic irrationality of Nietzsche but toward Reason.[6]

Joy invariably moves the characters and shapes the narrative in Lewis's stories. John of Puritania is driven on the road by his vision of a distant island and of the mountains in the West, and throughout the book, through despair and aimless wandering, John persists stubbornly in his desire for his island. The *Sehnsucht* that John experiences is the joy the Belfast boy had felt in seeing the Castlereagh Hills. Yet desire as Lewis depicts it is hardly unambiguous, for while it is on one hand rational and rooted in the desire for God, it is also easily corrupted by such allegorical sirens as Media Halfways into mere lust.[7] This ambiguity did not, in Lewis's mind, justify the attack on joy that had begun with Kant. Apart from the dwellers in the South who drowned joy in sentiment and reduced it to base desire, joy had two other enemies: the great moralists

---

[4]Lewis, *Surprised by Joy*, 221-22.

[5]Ruskin's description of the sanctity of nature, from *Modern Painters*, appears in an appendix to Rudolf Otto's *The Idea of the Holy* (New York: Oxford University Press, 1957) 215; G. K. Chesterton, *Autobiography* (London: Hutchinson, 1936) 49.

[6]Even during the period of his New Look, Lewis had "set a very great value on imagination in some high Coleridgean sense" (*Surprised by Joy*, 203).

[7]Lewis, *Pilgrim's Regress*, 40-45.

who did not understand that joy can be a guide to virtue, and the classicists who distrusted joy and indeed the whole romantic tradition. Virtue represents throughout most of *Pilgrim's Regress* the plight of those who, following Kant, must do good without any reason. The other enemies of joy whom Lewis gladly calls to account are Mr. Neo-Angular; Mr. Neo-Classical, and Mr. Humanist; that is, Eliot, T. E. Hulme, and Paul Elmer More.[8] Hulme's polemic against Romanticism, which he considered flawed by its denial of original sin, and More's Platonic humanism, had influenced Eliot deeply. All three considered desire to be not ambiguous, or as Lewis would have it, in its higher form a *preparatio evangelica*, but corrupt or at least profoundly untrustworthy. "My ethics are based on dogma, not on feeling," says Mr. Neo-Angular.[9] Eliot, More, and Hulme were not the only advocates of aridity Lewis had in mind. Karl Barth, who in the 1930s denied that revelation shared anything with reason, was also a dweller in Lewis's tableland, as were the Neo-Scholastics like Maurice De Wulf, who (in Webb's opinion) had denied the relation between philosophy and theology.[10]

It is difficult now to see Eliot or Hulme among the pale men of the North whom Lewis castigated in 1932. In 1928 Eliot had proclaimed himself a classicist (and an Anglo-Catholic), allegiances that brought him, in the imagery of *Pilgrim's Regress*, from a place somewhat south of the road, with the Imagists, Vorticists, and Bergson, to a place somewhat north of it.[11] Eliot had discovered Maritain, whom he considered a kind

---

[8]Ibid., 10. Lewis knew Paul Elmer More—who visited Oxford frequently in the 1920s, and was befriended by both Webb and J. A. Smith—better than he knew Eliot; and More, whom Lewis could have met in 1928 or 1931, was, with More's friends Irving Babbitt and Norman Foerster, the model for Mr. Humanist. More visited Oxford again in May 1933, after *Pilgrim's Regress* had gone to press, but before it was published. More was fascinated by Lewis's having found the faith that always eluded him. He befriended Lewis and was promised a copy of the book, which was duly sent; a cordial correspondence followed. See Arthur Hazard Dakin, *Paul Elmer More* (Princeton: Princeton University Press, 1960) 225, 301, 327, 333, 355n, 359. See also WJB, 22, 24 January 1925 [MS.Eng.misc.d.1117].

[9]Ibid., 97.

[10]Ibid., 10-11; Webb, Review of *Nature, Man, and God*, by William Temple, *Mind*, n.s. 10 (1935): 227.

[11]T. S. Eliot, *For Lancelot Andrews* (London: Faber and Gwyer, 1928) ix. Eliot's godfather was B. H. Streeter, who was pressed into service by the pastor who baptized Eliot at Finstock Church in the Cotswolds in 1927.

of antidote to his youthful enthusiasm for Bergson, and later wrote that he had become a Christian because Christianity found a place for values Eliot was bound to "maintain or perish, . . . the belief for instance in holy living and holy dying, in sanctity, charity, humility, austerity."[12] It is possible to see the author of the *Wasteland*, to use the words Lewis applied to the three pale men, as a poacher turned gamekeeper, but as Lewis confessed in the 1943 preface to *Pilgrim's Regress*, this hardly does Eliot justice. One misjudgment Lewis persistently made was his belief that the modern world was one in which the positive images of Renaissance and medieval literature could simply be refurbished. Eliot saw that poetry was *not* rooted in life, or was rooted in life that was a kind of death. Eliot's images are critical images that derive their power from an implicit tension between figures that display existence surrealistically against a background of unspoken hope that reveals the city for what it is. Because of his faith in all things human and his skepticism about the claims of modernity, Lewis trusted sweet desire, believing that in the most earthly of loves there was some root of goodness. Lewis, like Collingwood, considered Romanticism a living and fertile movement, joy the source of happiness, and invariably wrote as though the themes of the tradition were available and believable.

Reason, the armor-clad virgin of the *Regress*, was the second constant of Lewis's intellectual life. Difficult to discover clearly in what he has told us of the boy, the University scholar was from the first unable to doubt the fruitfulness of thought and the power of reason to touch reality. Thus Lewis would find the radical subjectivism of the new psychology an attitude his mind simply could not comprehend, and the poetry of the 1920s absurd and distasteful.[13] Even during the period 1919 to 1922 when he developed his New Look, a philosophy manly, realistic, void of self-pity and calculated to contain joy, Lewis was probably not a wholehearted realist. The New Look, as Lewis called it, was a "stoical monism" that had in the writings of Bradley a distinguished and philosophically sophisticated, if atheistic, pedigree. We accepted, Lewis later wrote, "as rock-bottom reality the universe revealed by the senses,"

---

[12]T. S. Eliot, "Christianity and Communism," *The Listener*, 16 March 1932.

[13]Lewis, *Surprised by Joy*, 209. For Lewis on the early poetry of Eliot, see Lewis, *Selected Essays*, xv-xvi; *Pilgrim's Regress*, 10, 47; Green and Hooper, *C. S. Lewis*, 130.

while at the same time "we continued to make for certain phenomena of consciousness all the claims that really went with the theistic or idealistic view." Abstract thinking gave "indisputable truth"; moral judgments were "valid"; and aesthetic experience was "not merely pleasing but 'valuable.' "[14]

The grounds of Lewis's personal commitment to this tempered realism were complex. Lewis the rebel considered idealism the dominant philosophy, and therefore relished his association with philosophical heresy. Realism, like Aristotle, satisfied Lewis's lifelong love for the objective: "I wanted nature to be quite independent of our observation; something other, self-existing, indifferent."[15] And events conspired to make Lewis long for the solid, reliable world of decent atheism. He had watched a friend who had flirted with theosophy, Yoga, and psychoanalysis go mad, and met an ancient parson who had forgotten God in an obsessive search for immortality. The new psychology had shown that imagination might be mere fantasy. In contrast, the philosophy of the New Look was a philosophy of common sense.[16] There were also personal reasons. E. F. Carritt, the University College tutor who had sent Collingwood to the lectures of the realists in 1909 and 1910, had identified Lewis as a highly promising scholar in 1916, when Carritt had examined Lewis for his scholarship. After Lewis returned to University College in 1919, Carritt, who was also Lewis's tutor in philosophy, persistently sponsored his search for a career in philosophy, generously writing testimonials to college after college, and finally giving Lewis his pupils in 1924 when Carritt was invited to lecture at the University of Michigan. Carritt obviously considered Lewis a candidate for a place in the rapidly developing realist succession, and the younger scholar duly recorded Carritt's determination that Lewis should meet H. A. Prichard. Lewis found Oxford's premier realist a mousy little man, but the meeting was the crowing effort in Carritt's lengthy attempt to secure a place in the university for one he obviously considered a disciple.[17]

---

[14]Lewis, *Surprised by Joy*, 208.

[15]Ibid., 209-10.

[16]Ibid., 201-203.

[17]LJ, 1, 23 June 1922; 9, 10 March 1924 [8:148, 196-98].

The summer of 1922 had been a time of crisis for Lewis. First there had been the Magdalen possibility, for which he wrote his "Hegemony of Moral Value," then the sinking realization that he would not succeed. It was also in the summer of 1922 that the realism he had learned from Carritt threatened collapse. Barfield had made Lewis see that if aesthetic experience were valuable, values must exist, and Lewis, haunted by reason, by the *Republic* and the *Metaphysics*, found the behaviorist theory of logic, ethics, and aesthetics increasingly incredible. The mind, he concluded, was "no late-come phenomena [*sic*], . . . the whole universe was, in the last resort, mental; . . . our logic was participation in the cosmic logos."[18] His monism became a good deal less stoical, a good deal more idealistic. There was perfection somewhere, and (at least) knowing it mattered. "What I learned from the Idealists (and still most strongly hold)," Lewis wrote in 1955, "is the maxim: 'it is more important that heaven should exist than that any of us should reach it.' "

Between 1922 and 1924 there was his work in the English School. There Lewis read *Piers Plowman* and *The Dream of the Rood*, Donne, Thomas Browne, and George Herbert. He was surprised to find that the best writers, those who really fed the intellect, were Christians. "The only non-Christians who seemed to me to know anything," he wrote, "were the Romantics; and a good many of them were dangerously tinged with something like religion, even at times with Christianity."[19]

Lewis's idealism, the period of his allegiance to Bradley and Bosanquet, began as he entered the English School in the fall of 1922. The months until he would finally find safe harbor at Magdalen in May 1925 were devoid of the rewards upon which the souls of aspiring dons feed, though he felt intellectually enriched. He ached for a fellowship, but none was offered. There was a chance at distant Reading, but Lewis would not leave Oxford, then openings at Exeter and St. John's were filled by other candidates. In July 1923, the end of the English School in sight, Lewis mentioned to his father for the first time the possibility that he might stay on for a research degree. The English School ended in No-

---

[18]LJ, 29 September 1922 [7:237]; Lewis, *Surprised by Joy*, 208-209.

[19]Lewis, *Surprised by Joy*, 210-11, 214.

vember, but Lewis, now armed with firsts in both Greats and English, still found no appointment.[20]

Carritt's sponsorship remained the only certainty, and in February that friendship at last produced a tangible result: Carritt had been invited to Michigan for the year 1924-1925, and asked Lewis to take his lectures at University and part of his pupils. The months June through August 1924 were spent in preparation. Lewis read Sidgwick, Bosanquet, Mill, Alexander, and McTaggart, and daily he repaired to the attic, where the fourteen lectures entitled "The Moral Good—Its Place Among the Values" were produced.[21] Lewis's method was historical, Locke, Hume, Leibniz, Kant, and Berkeley coming before his audience in succession. Lewis criticized Locke for having at the outset begged the question, for having assumed that "the mind can apprehend directly nothing but its own states." Lewis suggested that Kant's implicit idealism was naive and unwarranted. Nor would a physical theory rescue Locke's epistemology of impressions and ideas: "If we cannot see beyond our ideas, we cannot use some of those ideas as evidence for the method by which the others were produced." Again: "I am aware of the green. This proves that my awareness is a state of mind, not that the green is a state of mind." Furthermore, Locke had attempted—illegitimately, Lewis thought—to move from percept to concept, but this either implied the existence of the very innate universals Locke wished to deny or else left the knower with "an indeterminate number of unrelated percepts, none of which is knowledge."[22] Lewis was sufficiently rooted in classical metaphysics to insist that Locke's empiricism had failed, but enough of a realist to want no more of subjective idealism. Of Berkeley Lewis wrote in 1924,

> What Berkeley *really* seems to mean is that there is a common world of *sensibilia* which is directly accessible to us all; ideal only in the sense that there is no substratum below the *sensibilitas*. . . . What we actually

---

[20]LJ, 20 February, 6 March 1924 [8:183, 194].

[21]C. S. Lewis to Albert Lewis, undated, 1925, LPW [8: 225]; LJ, 14 March, 6, 14, 26 May, 3 June 1924 [8:202, 224, 229, 236].

[22]C. S. Lewis, "The Moral Good—Its Place Among the Values," 50-52.

> get in Berkeley is a series of private worlds only held together by the goodness of God.[23]

Against Hume, Lewis brought the typical criticism of the school of Green: "The self has disappeared under his dialectic, and we are left with nothing but ideas and impressions." Yet Hume is praised for his distinction between the *is* and the *ought*, an idea Prichard had made the fulcrum of his own moral philosophy.

In 1924 Lewis was indeed willing to use idealistic arguments to refute empiricism, but was clearly not an idealist in any systematic sense. His lectures at University as Carritt's proxy filled only part of a year spent as a professional philosopher. He attended the postgraduate society of philosophers and on one occasion read his "Hegemony of Moral Value." W. D. Ross, then Deputy White's Professor of Moral Philosophy, was present and praised the paper, urging Lewis to publish it in *Mind* or in *Hibbert Journal*. For months Lewis worked at revising the essay for *Mind*, but it was never published, and it finally made its way, at least in part, into the fabric of *The Abolition of Man*.[24]

His temporary appointment as Carritt's proxy ended, Lewis still had no fellowship. The scheme to take a D.Litt. was revived in February 1924 and on 6 March Lewis wrote his father that he was at work on a D.Phil. dissertation on the seventeenth-century Cambridge Platonist Henry More. The exercise produced no degree, but it once again brought before Lewis's mind the case in favor of Christianity. When another fellowship at Magdalen was announced in April 1925, Lewis wrote his father that he would of course put in for it, "but without any serious hopes." When at last, on 25 May, came the news that he had been elected, it was, he wrote, his reputation as a philosopher that had turned the tide. He would be expected to help out in philosophy as well as tutoring in English. He left philosophy, he wrote his father, without regrets. He had found the philosopher's life lonely, and disliked the perpetual questioning of the truths plain men found obvious. He was,

---

[23]Lewis, "The Moral Good," 75. Lewis had first read Berkeley—with delight—in 1917 (Hooper, ed., *They Stand Together*, 196). Cf. *Surprised by Joy*, 223.

[24]C. S. Lewis to Albert Lewis, March 1924 [8:198]; LJ, 12 May 1924 [8:228].

he wrote, conscious of a descent from the pure air of philosophy, but he entered his new work, and Magdalen, with an obvious sense of relief.[25]

"My adversary," Lewis wrote of the period beginning about 1925, "began to make His final moves."[26] These were five: Lewis reread Euripides' *Hippolytus*, and all the "world's end imagery" that he had rejected for the New Look rose before him. From Alexander's *Space, Time, and Deity*, Lewis learned the distinction between the object of thought and the emotion our contemplation of the thinking self arouses: "When we think a thought, 'thought' is a cognate accusative (like 'blow' in 'strike a blow')." This meant that the one essential property of love (or hate) was attention to its object, not attention to the emotional states left behind by our thoughts or acts. "I saw that all my writings and watchings for joy . . . had been futile attempts to contemplate the enjoyed." It is hard to overestimate the importance of this discovery for Lewis, who considered it an "indispensable tool of thought." He had used it often in the lectures of 1924, and had then raised the possibility in his notes on Berkeley "that all introspection always leaves out all the important things." After 1925 Lewis would find this skepticism regarding introspection reinforced by J. A., who had written in 1915 that reflection upon sensations led into the realms of pseudohistory. This principle was a serviceable weapon against the new psychology, and the refutation of the giant by Reason in *Pilgrim's Regress* is Lewis's vindication of Alexander's idea.[27]

The Adversary's third move "consisted merely in linking up this new éclaircissement about joy" with Lewis's idealism. Thus our longing for joy without (in this life) experiencing it fully could be explained, given an intellectual coherence. The fourth move was, Lewis wrote, "more alarming": "A tutor must make things clear. Now the Absolute cannot be made clear. Do you mean nobody-knows-what, or do you

---

[25]C. S. Lewis to Albert Lewis, 26 May 1925 [LJ 8:291].

[26]Lewis, *Surprised by Joy*, 216.

[27]J. A. Smith, "Are the Materials of the Senses Affections of the Mind?" "On Feeling," *PAS* 14 (1913-1914): 62-65. On 10 October 1911 Smith wrote Bosanquet that he considered "the non-existence of feeling as a . . . form of spiritual life," an "inexorable corollary" of his inaugural *Knowing and Acting* (Newcastle University, Bosanquet Papers, Trunk 1, A 7); Lewis, *Pilgrim's Regress*, 57-64.

mean a superhuman mind and therefore (we may as well admit it) a Person? After all, did Hegel and Bradley and all the rest of them ever do more than add mystifications to the simple, workable, theistic idealism of Berkeley? I thought not."[28]

At this crucial juncture, when Lewis's Hegelianism had failed, he read Chesterton's *Everlasting Man*, remarking that he then saw for the first time "the whole Christian outline of history set out in a form that seemed to me to make sense." What followed was the abandonment of the last vestiges of the New Look and the gradual transformation of idealism into pantheism. Idealism dominated Lewis's thought until 1929, becoming gradually more and more a full-blown belief in God. I could do nothing, Lewis recalled, "without continual recourse to what I called 'Spirit.' " But the fine philosophical distinction between this and what ordinary people called 'prayer to God' breaks down as soon as you start doing it in earnest."[29]

For Lewis, the real terror was that,

> If you seriously believed in even such a "God" or "Spirit" as I admitted, a wholly new situation developed. . . . I was to be allowed to play at philosophy no longer. It might, as I say, still be true that "Spirit" differed in some way from the God of popular religion. My adversary waived the point. . . . He only said, "I am the Lord"; "I am that I am"; "I am."[30]

So in Trinity term 1929 Lewis passed from pantheism into a clear and compelling belief in God, and knelt and prayed. "The hardness of God," he wrote, "is kinder than the softness of men, and his compulsion is our liberation."[31] The years 1925 to 1929, which Lewis entered as an idealist (still not quite free of his New Look), he left a believer. These were also his first Magdalen years, and there Jack Lewis had suddenly been surrounded by older men who believed that thinking led to the kind of metaphysics the realists had taught Lewis to suspect, and worse, to religion. Soon there was the habit of breakfasting with Canon Adam

---

[28]Lewis, *Surprised by Joy*, 222-23.

[29]Ibid., 223-24, 226; Lewis to Owen Barfield, 1930, *LCSL*, 141.

[30]Lewis, *Surprised by Joy*, 227.

[31]Ibid., 229.

Fox, Magdalen's dean of Divinity, and with J. A.[32] It was in these years that the friendship between Smith and Lewis developed, Smith becoming the sympathetic elder mentor Lewis had never found. Lewis carefully recorded in his journal in 1926 that although he had put questions to Smith on many occasions, he had never had a conversation with J. A. until the evening of 26 May.[33] And if J. A. was not much of a believer, he was certainly death on the philosophy of Cook Wilson and his disciples. As a devout theist Lewis prayed, dutifully examined his conscience, and attended chapel.[34] He was still not a Christian. The particularity of it all seemed scandalous and unnecessary, and like countless others before him, he asked why the death of one man, even one who claimed to be the Father's Son, could have brought peace with God.

What Lewis's conversion awaited, at least in an intellectual sense, was the realization that myth is—to use Tolkien's words—a refraction of the one great myth that fulfills every literary anticipation.[35] Webb had developed this idea in his Gifford lectures in 1915, in which he spoke of the Platonic myths as myths of truth, and Collingwood had written of "typical truth"[36] in "The Devil." This was generally the idea Tolkien and Hugh Dyson urged on Lewis as they stood on Addison's walk beneath the soft gray face of Magdalen on the night of 19 September 1931. Lewis had insisted myths were lies, "though lies breathed through silver." "No," said Tolkien, "they are not. . . . We have come from God, . . . and inevitably the myths woven by us, though they contain error, will also reflect a splintered fragment of the true light, the eternal-truth that is with God. Indeed, only by myth-making . . . can man aspire to the perfection he knew before the fall."[37]

---

[32]Adam Fox, "At the Breakfast Table," 90-92, 93.

[33]LJ, 14 June 1922 [7:157].

[34]Lewis, *Surprised by Joy*, 232.

[35]Humphrey Carpenter, *Tolkien: A Biography* (London: Allen and Unwin, 1977) 165.

[36]*God and Personality*, 167-80; Collingwood, "The Devil," 228.

[37]This account is based on Tolkien's poem "Mythopoieia" as it was interpreted by Humphrey Carpenter. See also Lewis to Dom Bede Griffiths, 21 December 1941, *LCSL*, 197.

It was just here, when Lewis saw that the relationship between the images of literature and the myth of truth was such that myths inevitably led "further up and further in," that the circle closed.[38] On 1 October he wrote to Arthur Greeves, "I have passed from believing in God to definitely believing in Christ—in Christianity. . . . My long night walk with Dyson and Tolkien had a great deal to do with it."[39] Lewis's conversion had of course its moments of emotional depth: the trip atop the bus during which he felt his lobsterlike armor dissolve; the night he knelt and knew that God was God; and through it all the sense that the hound of heaven was in pursuit.[40] But it had been an intellectual pilgrimage, a road along which he had been convinced progressively of the truth of Christianity. The final shove had come from the realization that, in something of Coleridge's sense, there was reason in imagination; that the great literary themes themselves constituted a rational testimony to the myth of truth; indeed, they drew their power from it.[41]

The conversion of C. S. Lewis was to have an impact on all Christendom, for Lewis possessed superb intellectual and literary gifts, and from the day in 1931 when he became a Christian until his death, he used his talents to explain and recommend what he had found. Though he would give a directly autobiographical account in *Surprised by Joy* in 1955, the book he wrote in the immediate aftermath of his conversion is a fuller guide to the ideas that made Lewis a Christian. *Pilgrim's Regress* was written in Ulster in two weeks in 1932, read in manuscript by Tolkien, and published in May 1933.[42] Though it is allegorical, not autobiographical, *Pilgrim's Regress* was written out of Lewis's own

---

[38]Lewis invented the "further up further in" metaphor in *The Great Divorce* (London: Macmillan, 1945) and used it as well in the Narnia tales beginning in 1950.

[39]Lewis to Arthur Greeves, 1 October 1931, in Hooper, ed., *They Stand Together*, 425.

[40]Lewis, *Surprised by Joy*, 224, 228; *LCSL*, 19.

[41]For Lewis's understanding of myth, see *Pilgrim's Regress*, 151-60; *Miracles* (New York: Macmillan, 1947) n. 139; "Myth Became Fact," *World Dominion* 22 (Sept.-Oct. 1944): 167-70; Austin Farrer, "Can Myth Be Fact?" In *Interpretation and Belief*, ed. Charles C. Conti (London: SPCK, 1976) 169-75.

[42]Warren Lewis, entries from 13 April, 2 June 1933, in Clyde S. Kilby and Marjorie Lamp Meade, eds., *Brothers and Friends: The Diaries of Major Warren Hamilton Lewis* (San Francisco: Harper and Row, 1982) 101, 103.

experience. John, the lad whose boyhood vision of the island in the West led him safely from Puritania through Zeitgeistheim to Mother Kirk, is Jack Lewis. The book was a regress because it traced Lewis's return to the Christianity of his youth and to the intellectual inheritance of the great tradition, and about it there was something of Chesterton's memorable figure, drawn in the opening lines of *Orthodoxy*, of the lost sailor who had gone round the world to find himself at last at home in England. The fundamental metaphor of the regress is a geographical analogy to the Aristotelian-Christian anthropology and its associated ethic: a single track leads along a safe path between a Northern land of rationalistic aridity and a Southern waste of swamplike and affective sentimentality. Lewis's two concerns, the extremes of his apologetic setting, are the sensuality and irrational affectivity of poetry (D. H. Lawrence), and the rejection of joy by the classicists (Eliot). That Lewis was by 1943 ashamed of the attack on Eliot's classicism ought not obscure the anxiety he felt in 1932 at the prospect that William Morris and Wagner might be discredited by the angular disciples of neo-orthodoxy and of classicism. Upon this image of the mean between reason wrung dry of joy and sentimentalism rampant was overlaid the distinctively Christian image of *the way*, a path through life beset by danger but leading finally across the chasm of the fall to the throne of God. So Mother Kirk's story, the story that explains the great chasm and the sense of a world saved (even as it decays) from catastrophe, is as important, indeed more fundamental, to *Pilgrim's Regress* than the tension between the men of the South and North.

Pilgrim's Regress had, in addition to its author's concern with the joy that is desire, three major themes: (1) the efficacy of reason; (2) the objectivity of value; and (3) the unity of history and its importance as *preparatio evangelica*. Desire is represented by the island in the West, and by the mountains, as a kind of invariable feature of the human landscape. Each of the others, reason, virtue, and history, is represented allegorically, and in the narrative each is powerfully opposed by figures taken from the world of art, literature, and politics that Lewis knew in 1932.

To understand what Lewis means by reason in *Pilgrim's Regress* is to have some insight into a fundamental category of his thought, for he was, in the best and classical sense, a rationalist. Yet reason as he uses the word does not refer to the quality of consistency in logical operations, but the ability, indeed the common experience, through which every man gains access to a transcendent ground of truth and discovers his unavoidable responsibility for shaping his nature and nature generally in this higher image. Reason in Lewis is the light with which we grasp reality, the *logos* of Philo and St. John, the judge of abstract truths as well as the foundation of practical reason, and hence of morality. It stands closer to what the classical tradition meant by wisdom, understanding, art, and prudence than does the thin talent for deductive consistency that sometimes passes for rationality. Lewis saw the major attack on the efficacy of reason as the work of the new psychology, which by 1930 was roughly equivalent to the psychology of Freud. In *Pilgrim's Regress* Freudianism is the complex of ideas that poisons the very wells of thought, a jailer set to teach imprisoned mankind that the fruition of joy is an illusion, that every noble deed is at best self-interested or at worst the rationalization of some baseness. Lewis believed that the new psychology was constructed around an overzealous attention to one's own subjective states, an attitude as destructive as it was (in fact) impossible. He was convinced that he had found the key to this problem in Samuel Alexander's careful distinction between enjoyment and contemplation. He concluded that

> to cease thinking about or attending to a woman is, so far to cease loving. . . . But to attend to your own love is to cease attending to the loved . . . object. In other words the enjoyment and contemplation of our inner activities are incompatible. . . .

Psychological introspection "finds precisely what is left behind by the suspension of our normal activities; and what is left behind is mainly mental images and physical sensations. The great error is to mistake this moral sediment or track for the activities themselves." Upon this insight Lewis would construct one of the unforgettable figures of *The Great Divorce*, the tragedian whose attention is riveted in pity upon himself.[43]

In *Pilgrim's Regress* John is thrown into a dungeon by the Freudian giant, whose eyes penetrate the skin to render the intestines and lungs of

---

[43]Lewis, *Surprised by Joy*, 217-18. Barfield, and perhaps Tolkien as well, thought that Lewis's reliance on this insight had dissociated his subjectivity from a kind of formally constructed personality. See Tolkien to Clyde S. Kilby, 20 October 1965, *LJRRT*, 363; Owen Barfield, in Jocelyn Gibb, ed., *Light on C. S. Lewis* (London: Geoffrey Bles, 1965) ix-xi; Lewis, *Great Divorce*, 108-17.

his prisoners visible. The giant obviously represents the psychology that studies the sediment of our activities and directs our attention from the world, insisting all the while that the emotional detritus of intentions past and present is their reality. The philosophical heart of *Pilgrim's Regress* is the three riddles Reason asks the Freudian giant, and which the giant cannot answer.[44] The first is: "What is the colour of things in dark places, of fish in the depth of the sea, of the entrails in the body of man; the third, "By what rule do you tell a copy from an original?" The first riddle is calculated to remind the Freudians that the thought they draw up from the dark places is not thought at all. The third is intended to call into question the claim of the new psychology that our images of the island are projections of an ultimately unreal desire. Might our desires not be taken, and with more cogency, as images founded upon and representing some transcendent original?

The second of Reason's riddles is a parable, the parable of the man who was required to decide whether to destroy the bridge over which his enemy would pass if by the act he would destroy the only route over which relief might come. Here Lewis probably had in mind all those defenders of Christianity who, like Schleiermacher and Barth, stood ready to abandon theology's claim to rationality, perhaps because they saw it used with apparent effectiveness by the scientific (in this case psychological) enemy.

Freud and irrational art were the enemies of Reason, but in Lewis's world Reason had allies as well. On the road John meets Wisdom and Contemplation, allegorical representatives of philosophy. Hegelian monism had taught that the island in the West was neither real nor an illusion, that we must see it as an island, as a continuation of the world we know, but that the island was yet not a place. As Lewis quickly realized, monism led to two possible interpretations of the moral world. According to the first, creaturely existence presupposed the failure of reality. If the rules were from the spirit who was somehow still each finite self, in Virtue's words, "The real disobedience to the rules begins with being in this country at all." This country was simply "*not* the island"; the spirit answers to the Landlord, the world to the black hole. On the other hand, since all that exists is an expression of Spirit, nothing could be evil:

---

[44]Lewis, *Pilgrim's Regress*, 57-64.

"Everything is this Spirit's imagination, and therefore everything properly understood, is good and happy."[45]

The difficulty was the poetic identity between God, the world, and the self. Still, idealism had its lessons. A caption in the 1943 edition assures the reader: "The Doctrine of the Absolute or Mind as such covers more the facts than any doctrine John has yet encountered."[46] For Lewis it surely had. But the philosophic tradition as he had received it lacked integrity. Wisdom's advice was fragmentary and flawed, and the daughters of the house of wisdom whom John saw at play in the moonlight were a quarrelsome lot. They feasted on the goods available locally: cold chicken from Mr. Mammon, hashish from the South, caviar from the theosophists, brandy from Savage's dwarfs, and plain fare from Claptrap. Marx fed on Savage's gift, while Rudolph Steiner, the theosophist who had captivated Owen Barfield, proposed a trip south to the magicians, and Herbert Spencer, the popularizer of Darwin, recommended Claptrap's plain fare. God is much in the thoughts of the philosophers. One shy girl—perhaps Evelyn Underhill—suggests that claret from Mother Kirk is available. Kant appears in the ambiguous character of a philosopher who had denied that thought can lead to belief, but who professes a high morality. Having little philosophic use for joy, Immanuel suggests that a few quiet hours in Puritania would cure Steiner's desire for magic, to which another of wisdom's children, aware undoubtedly of the role Kant's philosophy had played in England, retorted: "Chuck it, Immanuel, you might as well go to Mother Kirk straightaway." And the shy girl replied: "Bernard does." For the late Victorians the best of philosophy was Kant, and Bernard Bosanquet had been one of Kant's finest English disciples. John had seen Bosanquet drinking Mother Kirk's wine with great relish and taking refreshment by moonlight—importing wholesale into his philosophy the presuppositions of a Christian philosophy—but the waking Bernard maintained that Mother Kirk's wine was merely a bad, early attempt at the admirable barley water that his father sometimes brought out on birthdays and great occasions. "To this barley-water," he said, "I owe my health. It has made me what I am." Idealism owed its substance to the older tradition in which theology and

---

[45]Ibid., 139.

[46]Ibid., 134-35.

philosophy were related integrally, with faith considered not only possible but rational, but the Neo-Hegelians were committed to the view that the Christian revelation was a primitive version of some larger truth. Even in this dilute form the barley water of the older tradition had provided the only substance of the idealists' systems.[47]

Reason was the common possession of mankind, capable of freeing us from error in the name of truth, fed on one hand by the innate springs of rationality that would cause John to reject the nonsense of the giant (just as Mark Studdock would finally reject the spurious "objectivity" of N.I.C.E. in *That Hideous Strength*)[48] and nourished, at least to some degree, by a self-consciously intellectual philosophical tradition. But reason had another function as well, appearing in alliance with Virtue as that practical reason upon which the moral life is founded. In the allegory of the *Regress*, Virtue is John's companion on the way, and if Virtue, searching endlessly for an acceptable motive for righteousness, is throughout most of *Pilgrim's Regress* a sad or even tragic figure, he at the same time represents Lewis's own moral struggle and the weakness of the moral theory with which he was most familiar.[49]

In the "Hegemony of Moral Value," then more fully in *The Abolition of Man* (1943), Lewis argued that the first platitudes or natural law were not inventions but connatural in the human heart and universally attested by ethical tradition.[50] The reference was in one sense to Kant's moral law within and starry heavens without, or, more fundamentally, to the Pauline insight that the law was written on Gentile hearts and attested by all nature. The college had not liked it, and the paper has not been found, but its content is probably indicated by a surviving outline of the lectures on moral philosophy that Lewis gave in 1924 and perhaps subsequently. In those lectures he contrasted Kant, who believed that duty was unmoderated by anything empirical, with utilitarianism, the philosophy of men like Mill who thought that only some end or result was justifying. He concluded the series with the "Hegemony of Moral

---

[47]Ibid., 130-33.

[48]Lewis, *That Hideous Strength*, 254-58.

[49]Lewis, *Pilgrim's Regress*, 92, 112-14.

[50]C. S. Lewis, *The Abolition of Man*, 28-33, 51-61.

Value."[51] What Lewis meant in 1924 and had meant in 1922 was that moral values, the first platitudes, are objective, eternal, and incapable of any but the most carefully defined progress, and that not in themselves but with respect to us. Lewis insisted that the self knows the rules immediately, since the axioms of practical reason are seconded by moral tradition, by what in *The Abolition of Man* is called the Toa. These rules are both dictated to, and discovered within, conscience: "Every conflict between the rules and our inclinations is but a conflict of the wishes of my temporary and apparent self against those of my real and eternal."[52] As a convinced eudaemonist, Lewis was impatient with the Kantian rejection of desire. John's companion, Virtue, seeking the justification for good actions, is debilitated, struck blind, by the apparent and awful contradiction between a theistic ethic of reward and punishment—which because it is empirical can in Kantian terms be no ethic—and the Kantian philosophy of absolute duty, which though free of any self-interest, leads nowhere: "Without desire it [traditional morality] finds no motive: with desire no morality." The thought that desire was morally disqualifying, an opinion broadly shared by a generation brought to philosophy by Kant's *Foundations of the Metaphysics of Morals*, Lewis rejected. John shouts at his blind companion Virtue, "Oh go ahead, want something."[53] Lewis never doubted the objectivity of moral value; he did deny that this objectivity was established by the mere absence of motives. Indeed, without joy, what would have been the motive for life?

The biographical background of Lewis's appeal to history is perhaps less obvious than the appeal to reason and virtue, but no less important. There was of course the association with J. A. Smith—who by the time Lewis knew him well believed the major mistake of his career had been his neglect of history—and with Webb and Brightman, whose lives were given to historical studies. Lewis's own studies in the history of medieval

---

[51]Only the outline remains: "1. Introduction, 2. Objectivity of Value, 3. Statement of Problems, 4. Same Continued, 5. Philebus and Republic, 6. Critique, 7. Utilitarian Ethics, 8. Critique, 9. Kantian Ethics, 10. Critique, 11. Fundamental Errors of both these theories, 12. Practical Hegemony of the Moral Value, 13. Basis of Obligation, 14. Summary."

[52]Lewis, *Abolition of Man*, 28.

[53]Lewis, *Pilgrim's Regress*, 113.

and Renaissance literature, perhaps encouraged originally by his tutor in history, G. L. Stevenson, were extensions of the work begun by his older colleagues. Lewis had gradually freed himself from chronological snobbery.[54] His essays "Historicism" and "The Funeral of a Great Myth" were written many years later,[55] but by 1925 he had ceased believing in the myth of progress. Lewis's mature opinion of the value of history was nicely balanced between his optimistic practice as a historian of literature and ideas and a moderate skepticism that made him quick to insist that our knowledge of the past was partial, eclectic, even accidental. His historical method was Collingwood's, though he probably learned it from Smith. Both science and history were, Lewis believed, founded upon *supposals*, supposals being hermeneutic ideas or principles supported by evidence. Smith had used the term in his Gifford Lectures in 1929, and it passed quickly into the vocabulary of both Lewis and Collingwood, in whose writings such words as a priori imagination, supposition, hypothesis, presupposition, and absolute presupposition all refer—though of course with relevant distinctions—to the ability of intellect to provide some hermeneutic yielding intelligibility and reasonableness. When Lewis's "Historicism" was written in 1950, he knew the definition central to Collingwood's historical studies, the belief that it is the work of the historian "to 'interpret' the past in the sense of reconstructing it imaginatively." Periods (unlike dates) were not, Lewis noted, facts, but works of historical imagination.[56]

When *Pilgrim's Regress* was written in 1932, Lewis's philosophy of history was still not mature, but he clearly understood the distinction Collingwood would later draw between the real work of the historian and "scissors-and-paste" history, "facts" discovered or remembered and strung together uncritically. In book eight of the *Regress*, History is a hermit, a peddler in youth, who knows "all parts of this country . . . and the genius of places," a cosmopolitan unlike the citizens of Zeitgeistheim, who have traveled little.[57] The contrast is clearly between that his-

---

[54]Lewis, *Surprised by Joy*, 206; Lewis to Albert Lewis, 1 April 1927, *LCSL*, 112.

[55]"The Funeral of a Great Myth" was published in *Christian Reflections* (1967); "Historicism" in *The Month* 4 (October 1950).

[56]"Historicism," *Christian Reflections*, 100.

[57]Lewis, *Pilgrim's Regress*, 148-55.

torical understanding Collingwood would describe in his inaugural of 1935 and the positivistic, antihistorical attitude of the realists. The Hermit comprehends all times and places, or, as J. A. put it, all knowledge is historical knowledge. The task the Hermit undertakes is the task fulfilled in Lewis's own intellectual history by Chesterton's *Everlasting Man*, in which Lewis first found a convincing Christian reading of history.[58]

The Hermit's tale is woven around the contrast, first, between the stay-at-homes who cannot discern the unity and high significance of history, always giving to their own local misunderstanding a universal authority; and, second, the tension between the natural revelation made to imagination through images central to various civilizations and the revelation made through the written word, or rules. The first of these tensions History resolves for John by assuring him that history moves with an interior unity that requires insight, melioration, and correction rather than the provincial narrowness of tough-minded Northerners, who adopt the "strange ritual of always emptying out the baby along with the bath," or cutting off their noses in desperate imitation of the tailless fox the enemy had sent among them. The same unsympathetic provincialism motivated the contempt of the tough-minded for the sentimental and prurient Mr. Halfways, who was, History reminded John, merely "the local representative of a thing as widespread and as necessary (though, withal, as dangerous) as the sky!" The difficulty was, in the Hermit's words, endemic with stay-at-homes: "If they like something in their own village they take it for a thing universal and eternal, though perhaps it was never heard of five miles away; if they dislike something, they say it is a local, backward, provincial convention, though, in fact, it may be the law of nations." History itself had militated against this provincialism by bringing the Shepherd people (with their written rules) and the Pagans (with their diffuse images of the island) into the great tradition over which Mother Kirk presides.[59]

His exposition of the interplay between the pictures and the rules clarifies the view of history that Lewis held in 1932. Not only must men finally enjoy the unity represented by both Israel and Pagus, but within

---

[58]Lewis, *Surprised by Joy*, 223.

[59]Lewis, *Pilgrim's Regress*, 149, 151, 153-56.

history itself there is a providential government of imagination through which God has sent three great revelations: the first that diffuse image of the island that inspired classical poetry in Pagus; the second the Lady, an image given to late Roman civilization as a therapeutic for its seared imagination, and fulfilled by Dante; the third the Romantic image of nature, given just as the idea of nature was both threatened by the machine and sentimentalized by the Victorian poets. This theological history of imagination, brilliant in itself, is a primary witness to Lewis's belief in the unity of history's purpose. In none of his later writings did Lewis deal as seriously with history or as kindly with the Church of the Middle Ages, but in *Pilgrim's Regress* Lewis insisted that the Pagans themselves had been directed to God by images, and that the image of the Lady had not been nearly so badly misunderstood as subsequent [English] theologians maintained.[60]

The only figure in *Pilgrim's Regress* with magisterial powers of synthesis approaching those displayed by the hermit History is Mother Kirk. The Church of Lewis's imagination, at least in 1932, was an idealized Catholicism that comprehended the essential moral, intellectual, and historical content of Christianity.[61]

Among Christians of orthodox disposition, C. S. Lewis lives in the borderland of hagiography, still remembered by those lives he touched, by colleagues who loved or disliked him. Because—as he intended—he has touched so many, it is difficult to see him in his time and place, and what we see does not always clarify. Lewis was not universally appreciated at Oxford, and the reluctance of his university to give him a professorship was redeemed only by the action of Cambridge in offering him the newly created professorship of Medieval and Renaissance Literature in 1954. Somehow to see him in his college, in Oxford in the 1930s, seems impious. But it was a place he loved, and of all twentieth-century writers, Lewis would be least comfortable with the image of himself as an example of romantic singularity. His thought was, as he insisted, never novel. Historically it was the result in part of the recovery of orthodoxy begun in different ways by J. A. Smith, Collingwood, and Chesterton, caught by Lewis like an infection, perfected, and refracted.

---

[60]Ibid., 157-60.

[61]Ibid., 14.

Jack Lewis, led on by the joy that had never really forsaken him; unshakably certain of the efficacy of reason; dedicated to the proposition that morality was utterly objective; and convinced that history itself told a story that led men to Mother Kirk, had become a Christian.

Between 1932 and 1945 C. S. Lewis created the canon through which his apologetic and scholarly aims were realized. *Pilgrim's Regress* (1933) was followed by *The Allegory of Love: A Study in Medieval Tradition* (1936). The trilogy was begun in 1938 with *Out of the Silent Planet*. Lewis's controversy with E. M. W. Tillyard, *The Personal Heresy*, and *Rehabilitations* followed in 1939, *The Problem of Pain* the next year. *Screwtape*, perhaps his most popular work, appeared in 1942 as did his popular *Broadcast Talks*. In 1943 Lewis published *Perelandra, Christian Behavior*, and *The Abolition of Man*; in 1945 *The Great Divorce* and the third volume of the trilogy, *That Hideous Strength*. *The Abolition of Man* is a kind of philosophic reprieve of *Pilgrim's Regress*, a practical book written to gainsay a defective theory of language and criticism, to establish the objectivity of moral values, and to criticize the corrupt motives and uses that inform our engagement with science. It is a philosophic treatise that begins with a defense of the intelligibility of imagination and ends with a reflection upon the relation between love and technique. Lewis would live eighteen years after the war, but his intellectual apologetic was substantially complete in 1945.

There had been many notable advocates of the unity of the European mind, among them Hulme, Collingwood, and Eliot. But it was in Lewis's works that the quest for unity in its inescapable combination with Christianity passed out of the academy and into the lives of ordinary folk. In his works metaphysics lived; history found significant unity; and reason joined imagination. *Pilgrim's Regress* bears the influence of men who were never dons—Chesterton and George Mac Donald. But without the great Magdalen men, without J. A. and Clement Webb, without the long night walk with Tolkien, Lewis might not have become the great clerk whose apologies made Christianity reasonable in the absurd world of the mid-twentieth century. Certainly Lewis's conversion might never have occurred had he not learned to love a body of literature and thought reaching into the classical period, or if he had concluded with the realists that talk about God was necessarily insignificant. Lewis had gathered up the fragments of Eliot's *Wasteland*, the broken images and intellectual themes of England between the wars, and composed them as an intelligible whole with the framework of the European unity of mind Collingwood had sought.

There were limitations. One, a glory as well, was his love of England, and hence his Anglicanism. To Catholics the Anglicanism of one who in so many ways wrote as one of their own has seemed incongruous.[62] Lewis was in some respects more English than the English; loyalty to any other church was simply an impossibility. He was fond of quoting Charles Williams's remark that we have a duty to worship at the authorized altar,[63] by which they both meant in the Church of England. *Pilgrim's Regress* closes with a poetic reference to the "pang and tether of the particular." Perhaps Tolkien was right in insisting that Lewis's adaptation of Williams's Arthurian-Byzantine myth as the structure for the third volume of the trilogy written about 1944 was a turning point, a deliberate choosing of Britishness as the heart and limit of his apology. The point of *That Hideous Strength* is very much England. The pull of the very soil was something other poets felt. Eliot needs no citation, nor Hopkins's plea for "rare-dear England." But despite his imaginal betrothal to England, Lewis was, except from love of England, and history, no more an Anglican than anything else, given that Anglicanism tolerated and often encouraged that broad, clear reading of the central dogmas that he discovered in Scripture and tradition. His theology is always migrant; the mere Christianity he defended consists of those doctrines he shared with most of the men who met in the Eagle and the Child on Tuesdays. It had no home; it was in its way as idealistic as the philosophy of Bradley, but the vagabond has been a welcomed and comfortable guest almost everywhere.

It is also important to remember that Lewis never claimed to be a theologian. If theology is the attempt to explicate theological sources or to criticize gracefully the revealed image or images or to relate dogma to new philosophies, there is not much theology in any of Lewis's writings. Any novelty Lewis would have recanted instantly.[64] Even the fact of his conversion was not new. In the 1920s and 1930s conversions to Angli-

---

[62]C. S. Lewis to Sister Mary Rose, January 1950, *LCSL*, 223; Christopher Derrick, *C. S. Lewis and the Church of Rome* (San Francisco: St. Ignatius Press, 1981).

[63]Lewis, *Screwtape Letters*, 72.

[64]Tolkien to Dick Plotz, 12 September 1965, *LJRRT*, 361.

canism and Catholicism had been common among the literati; from Collingwood and Chesterton to Waugh and Eliot, Mother Kirk had claimed her own. The power of his writing comes not from the novelty of his theological ideas or from his situation, but from his having provided the world of English-speaking Christendom with two necessities at a time when others were silent. First, Lewis was perhaps the single most effective spokesman for supernatural religion in England or America after 1940. When lay readers often found around them only voices of confusion and accommodation, Lewis, a professor in a very great university, eloquent and convincing, was always there to speak for the tradition in a way that made people know that truth was not the name of a time.

Lewis's second contribution lay in the particular intellectual force of his apology. Webb was a philosopher of religion, interested in the analysis of the human experience of God, and in certain classical questions involving the relation between men and God, grace and nature, philosophy and theology. So was Collingwood, though Collingwood was less interested in the philosophy of religious experience than Webb. Lewis was an apologist, at times a philosophical theologian, who assumed the truth of mere Christianity and argued its intelligibility, power, and sufficiency in relation to history, reason, and human nature. The appeal of his writing was derived from his ability to range the intellectual witness of the entire tradition in favor of Christianity and the philosophy of Christianity; presupposed in such a way that belief became not only intellectually respectable but intellectually compelling. Since the death of John Richardson Illingworth in 1915, no one in England or America possessed of deep erudition had offered readers so winning an intellectual apology for the Christian faith. Lewis's older contemporaries had tried, men like Charles Gore and William Temple, but Gore's last book was written in 1930, and in Temple's beautiful, complex idealism the great intellectual themes of orthodoxy remained obscure. The ordinary reader did not attempt *Nature, Man, and God* or Webb's *God and Personality*. Not many read *Pilgrim's Regress*, for it was a difficult book, and not until the *Broadcast Talks* of 1939 and *Screwtape* (1942) was Lewis really popular. But as his method matured, it became clear that he had drawn together the intellectual patrimony of the romantics, and rendered it intelligible to that same audience whom Green and Newman had touched a half-century before. The inability of the Ruskinian tradition to come to terms with the supernatural had been repaired. The imprecision of the grand theosophies of idealism had been purified.

In his poem "Reason," Lewis asked of our search for wholeness of soul,

> Oh who will reconcile in me both maid
> and mother?
> Who make in me a concord of the depth
> and height?
> Who make in me imaginations dim exploring touch
> Ever report the same as intellectual sight?

Ultimately, the reconciler is of course God, but in the English-speaking world of the 1940s the means was C. S. Lewis, in whose life and writing reason and imagination had been conjoined, first by a decade of hard thinking, then by the gift of faith.

•CHAPTER VI•

Controversies, Contemporaries, Disciples

What we now call "the Romantic Movement" once was Mr. Wordsworth and Mr. Coleridge talking incessantly (at least Mr. Coleridge was) about a secret vision of their own.

C. S. Lewis,
The Four Loves, 1960

They lived in a world of intellectual crosscurrents and conflicts; there were influences upon them and influences exercised by them that came from and reached beyond their places and their acquaintances. In the 1930s Oxford was more and more a university at war with itself on fundamental issues. As Lewis liked to say, things kept coming to a point. The evident secularism of Oxford was matched by an obvious and unembarrassed Christianity represented by (among others) Lewis, Tolkien, and less blatantly, Collingwood. The philosophy of A. J. Ayer, who was a disciple of G. E. Moore, faced the philosophy of R. G. Collingwood: one atheistic, interested in the particular, in facts, and in the most precise and arid uses of language; the other theistic, Christian, persuaded of the unity of poetry and thought, and convinced that thought and action were necessarily related. These were issues that urbanity could not completely disarm, and the university was more and more an intellectual battlefield—lively, fragmented, dangerous to careers.

With the exception of Webb, they did not display much detachment. Lewis's *Abolition of Man* was written against the defenders of a literary aesthetic whose philosophic foundations he considered vicious; and despite his insistence that he intended no harm to schoolmasters trying to make a living, the book was a polemic against writers whose identities were obvious in Oxford.[1] Collingwood's *Autobiography*, in which he unburdened himself fully regarding his philosophical and political contemporaries, was considered scandalous by his enemies and regretted by his friends. The four were as enthusiastic on behalf of causes they approved as they were vociferously opposed to those they considered wrongheaded. Smith's regard for Benedetto Croce was notorious. Lewis took up first Tolkien, then Charles Williams.[2] Collingwood devoted as many pages to the thought of Michael Oakeshott, a Cambridge contemporary, as to Hegel in *The Idea of History*.[3] Enormously well read, they found little that did not touch them. They were men ever sensitive to the winds, and Collingwood's repeated assertions that he had ignored the opinions of his colleagues were in part the protestations of one who cared overmuch.[4]

For the most part the philosophic winds were against them, and their thought bears the stamp of controversy. When Lewis and Collingwood came into their own as scholars of stature, they found the field possessed by able opponents. The positivism of the 1930s was the fruition of the physical realism begun by Thomas Case in the 1870s.[5] The Cambridge phase of the movement, represented by G. E. Moore and Bertrand Russell, is better known, but Oxford had never been without its native realists. J. R. Illingworth complained in 1885 that since the death of Green, Oxford philosophers had been too busy with the particular to pay much

---

[1]The Green book, by Gaius and Titus, is *The Control of Language* (London: Longmans, 1941) by Alexander King and Martin Ketley. The work by Orbilius was E. G. Biaggini's *The Reading and Writing of English* (London: Hutchinson, 1936).

[2]Carpenter, *Tolkien*, 167-68; Tolkien to Michael Tolkien, November or December 1963, *LJRRT*, 341. Lewis and Tolkien once, on sudden inspiration, had their friend Canon Adam Fox elected Professor of Poetry. See Carpenter, *Inklings*, 163.

[3]Collingwood, *Idea of History*, 151-59.

[4]Collingwood, *Autobiography*, 44, 45, 53, 58-59.

[5]Ibid., 18, n. 2.

attention to the great themes of Green's philosophy.[6] Encouraged by Prichard and Joseph, Edwardian realism had become by 1925 the positivism of Gilbert Ryle and A. J. Ayer, intellectually confident and academically respectable.

Since Collingwood was the only one of the Magdalen group who was a practicing philosopher in the 1930s, he shouldered the responsibility for answering the positivists. Always protective of his desire to be a dispassionate and synthetic thinker, Collingwood had, even after he took Vico and Croce as his guides, avoided attacking the realists. In a display of optimistic evenhandedness, he had in 1916 praised Joachim's *The Nature of Truth*, Prichard's *Kant's Theory of Knowledge*, and Carritt's *Theory of Beauty* in the same paragraph.[7] For twenty years he corresponded sympathetically with Samuel Alexander, whose philosophy was of a decidedly realist cast.[8]

But by 1920 he had become an outspoken critic of the realists, and in the early 1930s he abandoned dispassionate criticism for righteous anger. Perhaps Gilbert Ryle's attack on his *Essay on Philosophical Method* was the cause of this change,[9] or perhaps it was the increasingly pointed opposition of A. J. Ayer, a young Oxford philosopher who at thirty-six had written *Language, Truth and Logic*, a work that served as a kind of platform for positivism.[10] Another occasion of his irritation may have been the publication in 1929 of I. A. Richard's *Principles of Criticism*, which presupposed Ayer's position. Whatever the case, by 1938, when the *Principles of Art* was published, Collingwood had become the vocal opponent of positivism, a philosophy he considered mistaken in matters metaphysical and ethically dangerous.

---

[6]J. R. Illingworth to Wilfrid Richmond, 12 May 1884, Agnes L. Illingworth, ed., *Life*, 88.

[7]Collingwood, *Religion and Philosophy*, n. 101.

[8]The Collingwood-Alexander correspondence spans the years 1920-1938. See van der Dusen, *CUM*.

[9]Gilbert Ryle, "Mr. Collingwood and the Ontological Argument," *Mind* 44 (1935): 136-51.

[10]A. J. Ayer, *Language, Truth, and Logic* (London: Golancz, 1936); Collingwood, *Essay on Metaphysics*, 163-68; *Principles of Art*, 201, n. 1.

Since the publication of his "Does Moral Philosophy Rest on a Mistake?" in 1912, H. A. Prichard had argued persistently that the facts of behavior and obligation should be separated from judgments about the good. As a result, the moral world was split into an objective realm of verifiable truth and a shifting and subjective domain of value that was unverifiable, problematic, personal. Soon there was an analogous aesthetic, developed at Oxford by Professor Richards, which distinguished two uses of language. One use involved references to facts existing in the world of verifiable experience; the other use concerned references to the subjective states of the poet. The poetic expression of belief could not, according to Richards' systematization, be a scientific use, but was "the clearest example of reference to attitude."[11] Poetry and belief were not scientific and therefore neither true nor false.

This vitiated the Croce-Smith-Collingwood aesthetic and ethic, which asserted that language (or any work of art) expressed imaginative truths; that feeling, while never identical with reason, was not blind, and that feelings themselves might be just or unjust, consonant with reality or not. Collingwood's rebuttal of Richards' position in *The Principles of Art* is surely among the masterpieces of twentieth-century philosophic *reductio ad absurdum*.[12] Lewis was at first unconvinced of the dangers of Richards' theory; however, by the time *The Abolition of Man* was written in 1945, Lewis believed Richards' theory encouraged a spurious division between a world of fact and an inevitably subjective realm of poetic diction.[13]

The tendency of the positivists was always to move reality away from the personal and metaphysical and toward the world of objects. The tool through which this was accomplished was the verification principle: it held that statements were meaningful only if the objects to which they referred could be called as witnesses to their significance. Statements about God, poetry, and morality then became emotive, subjective assertions, personally satisfying but unrelated to reality.

---

[11]I. A. Richards, *Principles of Criticism* (London: Kegan Paul, 1925) 273.

[12]Collingwood, *Principles of Art*, 262-68.

[13]Lewis, *Abolition of Man*, 22, n. 2. Lewis criticizes Richards' *Principles of Literary Criticism* as a "determined effort to construct a theory of value on the basis of 'satisfaction of impulses.' "

Unlike most of their colleagues, none of the four found the verification principle compelling or even useful. Lewis poked fun at it in the third volume of the trilogy, in which the National Institution for Coordinated Experimentation measures its progress with a "pragmatometer," and the unfortunate Mark Studdock endures the objectivity room of the pseudoscientists, along with their mistaken argument that thought is subjective, until he finds and trusts his reason.[14] H. J. Paton commented wryly that although it was considered bad form to point out that the verification principle was a splendid example of the very metaphysics the positivists were dedicated to destroying, he had still not had "the good fortune to come across a clear and convincing refutation."[15] Collingwood believed that reliance upon the verification principle had led the positivists into the fatal error of assuming that the truth of any proposition depended upon its existence as an object among objects.

> A concept or notion was thus the same thing as a class of facts and since facts were by definition observable (where to observe meant to ascertain by use of the senses) a concept or notion was valid only if the facts of which it was a class were observable.

This was, Collingwood believed, naive: "It was not very acute to think that the 'facts' of which a scientist speaks are observed by the mere action of our senses." Furthermore, the positivists assumed that the presuppositions of science were observable, which was of course nonsensical. What they called observing facts was really historical thinking, rendered possible by presuppositions that were usually unexamined.[16] Collingwood concluded that in metaphysics Cook Wilson had fathered an obscurantist movement based on the uncritical acceptance of Kant's doctrine that every event had a cause, that its cause is a previous event, and that both event and cause are known to us. The determination of causes then became not the complex imaginal act of historical thinking,

---

[14]Lewis, *That Hideous Strength*, 295-300.

[15]H. J. Paton, *The Modern Predicament* (London: George Allen and Unwin, 1959) 39; "The Alleged Independence of Goodness," Paul Schilpp, ed., *The Philosophy of G. E. Moore* (Evanston Il: Northwestern University, 1942) 111-24.

[16]Collingwood, *Essay on Metaphysics*, 146-50.

but a commentary on the (in principle) obvious antecedents of happenings.[17]

These errors in metaphysics Collingwood considered compounded by the irrationalist psychology that had appeared in the aftermath of the works of William James and Wilhelm Wundt. The former was an American who had reduced religion to experience, and the latter the German founder of the sensationalist, empirical psychological method.[18] Psychology, Collingwood believed, had been for thirty years progressively abandoning its role as the science of feeling and seeking a new place as a pseudoscience of thought. Under the cover of this new irrationalism, religion ceased to be the worship of the truth and became the worship of emotion. Scientific thought was belittled. Politics had given up the painstaking task of education and exploded into emotion-ladened action.[19] Here Collingwood wrote in precise agreement with Smith, who had denied in 1915 that feelings could be captured and studied at all.[20] He concurred also with Webb, who had written extensively against the notion that religion was an individual or group illusion.[21] Lewis's concerns were practical. Irrational man could only be trained, never convinced or converted. Psychoanalysts, he wrote repeatedly, were to be avoided.[22]

The other philosophical movement for which Webb and Lewis expressed distaste was Neo-Scholasticism, the movement begun on the Continent after Leo XIII recommended in 1879 that the study of St. Thomas and other medieval writers be renewed. Neo-Scholasticism had taken root in France, where it was centered at the University of Lou-

---

[17]Ibid., 338-40; *Autobiography*: "History did not mean knowing what events followed what. It meant getting inside other people's heads and looking at the situation through their eyes (5)."

[18]On William James, see Clement C. J. Webb, "Psychology and Religion," *JTS* 3 (1902): 46-58; Collingwood, *Religion and Philosophy*, 131, n. 1; *Essay on Metaphysics*, 232.

[19]Collingwood, *Essay on Metaphysics*, 106-11, 115-16.

[20]Smith, "Are the Materials of the Senses Affections of the Mind?"; "On Feeling," *PAS* 14 (1913-1914): 49, 63, 65.

[21]Webb, *Groups Theories*.

[22]C. S. Lewis to a Lady, 26 March 1940, *LCSL*, 179-82; Lewis, "Psycho-Analysis and Literary Criticism," *Selected Essays*, 282-300.

vain, and by 1920 Jacques Maritain and Etienne Gilson had emerged as champions capable of winning international consideration for the movement. To the degree that Neo-Scholasticism encouraged the study of medieval writers by a strictly historical method, it necessarily earned the approval of Lewis, Collingwood, and Webb. On the other side, whenever Neo-Scholasticism was presented as a system claiming philosophic certainty, or in its connection with Catholic dogma, the Oxford men found it biased and unhistorical. Smith wrote that in his studies of the Aristotelian text, St. Thomas had provided unexpected help, and had "attained what seemed to be a quite surprising grasp."[23] Smith had, on the other hand, only contempt for those who tried to make a system of what had been a living philosophy. In 1925 he wrote:

> I have, I believe, given, as compared with most of my colleagues in this university, an unusual amount of attention to the study of medieval philosophy and in particular the works of S. Thomas. I have the highest regard for the moral and intellectual qualities which rendered possible the construction of the encyclopedic system and welcome the renewal of attention to it in the works of modern scholars.

Yet Smith insisted that "we cannot construct philosophies and choose among them," moreover, "scholasticism was not *a* philosophy." To pursue these criticisms, justified perhaps by the rapid decay of textbook neo-Thomism after 1960, is to follow Smith's own presuppositions to their roots. Philosophy was not, and could not be, knowledge of some ahistorical truth: "The most neo-scholastic thinkers can do is to enlarge their acquaintance with the history of medieval philosophy and to correct in themselves and others ignorant or intolerant mistakes about it."[24]

For Lewis, Eliot was part of the problem. Eliot had, under the influence of Maritain, become something of a Thomist around 1927, gaining thereby the place assigned him by Lewis. Since he had become a Christian Lewis had learned to value the truth of idealism, and to fear that Eliot among Anglicans and Maritain among Catholics would use the reaction against nineteenth-century philosophy to make Christianity into

---

[23]J. A. Smith, "Art and the Beautiful in the Philosophy of St. Thomas," SPM, 1:8. Smith's point was that St. Thomas had no philosophy of art.

[24]J. A. Smith, "Neo-Scholasticism," SPM, 1:23.

an intellectual fad.[25] Both Lewis and Webb probably considered Neo-Scholasticism an arrogant rationalism bound too closely to Rome. Webb believed that Neo-Scholasticism was reactionary, embodying two obvious mistakes: the belief that some system could deliver propositions by nature sufficiently final to command the obedience of the intellect; and a mistaken tendency to sever theology and philosophy.[26] In the 1940s Webb lambasted the Anglican Thomist E. L. Mascall for his claim to orthodoxy. He is, Webb wrote, "always the man who had found the right explanation, not the seeker after truth."[27]

Clement Webb was somewhat more sympathetic toward the amiable Gilson, though he did not find Gilson's Gifford Lectures of 1930 faultless, and tended on the whole to consider his influence unfortunate.[28] Lewis believed Neo-Scholasticism was one of those "high and dry" states of mind like Barthianism, the humanism of the Americans More and Babbitt, and the classicism of Hulme and Eliot. In 1934 Lewis advised a religious to stick to Gilson, a safe historian, and "to beware of the people who are at present running what they call 'neo-scholasticism' as a fad."[29] Collingwood quietly ignored Neo-Scholasticism while profiting from its advocacy of medieval Christian literature. By 1942 he believed that the Christian Fathers were essential to understanding European civilization, and Knox thought Collingwood's reading of the Scholastics had contributed to the dogmatism of the *Essay on Metaphysics*.[30]

Though the interests of Oxford philosophers were increasingly irrelevant to Lewis and the others after 1930, there were at least two movements upon which they depended to some degree: Chesterton, and the revival of mysticism.

---

[25]Lewis to Bede Griffiths, ? June 1931, LPW.

[26]Clement C. J. Webb, Review of *Scholasticism Old and New*, by Maurice de Wulf, *Mind* 18 (1909): 616; Review of *The World and God: The Scholastic Approach to Theism*, by Hubert J. Box, *Philosophy* 10 (1935): 248-49; Review of *Nature, Man, and God*, 227.

[27]Clement C. J. Webb, Review of *He Who Is*, by E. L. Mascall, *JTS* 45 (1944): 114. Catholic scholars reciprocated Webb's distrust. See George Hayward Joyce, *Principles of Natural Theology* (London: Longmans, Green, 1924) 16n.

[28]Webb, Review of *Nature, Man, and God*, 227-28.

[29]Lewis to Sister Madeleva, 7 June 1934, *LCSL*, 157.

[30]Knox, *DNB* 1941-1950, 170.

To consider Gilbert Keith Chesterton a one-man movement in English intellectual history may seem extreme. Nonetheless, he seemingly appeared from nowhere, a solitary genius, a would-be artist and journalist whose thought changed the course of English theology, and perhaps of English Catholicism. No account has ever been given of the particular psychological and intellectual events that led to the writing of *Orthodoxy* in 1909, but the repercussions were immediate and immense. The book was, like similar works by Illingworth and Charles Gore,[31] a reply to the new theology of R. J. Campbell. Unlike those works, though, it breathed a compelling freshness and exercised an influence matched by nothing written by the professional philosophers. Chesterton had been a member of the Synthetic Society, and had heard enough of late-Victorian idealism and of Modernism to know what these were. When he began to write on the Christian religion, he brought to the task a clarity largely lacking in the Edwardian academic philosophers, and an intellectual depth that would justify Etienne Gilson's judgment that Chesterton was a great metaphysical intellect.[32]

Chesterton influenced directly only one of the Magdalen group, but on Lewis his influence was decisive. When Lewis was recuperating in 1918, he read a volume of Chesterton's essays, perhaps *Heretics*. Writing in the 1950s, Lewis remarked that he still could not understand why Chesterton had made such an immediate conquest of him, adding that Chesterton's humor—the "bloom" on the dialectic itself—and his manifest goodness had certainly been part of the appeal. Then about 1925 Lewis had read *The Everlasting Man*, and had seen for the first time "the whole Christian outline of history set in a form that seemed to me to make sense."[33] Later Lewis commented that Chesterton's influence had been intellectual rather than literary or imaginal.[34]

Without the influence of Chesterton, Lewis's own interpretation of history would be a good deal more difficult to explain. Collingwood, of

---

[31]See J. R. Illingworth, *The Gospel Miracles* (London: Macmillan, 1911); Gore, *The New Theology and the Old Religion*.

[32]Maisie Ward, *Gilbert Keith Chesterton* (New York: Sheed and Ward, 1943) 620.

[33]Lewis, *Surprised by Joy*, 223.

[34]C. S. Lewis to Charles A. Brady, 29 October 1944, *LCSL*, 205.

course, believed in the unity of history and in its sufficiency as a way of knowing, but he never offered a historical apology for the use of the Christian presupposition upon which his work rested: to do so would have taken him beyond philosophy. Webb tended to see the same unity in the human experience of religion, but never in the history of the Church. In *Pilgrim's Regress*, all of history finds its intelligibility in Mother Kirk, and that is a distinctly Chestertonian move.[35]

Even more important may have been Chesterton's influence on behalf of the view that revelation could convey truths in human language that were both final and binding upon intellect. It was just here that Lewis—and with a less dramatic obviousness, Collingwood—parted ways with Webb, who tended to see revelation as progressive, a series of perceptions to which human language inevitably failed to do justice, and a process that must remain provisional. Of course, with Webb one must be certain that he is speaking theologically. No one at Oxford in the first half of the twentieth century claimed that philosophy delivered final truths. But time after time Webb insisted that in this life there is no voice of certainty.[36] Lewis was inclined to believe that there was, or at least that Reason (and in matters theological, a reason obedient and enlightened by grace) could indeed discover truths to which intellect might be bound. The figure of the bishop from *The Great Divorce*, along with Mr. Sensible and Mr. Broad from *Pilgrim's Regress*, represent the idealistic view that thinking can yield no conclusions commanding more than provisional assent, or capable of requiring universal obedience from those who understand their terms.[37] Lewis had learned, from Chesterton among others, that once thinking begins, conclusions come that can be avoided only by deliberate intellectual failure, the suicide of the mind.[38]

One other collateral movement that influenced the Magdalen group was the newly recovered interest in mysticism. This revival owed something to Anglo-Catholic spirituality; something to the broad interest in

---

[35]Lewis, *Pilgrim's Regress*, 78-81.

[36]See, for example, Webb's defense of Leonard Hodgson's statement that "no one, not even our most Christian selves, can have the whole truth," in Webb, Review of *Christ, the Christian, and the Church*, 56.

[37]Lewis, *Pilgrim's Regress*, 82-87, 116-20; *Great Divorce*, 37-46.

[38]Chesterton, *Orthodoxy*, 52-60.

medieval texts; something to the renewed enthusiasm for the "spiritual" aspects of reality that accompanied both Hegelianism and Platonism in early twentieth-century England; something to Rudolf Otto;[39] and a great deal to Baron von Hügel and his sometime pupil Evelyn Underhill. It was after Webb met von Hügel in 1896 that his interest turned from history to the philosophy of religion and of religious experience. The typical English scholar who knew mysticism at all before 1914 probably owed his knowledge to Evelyn Underhill's *Mysticism* (1910).

In *Mysticism*, Underhill was taken up with the unitive life as a way common to mystics of every kind though focused in Christianity. The book offers the best of the spiritual side of idealism, though in it there is still a lingering interest in magic and a tendency to see union with God as the annihilation of the self.[40] She had discovered von Hügel's study of St. Catherine of Genoa before 1910, calling it "indispensable," "the best work on Mysticism in the English language."[41] About 1917 she began a five-year period under von Hügel's spiritual direction, and gradually the carelessness that made her identify the Christian God with the world-soul was replaced by a precise regard for the integrity of creatures, and an understanding that God's relation to creatures was "free, distinct, many-graded, sacramental."[42] Evelyn Underhill's translations, and perhaps her treatises, would have been hard for Lewis to miss. Charles Williams, who had edited Underhill's letters in 1942, and who from 1939 to 1945 was perhaps Lewis's closest friend, was a link between them. Underhill wrote to Lewis enthusiastically when *Out of the Silent Planet* appeared in 1938, and again when she read *The Problem of Pain* in 1942.[43]

To document the influence of the Magdalen metaphysicals on individual philosophers in England and America is impossible, but there

---

[39]The English translation of *Das Heilige* (1917) appeared in 1923.

[40]Evelyn Underhill, *Mysticism: A Study in the Nature and Development of Man's Spiritual Consciousness* (New York: E. P. Dutton, 1910) 530.

[41]Ibid., 580.

[42]Evelyn Underhill, "Finite and Infinite: A Study in the Philosophy of Baron Friedrich von Hugel," in *Mixed Pasture* (New York: Longmans, Green, 1933) 211.

[43]Evelyn Underhill to C. S. Lewis, 26 October, 3 November 1938, 13 January 1941, Charles Williams, ed., *The Letters of Evelyn Underhill* (London: Longmans, Green, 1943) 268-69, 300.

were colleagues and disciples whose own contributions to twentieth-century philosophy were obviously dependent upon one or another of the four.

An important Oxford contemporary upon whom J. A. Smith exercised great influence was Harold Henry Joachim (1865-1939), who came to Balliol as Smith's colleague in 1893. Between the two the bonds of intellectual friendship were strong and enduring, with Smith invariably dominating the relationship. Smith had been anxious for Joachim to stand for the Waynflete Chair in 1909, and would probably have been content to see his protégé appointed.[44] In 1919 Smith worked assiduously to secure Joachim's election to the Wykeham professorship, writing to F. S. Marvin on 19 July, "Today I have been engaged in a complicated endeavor to stave off what I regard as an imminent misfortune in regard to the election of a successor to Cook Wilson (this in strict confidence for your private ear)."[45] The misfortune would have been the election of one of Wilson's disciples, Prichard or Joseph, but Smith was successful. A few days later Joachim—as Joseph later remarked, "a convinced disciple of the school which Wilson opposed"—was duly elected Wykeham professor.[46]

When H. H. Joachim was elected to his professorship, he had already written *The Nature of Truth*, a work intended to restate the idealist theory of knowledge in a fresh way, answering Bertrand Russell (who read the manuscript) while scrupulously avoiding the subjectivism the enemies of idealism persistently charged against it. By 1919 Joachim was also a formidable Aristotelian scholar, and an expert on Spinoza and Descartes. J. A. Smith, in a manuscript entitled "On Joachim's Philosophy," suggested that Joachim had passed from the influence of Spinoza to the influence of Bradley. Furthermore, he claimed that from the time of Joachim's first reading of *Appearance and Reality* in 1897, he "never entered upon a course of independent speculation on any philosophic topic without first ascertaining and spreading before his mind what Bradley had said about it." H. W. B. Joseph noted succinctly that to

---

[44]J. A. Smith to Mrs. A. J. Carlyle, 7 February 1910 [MS.Eng.lett.c.482].

[45]J. A. Smith to F. S. Marvin, 3 July 1919 [MS.Eng.lett.166] (208).

[46]Joseph, "Harold Henry Joachim," 405.

Bradley "and to J. A. Smith he [Joachim] paid a deference in matters of philosophy he paid to no one else," and the writer of his obituary (perhaps Joseph again) noted that Joachim reached no conclusion in his studies of Aristotle without consulting Smith.[47] The alliance between Smith and Joachim never weakened. Instead, their friendship remained one of the compensations for the isolation both suffered as their philosophy became increasingly unfashionable. Joachim taught as Smith's assistant at Balliol from 1894 to 1897, and from 1924 to 1935 Joachim and Smith shared a course on a selected Greek text.

Before Joachim's election to the Wykeham professorship, he had already touched the life of the pupil whose praises would secure this most diffident philosopher a place in the history of English letters. In 1914 Thomas Stearns Eliot had come to Oxford to finish his doctoral dissertation, work already partly completed under the title "Meinong's *Gegenstands Theorie* Considered in Relation to Bradley's Theory of Knowledge." Eliot had intended to study with Bradley, whose *Appearance and Reality* Eliot had read in 1913,[48] and whom Eliot had followed in his subsequent attempt to maneuver between the positions of his Harvard teachers, Josiah Royce, perhaps the greatest American idealist, and Ralph Barton Perry, a convinced exponent of the New England version of Cook Wilson's realism. Conflict was as intense on the Charles as on the Cherwell.

In 1910 Perry and five colleagues had published "The Program and First Platform of Six Realists," defending pluralism and the objectivity of knowledge, and denying the idealist axiom that beings are conditioned by being known.[49] Eliot, whom Joachim inherited when Bradley proved unavailable, had already rejected the philosophy of Perry and Russell. Though he liked "manipulating those curious little figures," he doubted that Russell's philosophy had anything to do with reality and later wrote that Russell's Harvard lectures had "presented the spectacle

---

[47]Ibid.; G. R. G. Mure, "Harold Henry Joachim (1863-1938)," *DNB* (1931-1940) 487, mentions Joachim's "lifelong deference to the views of J. A. Smith."

[48]Richard Wollheim, "Eliot and F. H. Bradley," in *Eliot in Perspective*, ed. Graham Martin (New York: Humanities Press, 1970) 172.

[49]"The Program and First Platform of Six Realists," *Journal of Philosophy* 7 (1910): 393-401.

of a powerful mind (not at all inferior to Bradley's) at war with itself: destroying not so much other men's systems (though Russell has laid flat a good many) as his own."[50] In Bradley, Eliot found a brilliant thinker, a master of English style, whose philosophy radiated "the sweetness and light of the medieval schoolmen."[51]

Of all the aspects of Eliot's intellectual development, his studies at Harvard and Oxford have perhaps been examined most exhaustively in recent scholarship. In H. H. Joachim, Eliot had as tutor a protégé of J. A. Smith, and an expert on Aristotle, Spinoza, and Bradley. Yet even Joachim's studies of Bradley's thought were based not on personal contact—not even Joachim saw Bradley much—but on his books. Joachim may never have read Eliot's dissertation, which was after all produced for Harvard. But the paper does tell us something of Eliot's philosophical development in 1915. *Knowledge and Experience*, the title finally given Eliot's dissertation, is an attempt to come to terms with the problems raised by the realist theory of knowledge and the new psychology, problems that by 1915 had become critical for the future of metaphysics. *Mind* and the *Proceedings of the Aristotelian Society* were full of discussions of the relation between knower and the known, and Eliot shows himself a master of the extensive literature. The most striking single characteristic of Eliot's thesis, which Royce claimed to be "the work of an expert,"[52] was the intensely phenomenological quality that leads Eliot to the conclusion that knowing, though it has much of the character accorded it by the older idealists, cannot itself be known. It is not a relation; it is "inextricably intertwined with . . . processes which are not knowing," and knowing "is only an aspect in a continuous reality." Though nothing can be said of Smith's influence on Eliot, perhaps by way of Joachim, Eliot's epistemology was much like Smith's. Smith would have agreed that knowledge itself is "composed of ingredients

[50]Brand Blanchard, "Eliot in Memory," *Yale Review* 54 (1964-1965): 637; T. S. Eliot, "A Prediction in Regard to Three English Authors," *Vanity Fair* 21:6 (February 1974): 29.

[51]T. S. Eliot, Review of *Ethical Studies*, by F. H. Bradley, *Times Literary Supplement*, 24 December 1927; rpt. "Francis Herbert Bradley," *Selected Essays* (London: Faber and Faber, 1932) 444-45.

[52]Wollheim, *Eliot in Perspective*, 172.

which are themselves neither known nor cognitive, but which melt in the whole called experience."[53] Although Eliot was never under Croce's influence, he was evidently influenced by the new idealism.

When his dissertation was at last published in 1963, Eliot remarked that he no longer understood what he had written. But there was an earlier Eliot, an aspiring philosopher who considered Bradley the greatest metaphysical mind of modern times,[54] and several critics have argued persuasively that Eliot's encounter with the metaphysics of Bradley, Royce, and Joachim influenced his poetry and criticism.[55] At least he had learned what success in philosophy would mean. The purpose of philosophy, Eliot wrote in 1956, was insight and wisdom; and knowledge of philosophy was impossible without some knowledge of the history of philosophy. Eliot had come away from his philosophical studies convinced that the arts "without intellectual content are vanity."[56] The men who had been formed by the Greats curriculum in the 1880s and 1890s occupied the important chairs in 1915, and naturally considered literature a kind of philosophy. Eliot would later write that H. H. Joachim (along with Aristotle) had taught him whatever mastery of English prose style he possessed.[57]

As a pupil of Joachim and hence indirectly of J. A. Smith, and a member of the idealist connection, it is not surprising that Eliot knew Collingwood's work. Collingwood, and men of the older generation like Webb and Rashdall, were occasionally mentioned in the *Criterion*. One result was the quiet partisanship that developed between Eliot and Collingwood. Eliot had reviewed *Religion and Philosophy* in 1917, pronouncing "the philosophical interpretation of the Incarnation, of the

---

[53]Eliot, *Knowledge and Experience*, 156-97.

[54]Ibid., 9; Review of *Ethical Studies*; rpt. "Francis Herbert Bradley."

[55]E. P. Bollier, "T. S. Eliot and F. H. Bradley, A Question of Influence," *Tulane Studies in English* 12 (1962): 87-111; Lewis Freed, *T. S. Eliot: The Critic as Philosopher* (West Lafayette IN: Purdue University Press, 1979). For a summary of Eliot's dissertation, see George Whiteside, "T. S. Eliot's Dissertation," *English Literary History* 34 (1967): 400-24.

[56]Joseph Pieper, *Leisure the Basis of Culture*, trans. Alexander Dru (London: Faber and Faber, 1952) 15.

[57]Eliot to the *Times*, 4 August 1938; Eliot, *Knowledge and Experience*, 9.

Atonement and of miracles" extremely adept, and between 1927 and 1931 Collingwood published five reviews in the *Criterion*.[58]

A better index to the esteem that existed between Eliot and Collingwood was the singular use Collingwood made of England's "one great poet" at the climax of the argument of *The Principles of Art* (1938).[59] There Collingwood asks whether artistic competence will be "directed backward into the blind alley of nineteenth-century individualism, where the artist's only purpose was to express 'himself,' or forwards into a new path where the artist, laying aside his individualistic pretensions, talks as the spokesman of his audience." "In Literature," Collingwood continued, "those who chiefly matter have made the choice and made it rightly. The credit for this belongs chiefly to one great poet, who has set the example by taking as his theme the decay of our civilization. Apart from one or two trifles, Mr. Eliot has never published a line of pure literature."[60] What follows is a masterly and poetically successful interpretation of Eliot's intention in the *Wasteland*, set down in a way that the author of the impersonal theory of art would have found gratifying. Eliot's familiarity with Collingwood's *Principles of Art*, and his sympathy toward Collingwood's argument that sensation (and hence imagination) and thought are inseparable, is attested by Eliot's preface for Leone Vivante's *English Poetry* (1950).[61] Lewis, who had known Eliot since about 1930, came finally to appreciate the great poet whose attacks on romanticism he had resented in 1925.[62]

Another philosopher whom Smith influenced was H. J. Paton (1887-1969), a graduate of Corpus Christi who was White's professor from

---

[58]Eliot, Review of *Religion and Philosophy*, 543. Collingwood reviewed (in chronological order) *Plato: The Man and His Work*, by A. E. Taylor, *Etude sur le Parménide de Platon*, by Jean Wahl, *Epicurus: the Extant Remains*, ed. C. Bailey, and *Epicurus: His Morals*, trans. W. Charleton, 6 (1926-1927): 369-72; *Plato's Theory of Ethics*, by R. C. Lodge, 8 (1928-1929): 159; *The Intelligible World*, by W. M. Urban, and *The Idea of Value*, by John Laird, 9 (1929-1930): 320-21; *The Philosophy of the Good Life*, by Charles Gore, 10 (1930-1931): 560-62; *The Nature of Belief*, by M. C. D'Arcy, 11 (1931-1932): 334-36.

[59]Collingwood, *Principles of Art*, 333.

[60]Ibid.

[61]Leone Vivante, *English Poetry and Its Contribution to the Knowledge of a Creative Principle* (London: Faber and Faber, 1950) vii.

[62]Lewis, *Selected Essays*, xvi.

1937 until 1952.[63] Collingwood's contemporary, Paton had been tutored in philosophy by J. A. Smith at Balliol just before Smith's election to his professorship. The friendship between Smith and Paton lasted Smith's lifetime, and Paton was convinced that Smith was the best teacher he had ever known.[64] The side of his undergraduate education that Paton developed was his historical and systematic interest in Kant—an interest Collingwood, Smith, and Webb wholeheartedly shared. Before 1950 Paton produced *The Good Will* (1927), *Kant's Metaphysic of Experience* (1936), *The Categorical Imperative* (1947), and *The Moral Law* (1948), the last a new translation of the *Foundations of the Metaphysics of Morals*.

After 1945 Paton turned from historical studies of Kant to the philosophy of religion, taking up many of the problems Webb had discussed in the 1920s and 1930s, though apparently apart from any immediate influence by Webb. In the Forswood Lectures, delivered at the University of Liverpool in 1949, and again in the Gifford Lectures of 1950 and 1951, Paton discussed the relation between religion and philosophy, producing thorough and evenhanded treatments of the possibilities and difficulties of the philosophy of religion.[65] By the late 1950s "the linguistic veto," the positivists' refusal to allow the use of words that violated the verification principle, was much in evidence.[66] Paton argued against it, but he was never doctrinaire, and was as anxious to put down religious presumptions regarding reason as to maintain the possibility of a significant theological language.[67] Because of Paton, the tradition of philosophic reflection Webb had established remained an influence at Oxford throughout the 1940s. When his collected essays were published in 1951, Paton included a piece the idea for which had been given him by J. A. Smith forty years before.[68]

---

[63]Paton, "Fifty Years," *CBP* (3), 337-54.

[64]Ibid., 341-42, 344.

[65]H. J. Paton, *The Modern Predicament* (London: George Allen and Unwin, 1955).

[66]Ibid., 33-46.

[67]Ibid., 47-58.

[68]H. J. Paton, *In Defense of Reason* (London: Hutchinson's University Library, 1951) 255, n. 1. Paton wrote in 1927 that "both as tutor and friend" J. A. Smith had been "a continual source of philosophical inspiration" [*The Good Will: A Study in the Coherence Theory of Goodness* (London: George Allen and Unwin, 1927) preface].

Two somewhat younger men who perpetuated the thought of the Magdalen metaphysicals were Austin Farrer and Willmoore Kendall. The first was a devoted friend of Lewis, the second an American whom Collingwood had tutored at Pembroke in 1934 and 1935. Austin Farrer's estimate of C. S. Lewis was set down in "The Christian Apologist," an essay in the volume inspired by Barfield; and Lewis had stated his admiration for Farrer in the preface to *A Faith of Our Own*.[69] They had surely met by 1935 when Farrer had become chaplain of Trinity, a post he would hold for twenty-five years. During the 1940s Lewis and the Farrers had grown close, perhaps because their agreement on matters theological was almost complete. The Farrers came to the Socratic Club, Austin Farrer to the Inklings, and after Lewis's marriage to Joy Davidman in 1956, the Lewises and Farrers were fast friends.

The central insight in Farrer's writings, and the one that related his thought most closely to that of Lewis and Collingwood, is his insistence that knowledge is a poetic unity involving reason and imagination, and in the case of knowledge of God, revelation. Farrer was a romantic in Lewis's sense: "I count poetical vision and even amatory passion the friends of religion," he wrote, "for though poetry may breed fancifulness and egoism, and love animality, the lover and the poet can at least see the world."

> The chief impediment to religion in this age is that no one ever looks at anything at all, not so as to contemplate it, to apprehend what it is to be that thing and plumb, if he can, the deep fact of its individual existence. The mind rises from the knowledge of creatures to the knowledge of their creator, but this does not happen through the sort of knowledge which can analyze things into factors or manipulate them with technical skill. . . . It comes from the appreciation of things which we have when we love them and fill our minds and senses with them, and feel something of the silent force and great mystery of their existence. For it is in this that the creative power is displayed of an existence higher and richer and more intense than all.[70]

---

[69]Austin Farrer, "The Christian Apologist," *Light on C. S. Lewis*, ed. Jocelyn Gibb (London: Geoffrey Bles, 1965) 23-43; C. S. Lewis, preface, Austin Farrer, *A Faith of Our Own* (Cleveland: World Publishing Company, 1960) 7-10.

[70]Austin Farrer, "Poetic Truth," in Charles C. Conti, ed., *Reflective Faith* (London: SPCK, 1972) 37-38.

In this text rings the concrete method of the *Lux Mundi* group; Webb's defense of knowledge as a personal act; the idealist assertion that in the act of knowledge both knower and known are changed; Chesterton's unforgettable essay on appreciating the dandelion; and Lewis's defense of Augustine's *ordo amoris*.[71]

E. L. Mascall believed that Farrer's greatest contribution was to natural theology, and certainly there is in modern English scholarship no more compelling defense of theism than Farrer's *Finite and Infinite*, nor a more persuasive refutation of determinism than his *Freedom of the Will*.[72] It was in the writings of Farrer (and Mascall) that the questions of natural theology, analogy, and the existence of God had their first careful English formulation. Farrer was something of a Thomist; at least he treated Aquinas as an authority of great weight.[73]

Farrer's other important contributions to scholarship were his studies of the Apocalypse. These were attempts to understand one of the most difficult books in Scripture as literature and to explain the work as a repository of the images that form the Christian view of history. *The Glass of Vision* and *The Rebirth of Images* are in fact contributions toward a new methodology for the study of the Bible, one that begins with careful reading and an understanding of the nature of poetry.[74]

Collingwood is probably the twentieth-century English philosopher whose thought has been studied most since about 1960. Like Webb, he did not have many pupils who went on as professional philosophers to develop his thought, or who confessed themselves his disciples on cardinal metaphysical points. Van der Dussen says that T. M. Knox might be called Collingwood's "only real pupil";[75] but this must be qualified

---

[71]Chesterton, *Autobiography*, 328-32; Lewis, *Abolition of Man*, 10. Lewis is here citing Augustine [*De civ. Dei*, xv] in support of the common classical and medieval opinion that our affections are subject to a right order.

[72]Conti, ed., *Interpretation and Belief*, xiii, xiv; Austin Farrer, *Finite and Infinite* (Westminster: Dacre Press, 1943); *Freedom of the Will* (London: Adam and Charles Black, 1958).

[73]Farrer, *Finite and Infinite*, 26ff.

[74]Austin Farrer, *The Glass of Vision* (Westminster: Dacre Press, 1948); *The Rebirth of Images* (Westminster: Dacre Press, 1949).

[75]*CUM*, 363.

at least by the addition of Willmoore Kendall, Oklahoma-born, who became one of the most important American political philosophers of the post-World War II era, pursuing a brilliant career at Yale and the University of Dallas.

Kendall was at Oxford from October 1932 to April 1935, when he took a second in Philosophy, Politics, and Economics—Modern Greats. His tutor in moral and political philosophy was Collingwood, whom Kendall would have known at the end of his Pembroke career and at the height of his powers. From his Oxford studies Kendall gained a lifelong admiration for Collingwood. Also during this time he formed a lifetime friendship, attested by a considerable correspondence, with R. B. McCallum, his tutor in history and government, and later master of Pembroke.[76] His Oxford years remained for Kendall a golden age, and whenever his brilliance, candor, and stubbornness brought his career to a temporary standstill, Kendall would write to McCallum, leaving the unmistakable suggestion that a chance to return to Oxford would be welcomed.

From Collingwood, Kendall gained an interest in the painstaking reading of texts and the hermeneutic of question and answer that made possible a kind of methodological revolution: the reading of Locke in the context of his own presuppositions. Collingwood's *The New Leviathan* remained a source for Kendall, along with Collingwood's conviction that education, the mediation of tradition, is the alternative to the tyrannical rule of the mob.[77]

Willmoore Kendall owned two copies of *The New Leviathan*. An exclamation point stands beside the proposition that became one foundation of Kendall's political philosophy: Collingwood's denial that there exists such a thing as human nature having the rights the eighteenth cen-

---

[76]For Kendall's biography, see *Encyclopedia of American Biography* 39 (West Palm Beach FL: American Historical Company, 1969) 358-60.

[77]Kendall was just beginning to make his mark in the United States when Collingwood died, but Kendall often took an opportunity to express his debt to Collingwood. See Nellie D. Kendall, ed., *Willmoore Kendall Contra Mundum* (New Rochelle NY: Arlington House, 1971) 198, n400, 423, n500. See also Collingwood to Kendall, 15 January 1934; McCallum to Kendall, 2 December 1963, 6 November 1965; McCallum to Nellie D. Kendall, 27 April 1972, Kendall Papers.

tury so easily discovered.[78] Kendall was also deeply interested in Collingwood's notion that a political system is dialectical, not combatant, that aristocracy cannot exist without democracy or democracy without aristocracy. Civilization, then, becomes men locked together in deliberative argument, not purely rational, for men are not purely rational, but reasonable and patient. He was decisively influenced by Collingwood's distinction between a "society" based on force, and the traditional form of society denoting joint will. He looked also to education as the means through which "society" moves, dialectically, toward society.[79] Collingwood had agreed that there could be no nonsocial community in which babies are born free, as Rousseau would have it. To be a member of society is not a product of free will. Rousseau found the state of nature into which babies are born an immense tyranny. Collingwood and Kendall found it a fact. Certainly it was from Collingwood that Kendall learned his dislike for abstract legality and abstract doctrines on the natures of things.[80]

One certain index to Collingwood's influence is the works Kendall owned and used. Kendall possessed every philosophy book Collingwood had written, with the exception of *Religion and Philosophy* and *An Autobiography*. All but *Speculum Mentis* and the *Principles of Art* Kendall read with a pencil. As Kendall's marginal notations suggest, he was fascinated with the logic implicit in the *Essay on Philosophical Method*, especially the chapter entitled "The Overlap of Classes." He put the exclamation mark he used to reflect his deep agreement after the sentence in which Collingwood had warned that philosophical starting points were constantly to be revised in the light of conclusions. In the chapter "Philosophy as a Branch of Literature," Kendall noted as important Collingwood's conclusion that the reader must listen to the text and pay attention to his own condition as a reader. Kendall was especially interested in Collingwood's belief that a good reader must first "keep quiet and refrain from obtruding his own thoughts," and then exercise

[78]See Willmoore Kendall, "The Bill of Rights and American Freedom," "Equality and the American Political Tradition," Kendall, ed., *Kendall Contra Mundum*, 303-25, 347-61.

[79]Collingwood, *New Leviathan*, 19.1-23.97.

[80]Ibid., 23.9-23.97.

the obligation of criticism. "So understood, the function of the critic is to develop and continue the thought of the writer criticized."[81] From this interest, later encouraged by Kendall's fascination with the thought of Leo Strauss, came Kendall's own essays on "How to read Milton's *Areopagitica*" and "How to Read *The Federalist*."[82]

The marginalia in Kendall's copy of the *Essay on Metaphysics* suggest his agreement with Collingwood's belief that psychology was a pseudoscience. In the *Idea of History*, Kendall's pencil could not resist indicating his approval of the sections entitled "Historical Evidence" and "History and Freedom," both fragments of Collingwood's 1939 manuscript "The Principles of History," as well as essays belonging originally to 1936: "History as Re-enactment of Past Experience" and "The Subject Matter of History." Among the points Kendall most obviously approved was Collingwood's insistence that the historian must reenact the past in his own mind; that all history is the history of thought; that rational activity is free from the domination of nature; and that history is a process of question and answer in which evidence is always permissive, not coercive.[83]

Kendall's biography has not been written, but it will finally display a man on fire with ideas, a child of the parsonage who became a Rhodes Scholar and a Roman Catholic. In addition, Kendall was a conservative, but not a conservative tolerable to American economic conservatives. Jeffrey Hart wrote that Kendall was "for all the immense sanity of his genius, a strange and solitary figure, isolated not only from the academic establishment—though he was a great teacher, and profoundly changed the lives of some of his students—but from any establishment whatever."[84] Kendall's strangeness was the strangeness of genius in an academic environment that sometimes found the single-minded pursuit of intellectual principles exotic. Solitude was the penalty levied upon a man

---

[81]Collingwood, *Essay on Philosophical Method*, 216-17.

[82]Kendall came under the influence of Leo Strauss in the 1950s. For Kendall's bibliography, see Nellie D. Kendall, ed., *Kendall Contra Mundum*, 5-6. A complete bibliography is in the Kendall Memorial Library, University of Dallas.

[83]Collingwood, *The Idea of History*, 249-90.

[84]Jeffrey Hart, "Willmoore Kendall: American," in Kendall, ed., *Kendall Contra Mundum*, 9.

who, like Collingwood, persisted in raising unfashionable questions, which if heeded, might lead to actions disruptive to a superficial and implicitly anti-intellectual consensus.

Nobody can hope to catalog even the major influences of the Magdalen metaphysicals, nor all the influences that helped shape their thought. Some omissions are obvious. Joachim was partly responsible for inspiring Bertrand Russell, his sister's nephew, to make philosophy his vocation; and although Eliot would be Joachim's most famous pupil, he was also an important influence on another American, Brand Blanshard, whom Joachim tutored in 1915. Both Charles Williams and Tolkien were important influences on Lewis during the 1930s and 1940s, as was Owen Barfield. It was Tolkien's understanding of myth that had touched Lewis in 1932. Beginning in 1939 Lewis was fascinated by Williams' Platonic doctrine of real forms or ideas, itself a kind of literary absolute idealism. There was also George MacDonald, who taught Lewis that imagination might lead further up and further in. The influence of Collingwood on Sir Malcolm Knox and G. R. G. Mure was also significant. The list could be expanded indefinitely, and though it never included many of their fellow professionals, the influence of the Magdalen metaphysicals was diffuse and deep.

The educated middle class, professional or not, made the works of Lewis and Collingwood publishing successes quite unlike anything written by Oxford academics in the twentieth century. *Screwtape* alone sold half a million copies. Every one of Collingwood's books on philosophy is in print.

•CHAPTER VII•

1945

The future is impenetrable especially to the wise; for what is really important is always hid from contemporaries, and the seeds of what is to be are quietly germinating in some dark corner.

J. R. R. Tolkien to Christopher,
22 August 1944

"Dear old J. A. is dying," Webb wrote in his journal in December 1939. Joachim had gone the summer before, and Collingwood's life was the race of a brave man against time. The strokes had come with ever-greater frequency, but the deterioration had simply spurred him to complete his work. The *Autobiography* had been finished in October 1938, the *Essay on Metaphysics* in April 1939, and *The New Leviathan* would be sent to the printer in 1941.

When Collingwood returned to England from a year-long leave in May 1939, the professorial community was in an uproar over his autobiography. Webb had heard in February that in the book Collingwood had professed himself a Marxist, and when the author returned with a beard, the worst seemed confirmed.[1] H. W. B. Joseph answered Collingwood's book in the *Oxford Magazine* with bitterness, insisting that certainly not *all* the realists had contributed to the rise of the idea that

[1]WJB, 18 February, 2 May 1939 [MS.Eng.misc.e.1175].

moral philosophy was useless. Disapproval lingered into the 1960s, when a critic explained that Collingwood had "expressed himself with a degree of exaggeration," which, to put it mildly, "was uncommon in English academic philosophy."[2] The *Autobiography* confirmed in the mind of a great many of Collingwood's contemporaries the notion that he was an intemperate, and therefore an inconsiderable, man. But it also represented Collingwood at his best, writing history as he saw it.

Lewis was also experiencing, perhaps for the first time, the freeze that would prevent his ever winning a professorship at Oxford. He had become, he wrote to J. M. Thompson, "a prig and a spike": that is, he had not only been converted, but had become an apologist, behavior that by 1940 was already considered a violation of academic politeness.[3] These feelings of resentment on the part of other academics reached a climax in 1951 when one elector voted against Lewis when the poetry chair was to be filled because Lewis had written *Screwtape*.[4]

The sense of isolation that Lewis and Collingwood both felt by 1940 was mitigated by personal friendships. Collingwood was invited to sail the Aegean with undergraduates in 1939. Lewis, surrounded by an admiring circle of Inklings and sustained by the unvarying friendship and assistance of his brother, was not lonely; nor was J. A., who kept on writing long philosophical letters from Norham Gardens until the end. Their isolation was merely a punishment inflicted professionally on men who had somehow violated the rules of scholarship as they then existed. Lord Haldane, Webb had noted in 1924, had left the meeting before J. A. Smith delivered his impassioned British Academy lecture against Samuel Alexander; and philosophy tutors, McCallum wrote in 1943, "were distrustful of Collingwood's philosophy,"[5] as were theologians of Lewis's mere Christianity.

The cause of this distrust is not hard to find. Lewis and Collingwood were dangerous on the grounds that they believed thought led to truth

---

[2]H. W. B. Joseph, Review of *An Autobiography*, by R. G. Collingwood, *Oxford Magazine* 58:1 (28 October 1939): 34; Lewy, "*Mind* under G. E. Moore," 42.

[3]Lewis to J. M. Thompson, 25 July 1940 (MS.Eng.lett.c.496) BLW.

[4]Lewis, *Brothers and Friends*, 240-41.

[5]WJB, 5 November 1924 [MS.Eng.misc.e.1167]; McCallum, "Collingwood," 167.

and truth to action. The implication was that their ideas were right, or at least reasonable, and that men of good will should tolerate them graciously, agree with them, or enter into a conversation that would establish alternatives. Their philosophic style, though not their conclusions, was a throwback to the school of Green, indeed to Ruskin, who thought lectures on art not unrelated to building a road at Hinksey. This style was also reminiscent of Plato, who considered a good conscience more precious than life. If one thought like Lewis and Collingwood, if one allowed great questions to arise, one might at any moment meet God in the angle of the stairs. The whole thrust of the Wilson-Prichard school had been to preclude such questions systematically by severing the nerve relating fact to judgment, rendering the first rigidly empirical, the second utterly subjective. In an Anglo-Saxon world ruled by the iron hand of secular respectability, the positivists utilized tactics which implied that questions about truth and God were not only impossible but tasteless and jejune.

Collingwood was, of course, more exposed than Lewis, whose kinder colleagues could—if they chose—consider his Christianity an unfortunate adjunct to his obviously competent work in the English faculty. Not so with Collingwood, who thought art, religion, history, and philosophy were of a piece, and who resisted the charitable impulse of well-wishers to declare him an expert in one discipline, an amateur in the others. Clement Webb noted in his journal on 11 March 1926 that he had had a conversation with A. E. J. Rawlinson, a member of The Group, and a distinguished Anglican intellectual, about Robin Collingwood. Rawlinson thought Collingwood "very full of pride of intellect."[6] Webb added, "He is, of course, a man of most extraordinary gifts and accomplishments." But those gifts, which themselves seemed a scandal against the ideal of the expert, were held by a man who believed thought led to conclusions.

By 1940 fortune had turned different faces toward Lewis and Collingwood. Despite his professional loneliness, Lewis was, if letters and the testimony of friends signify, at peace with himself, a believer, a popular author, respected scholar, and successful teacher. Collingwood was ill; his marriage of twenty years to Ethel Graham was in dissolution; and

---

[6]WJB, 11 March 1926 [Ms.Eng.misc.d.1119].

the press of work he feared he would never complete had become burdensome. In 1941 he resigned the Waynflete Chair; married Katherine Frances Edwardes; returned to Lanehead, which he had inherited in 1932; and in January 1943 succumbed to the strokes that had plagued him since 1933. His sister Barbara Gnosspelius wrote in her diary on 12 January:

> Funeral at Coniston, 2:30 p.m. A frightful day of dark and rain. . . There were no flowers, and no wreaths but ours. The Churchyard was muddy and wet; it poured steadily. The grave had been dug beside his parents' and with great difficulty. He had an unpolished coffin, and on the plate was the only name he came into the world with, Robin Collingwood. (by my instructions)

John Coatman, who worked for the B.B.C. in Manchester, represented the university; there were no other mourners but the widow, Collingwood's sisters Barbara and Ursula, a few other family members, and the representatives of the Cumberland and Westmoreland Antiquarian Society, for which Collingwood and his father had worked and lectured for decades.

When the war ended in 1945, Clement Webb was very much alive, and to honor him on his eightieth birthday, 25 June 1945, his friends published an address he had given at Oriel the preceding year.[7] Lewis was riding a crest of popularity—*The Great Divorce* and *That Hideous Strength*, the last volume of the trilogy, had been published in 1945—darkened only by the death of Charles Williams on 15 May. Already Lewis's reputation, great in Britain and prodigious in America, was proving something of an embarrassment at Oxford, and a thorn in the flesh of theologians like Norman Pittenger, who found his thought simplistic.[8]

The world dealt variously with the Magdalen metaphysicals after the war. The esteem shown Clement Webb in 1944 was for his person as much as his philosophy, and for the most part the men who subscribed the volume published in his honor were his near contemporaries and older pupils: Leonard Hodgson, the distinguished idealist and sometime

---

[7]Webb, *Religious Experience*, 25.

[8]W. Norman Pittenger, "Apologist versus Apologist: A Critique of C. S. Lewis as 'Defender of the Faith,' " *Christian Century* 75 (1 October 1958): 1104-07.

dean of divinity at Magdalen; L. P. Jacks, the longtime editor of the *Hibbert Journal*; the modernist pillars A. L. Lilley and H. D. A. Major; Father Martin Cyril D'Arcy; G. L. Stevenson; E. F. Carritt, H. A. Prichard, and W. D. Ross, like Webb, philosophical survivors from late nineteenth-century Oxford; H. J. Paton; Canon Adam Fox, Magdalen's dean of divinity; Webb's contemporaries at Magdalen, P. V. M. Beneke and C. T. Onions.[9] At forty-seven C. S. Lewis was possibly the youngest don among the subscribers. Oxford's love for Clement Webb was in part an affection for its own past, since Webb's own philosophical position was increasingly neglected. Eleanor Joseph Webb had died in 1942. Clement Webb lived until 1954, and wrote occasionally, but his philosophy of religion had little place in postwar Oxford, so that Webb and his work went largely unnoticed for a quarter century.[10]

The war and the new philosophy obliterated the memory of John Alexander Smith among professional historians and philosophers. His biographer, W. D. Ross, offered two explanations that have been cited frequently since 1939, suggesting that Smith failed to influence Oxford philosophy in a lasting way because he did not write and because his versatility prevented his developing a system.[11] The first of Ross's reasons is true only to the degree that Smith's failure to write a long systematic treatise is relevant. Smith's impressive bibliography may still be incomplete because he wrote so much on philosophy, theology, history, economics, language, and the text of Aristotle in so many different journals. The outline of his philosophy was set down with considerable clarity in the Muirhead series in 1924, and there is no evidence that his contemporaries considered his views obscure. That this versatility inhibited his influence in the 1920s and 1930s seems unlikely, but the notion of the professional philosopher did overtake Smith, and new ideals of philosophic writings and conversation did make his thought seem eclectic and old-fashioned. By 1945 he seemed to have influenced nobody. Collingwood himself noted his debt to Smith, but Smith's biographer made

---

[9]Webb, *Religious Experience*, 7-12.

[10]Langford, *English Theology*, 73-77, 271-73.

[11]Ross, "John Alexander Smith," *DNB* 1934-1940, 819.

nothing of it. Nothing was written about J. A. Smith after his obituaries.[12]

In the decade following Collingwood's death in 1943, the events that made his thought part of contemporary philosophy were the publications of *The Idea of Nature* in 1945 and the *Idea of History* in 1946 by his literary executor T. M. Knox. Then for almost a decade Collingwood was largely ignored. A trickle of articles about his thought did appear. Alan Donagan began to make Collingwood's philosophy a major part of his own scholarly work,[13] and there were important studies by E. W. F. Tomlin and Errol E. Harris.[14] By 1964 Lionell Rubinoff had begun to write about the importance of religion for Collingwood's thought.[15] During the 1970s Collingwood became an acceptable subject for dissertations and monographs, and finally a kind of intransigent anomaly in the history of contemporary English thought, the metaphysician who refused to stop thinking his own thoughts, which were too important to ignore and yet too unfashionable to receive with much enthusiasm.

Clive Staples Lewis was the only one of the four who completed a major portion of his work after 1945, but his approach remained unchanged. The place of Lewis in contemporary thought had in large measure been determined by the appreciations that began to appear several years before his death. These reflect, for the most part, the efforts of those who remembered Lewis as a defender of Christianity. While several critical studies discussing the literary qualities of his apologies have

---

[12]Neither Smith nor Joachim appears in G. J. Warnock, *English Philosophy Since 1900* (London: Oxford University Press, 1958); in Rudolf Metz, *A Hundred Years of British Philosophy*; or in John Passmore, *A Hundred Years of Philosophy*.

[13]See especially Donagan, *The Later Philosophy of R. G. Collingwood*.

[14]Tomlin, a pupil of Collingwood, published the first monograph, *R. G. Collingwood* (London: Longmans, 1961), and the important article "The Philosophy of R. G. Collingwood," *Ratio* 1 (1958): 116-35. Errol E. Harris published "Collingwood on Eternal Problems," *Journal of Philosophy* 1 (1950): 228-41; Donald S. Mackay, "On Supposing and Presupposing," Review of *Metaphysics 2* (1948) 1-20.

[15]Rubinoff came to the study of Collingwood by way of editing F. H. Bradley's *Presuppositions of Critical History* (Chicago: Quadrangle, 1968), and subsequently collected and edited Collingwood's writings on religion under the title *Faith and Reason* (1968). *Collingwood and the Reform of Metaphysics* (Toronto: University of Toronto Press, 1970) is a comprehensive study of Collingwood's thought.

been written, the philosophic presuppositions of his arguments and the history of those presuppositions have remained unexamined.[16]

The tendency of scholarship has been to present Collingwood primarily as a philosopher of history in whose thought Christianity remains inchoate or problematic, while Lewis is usually considered an apologist and his relation to philosophy ignored. These interpretations deprive Collingwood of the single presupposition on which all his thought depended and rob Lewis of the philosophic insights that constitute the very texture of his apologetic. Forgetting Smith and Webb, and other Oxford philosophers of the 1920s and 1930s, causes Lewis and Collingwood, as well as others of their Oxford generation, to appear without context or background.

The reasons for this eccentric interpretation of the Magdalen metaphysicals in the period after 1945 are partly evident. That the Magdalen metaphysicals do not appear as a school is understandable, for in the ordinary sense they were not. Still, it is odd that, taken together with their pupils like Paton and Farrer, the philosophic approach they represented has until now been given little or no place in the historiography of twentieth-century thought. In 1976 the personal statements begun by J. H. Muirhead in 1924 went into a fourth series.[17] The volume gives no clue that metaphysics ever existed as anything other than a misunderstanding of language, and no contributor concedes that religion is an activity to which philosophy might prove relevant.

The apparent defeat of idealism by the realists in the 1920s and positivists in the 1930s was unlike other philosophic wars because it meant the denial not of discrete conclusions but of the possibility of metaphysics. A. J. Ayer modestly proposed that the kind of thinking Plato and Aristotle called philosophy be abandoned as nonsensical and Hume, or certain texts selected from Hume, be taken as the foundations of philos-

---

[16]See Gilbert Meilander, *The Social and Ethical Thought of C. S. Lewis* (Grand Rapids MI: William B. Eerdmans, 1978); Robert H. Smith, *Patches of Godlight: The Pattern of Thought of C. S. Lewis* (Athens GA: University of Georgia Press, 1981); William Luther White, *The Image of Man in C. S. Lewis* (Nashville: Abingdon, 1969).

[17]*Contemporary British Philosophy*, ed. H. D. Lewis, ser. 4 (London: George Allen and Unwin, 1976).

ophy.[18] Collingwood and his contemporaries understood the radical nature of the proposal and sensed that Ayer had imported in full-blown rigor the "Moorism" of Cambridge, which when grafted to the native realist stock, would cause a revolution. Paton wrote that when he returned to Oxford in 1937, he came back to a world radically different from the university he had left in 1914.[19] Lewis wrote in 1943 that "the world inhabited by philosophical students of my own generation had become as alien to our successors as if not years but centuries had intervened."[20] In 1954 he wrote Dom Bede Griffiths, "The gap between Professor Ryle and Dante is wider than that between Virgil and Dante." This notion would grow into his Cambridge inaugural, *De Descriptione Temporum*.[21]

The thought of the Magdalen metaphysicals is in fact unassimilable to the major tradition of academic philosophy in the 1960s and 1970s. Their understanding of language, of the relation between knowledge and duty, and of the place of reason in personality—though assumed by many of the ordinary people for whom they wrote—all make their thought an unruly guest at the house of professional philosophy. Of all the positions shared by the Magdalen four, the single proposition that goes most against the grain is their affirmation that thought may lead to belief in God. As Lewis wrote in 1943, the attempt "seriously to live by philosophy . . . turns into religion."[22] Collingwood had realized by 1915 what was at stake, and had argued in *Religion and Philosophy* that theology was genuine knowledge. Webb had devoted a scholarly lifetime to defending the existence of an integral relation between philosophy and the philosophy of religion; and Lewis, having been converted by thinking, had gone on to write a series of brilliant apologies that drew much of their power from the metaphysics he presupposed. The importance of this conclusion is obvious. Reason had led to skepticism throughout

---

[18]A. J. Ayer, ed., *Logical Positivism* (Glencoe IL: Free Press, 1959) 10-15; *Part of My Life* (Oxford: University Press, 1977) 54, 125, 149-50.

[19]Paton, "Fifty Years," 349.

[20]Lewis, *Pilgrim's Regress*, 5.

[21]C. S. Lewis to Bede Griffiths, 1 November 1954, *LCSL*, 258.

[22]Lewis, *Pilgrim's Regress*, 143.

much of the nineteenth century. Defenders of belief had denied its relation to reason or rationalized it beyond its character. The Magdalen metaphysicals had undertaken the task of righting the ancient relationship. In Oxford between the wars, for a few whose thought has proved fruitful for the late twentieth century, idealism—the belief in thought itself—had led to orthodoxy.

This movement did not stem from some necessity intrinsic to idealism as a philosophy. Belief in ideas that are more than things, in reason itself, may lead to faith. However, it may also lead into the morass of "spiritual" religion that compasses on one hand the righteous and intellectual God of deism and degenerates on the other into the popular cant of folk gnosticism. The vital forces—from Bergson's élan vital, through Teilhard's world process, to general faith in a progressive force that guides history—undergird in Anglo-Saxon imagination a pervasive belief in an abstract but inevitable goodness that is father of our kindness and our viciousness, of our optimism, our easy belief, and our cynicism. The nineteenth-century idealism that formed the background for the thought of the Magdalen metaphysicals considered orthodoxy and skepticism extremes that only an enlightened philosophic religion could avoid.[23]

T. M. Knox, with Mure and Paton the last of the Oxford idealists, found himself in his seventy-eighth year, perhaps to his surprise, delivering the Margaret Harris lectures at Dundee. In them he argued the great idealist principle that reason is the friend of faith, and numbered both Barth and Wittgenstein, the great irrationalists, "among those who have contributed to the eclipse of European civilization in my lifetime."[24] Knox had found his own faith returning in his old age, but the faith he recovered was still the orthodoxy of idealism, the faith of Thomas Hill Green and Edward Caird. Revelation was an experience, never truth. Knox did indeed believe that man is a spiritual being, a candle of the Lord, a dwelling place of the Holy Spirit. He believed as well that Jesus had revealed the Father; but Knox wrote quite candidly that he did not believe in the atonement, the Virgin Birth, Eucharist, or baptismal re-

---

[23]This had been Bradley's position, and it was recited in the 1970s by Mure and T. M. Knox. See Bradley, *Appearance and Reality*, 5-7.

[24]T. M. Knox, *A Heretic's Religion* (Dundee, 1976).

generation. Mure's last book, *Idealist Epilogue* (1979), offered an almost identical analysis. In it Mure wrote frankly that his Hegelianism had been a philosophic way that preserved Western values without involving a historically useful but intellectually discredited religion. The religion to which idealism led most effortlessly (one might almost say the religion into which idealism naturally degenerated) remained after a century a religion to which the deep things—grace, glory, sanctity, the virtues, the vision of God, sin, Jesus, his cross, his resurrection and ascension—were strangers. Idealism had been capable of inspiring a search for truth and for God in the lives of men like Lewis, Webb, and Collingwood. It was equally likely to produce an atmosphere of high-minded gnosticism and abstracted natural piety. Paul Van Buren's *The Secular Meaning of the Gospel* (1963), and J. A. T. Robinson's *Honest to God* (1964), which alarmed orthodox Anglicans in the 1960s, were in one sense merely recent manifestations of a theology which, because of its philosophic presuppositions, must always tend to belief in an impersonal God who is partially manifest in everything historical, but never really incarnate.

Of course, in the end every philosophy, displayed in the light of revelation, has about it a profound ambiguity, as well as an apparent necessity. Philosophy is necessary, and good, because reason exists and because men must seek the invisible realities to which the visible world bears witness. Philosophy is ambiguous because, taken in abstraction from the divine wisdom toward which it tends, it is fatally flawed and fragile. Christian intellectuals never simply take over a philosophy as it stands, for no philosophy stands perfected in this world. Collingwood, Lewis, and Webb did with Oxford idealism what Augustine had done with Plato and Aquinas with Aristotle, taking a current philosophy in which much was true and transforming it by bringing it into an integral and subordinate relation to revealed wisdom. And it is precisely the integral relation between their metaphysics and Christian revelation that makes them hard to locate. They were not in the long run idealists, or if they were idealists, they were such as Augustine had been a Platonist. More accurately, they were intellectuals of a kind almost unknown to English scholarship since Berkeley: Christian philosophers, men who could not philosophize apart from revealed truth, but who at same time remained philosophers and as such were unwilling to sacrifice thought to any apologetic purpose. In these dispositions they differed radically from most of their contemporaries, who tended, like the realists, to find

Christianity intellectually irrelevant, or else, like Charles Gore and J. R. Illingworth, simply assumed the truth of faith and the apologetic usefulness of philosophy. The Magdalen metaphysicals were Christian philosophers, men who followed philosophic method rigorously but who likewise considered revelation an indispensable knowledge apart from which the philosophic enterprise would fail.

Clearly this claim that the Magdalen metaphysicals and their pupils were a distinctive and fruitful school of Christian wisdom can be countered in the case of Webb with the assertion that he was not really a dogmatic Christian, in the case of Smith with his rationalism, in the case of Lewis with the plea that he was not really a philosopher, and in the case of Collingwood with the observation that he had no zeal for religion. Still, the fact is that Webb, Lewis, and Collingwood all became Christians as adults, self-consciously and after much of the dryest kind of thinking. Moreover, they chose throughout their lives to make the faith they considered true indispensable to their thought. Lewis could not stand outside his faith when he wrote. Webb considered Christianity, at the last, unique. Collingwood was, at the end, unable to discover any basis for either philosophy or history other than the absolute presuppositions belonging to revelation.

If their thought had carried them beyond the idealism of their teachers, their debt to it was nevertheless acknowledged. Idealism had, Lewis wrote, taught him the importance of heaven existing even if none of us should reach it.[25] For Collingwood the Greats philosophy of his teachers had been the source of moral responsibility and political maturity, and its abandonment had made the young prey to charlatans.[26] When Webb addressed his friends and former pupils in 1944, he noted that in his first years at Oxford, Christianity had been fed by the idealistic demonstration of its consonance with reason, and regretted the severing of the relation between faith and reason that had marked recent philosophy. If idealism had posed dangers for faith, it had also offered opportunities.

Long before Webb died in 1954, Anglo-Saxon philosophy had taken the path marked out by Cook Wilson, Joseph and Prichard, and developed by Ayer and Ryle; and from the point of view of this decade, pos-

---

[25]Lewis, *Surprised by Joy*, 211.

[26]Collingwood, *Autobiography*, 48-50.

itivism, though past its triumphalist phase, seems as unshakable as had the iron rule of idealism in 1910. Idealism had seemed secure; it had gone down like the Bastille. In its demise there may be lessons for the present philosophical fashion, for it too will prove transitory, and interest in the perennial problems, in justice, in goodness, in beauty will not forever be forestalled. The philosophy of the Magdalen Metaphysicals will then have a better reputation. It will not at any point provide some final answer. It will fail to do so not because it knows no truths to tell, but because philosophy is a way, and every generation, indeed every man and woman, must think independently. But as surely as life is an adventure in company, so philosophy is the enterprise of companionable scholarship, in which the masters of the past appear as our teachers, foils, and fellow travelers. The threads of reflection will be picked up where they can be grasped, in the writings of Lewis, Collingwood, Farrer, Kendall, and those others for whom the heritage of Plato, Aristotle, Vico, Kant, and Green was a highroad to fruitful thought about the world and to the reasonableness of the Christian intellectual patrimony. To say that their defense of the truth of a faith their colleagues often wished to explain into the shadows had much to do with their place, with Oxford as it was from the death of Victoria to the birth in 1945 of a world liberated from its past, would be hard to establish. But perhaps the American who wrote his *Pages from an Oxford Diary* in 1925[27] had sensed a coherent theme:

> Oxford is a creation of the Church and her beauty witnesses to the excellence of religion. The mark was put upon her once for all, wonderful city!

---

[27] Paul Elmer More, *Pages from an Oxford Diary* (Princeton: University Press, 1935) 1.

•BIBLIOGRAPHY•

I. Biographies, Intellectual Biographies, and Autobiographies Relevant to the History of Philosophy and Theology at Oxford, 1901-1945

Armstrong, Christopher J. R. *Evelyn Underhill (1875-1941)*. Grand Rapids MI: William B. Eerdmans, 1976.

Ayer, A. J. *Part of My Life*. Oxford: University Press, 1977.

Campbell, R. J. *A Spiritual Pilgrimage*. London: Williams and Norgate, 1916.

Carpenter, Humphrey. *The Inklings: C. S. Lewis, J. R. R. Tolkien, Charles Williams, and Their Friends*. Boston: Houghton Mifflin, 1979.

______________. *Tolkien: A Biography*. Boston: Houghton Mifflin, 1978.

______________, ed. *The Letters of J. R. R. Tolkien*. Boston: Houghton Mifflin, 1981.

Carritt, E. F. *Fifty Years a Don*. Oxford: The Author, 1960.

Chesterton, G. K. *Autobiography*. London: Burns and Oates, 1937.

Como, James T., ed. *C. S. Lewis at the Breakfast Table*. New York: Macmillan, 1979.

Cropper, Margaret. *The Life of Evelyn Underhill*. New York: Harper and Row, 1958.

De La Bedoyère, Michael. *The Life of Baron von Hügel*. New York: Charles Scribner's Sons, 1951.

Farquharson, A. S. L., ed. *Statement and Inference with Other Philosophical Papers by John Cook Wilson*. Oxford: Clarendon Press, 1926.

Fox, Adam. *Dean Inge*. London: John Murray, 1960.

Griffiths, Bede. *The Golden String*. New York: P. J. Kennedy, 1954.

Harrod, R. F. *The Prof: A Personal Memoir of Lord Cherwell*. London: Macmillan, 1959.

Holland, Henry Scott. *A Bundle of Memories*. London: Wells Gardner, Darton, 1915.

Illingworth, Agnes L., ed. *The Life and Work of John Richardson Illingworth*. London: John Murray, 1917.

Jacks, L. P. *The Confessions of an Octogenarian*. London: Macmillan, 1942.

Jones, Henry. *The Life and Philosophy of Edward Caird*. Glasgow: MacLehose, 1921.

Kilby, Clyde S., and Marjorie Lamp Meade, eds. *Brothers and Friends: The Diaries of Major Warren Hamilton Lewis*. San Francisco: Harper and Row, 1982.

Knox, Ronald Arbuthnot. *A Spiritual Aeneid*. London: Longmans, 1918; rpt. Westminster MD: Newman Press, 1948.

Langstaff, John Brett. *Oxford 1914*. New York: Vantage, 1965.

Levy, Paul. *Moore: G. E. Moore and the Cambridge Apostles*. Weidenfeld and Nicholson, 1979.

Matheson, Percy Ewing. *The Life of Hastings Rashdall*. London: Oxford University Press, 1928.

Muirhead, John Henry. *Reflections of a Journeyman in Philosophy*. London: Allen and Unwin, 1942.

______________, ed. *Bernard Bosanquet and His Friends: Letters Illustrating the Sources and Development of His Philosophical Opinions*. London: Allen and Unwin, 1935.

Mure, G. R. G. *Idealist Epilogue*. Oxford: Clarendon, 1979.

Petre, Maude D. *Von Hügel and Tyrrell: The Story of a Friendship*. London: J. M. Dent, 1937.

Prestige, G. L. *The Life of Charles Gore: A Great Englishman*. London: William Heinemann, 1935.

Russell, Bertrand. *My Philosophical Development*. London: Allen and Unwin, 1959.

______________. *Portraits from Memory*. New York: Simon and Schuster, 1956.

Sidgwick, Eleanor M. *Henry Sidgwick*. London: Macmillan, 1934.

[Smith, Mary Baird]. *Arthur Lionel Smith, Master of Balliol (1866-1924): A Biography and Some Reminiscences by His Wife*. London: John Murray, 1928.

Tyrrell, George. *Autobiography and Life of George Tyrrell*. 2 vols. Edited by Maude Petre. London: Longmans, Green, 1912.

Williams, Charles, ed. *The Letters of Evelyn Underhill*. London: Longmans, Green, 1943.

Wollheim, Richard. *F. H. Bradley*. Harmondsworth, Middlesex: Penguin Books, 1959.

II. Histories of Philosophy, 1901-1945

Ayer, A. J., ed. *Logical Positivism*. Glencoe IL: Free Press, 1959.

Carr, H. Wildon. "The New Idealist Movement in Philosophy." *The Scientific Approach to Philosophy*. London: Macmillan, 1924.

Cunningham, G. Watts. *The Idealistic Argument in Recent British and American Philosophy*. New York: Century, 1933.

Ewing, A. C. *The Idealist Tradition: From Berkeley to Blanshard*. New York: Free Press, 1958.

Geoghehan, William D. *Platonism in Recent Religious Thought*. New York: Columbia University Press, 1958.

Hoernlé, R. F. Alfred. *Idealism as a Philosophy*. New York: Richard R. Smith, 1930.

Jenks, Craig. "T. H. Green, the Oxford Philosophy of Duty and the English Middle Class." *British Journal of Sociology* 28 (1977): 481-97.

Laird, John. *Recent Philosophy*. London: Thornton Butterworth, 1936.

Lewis, H. D., ed. *Contemporary British Philosophy: Personal Statements*. Ser. 3. London: Allen and Unwin, 1956.

Metz, Rudolf. *A Hundred Years of British Philosophy*. Trans. J. W. Harvey, T. E. Jessop, and Henry Sturt. New York: Macmillan, 1938.

Muirhead, J. H., ed. *Contemporary British Philosophy: Personal Statements*. Ser. 1. London: Allen and Unwin, 1924.

______________. *Contemporary British Philosophy: Personal Statements*. Ser. 2. London: Allen and Unwin, 1924.

Mure, G. R. G. "Benedetto Croce and Oxford." *Philosophical Quarterly* 4 (1954): 327-31.

______________. "Oxford and Philosophy." *Philosophy* 12 (1937): 291-301.

Passmore, J. A. *A Hundred Years of Philosophy*. London: Duckworth, 1927.

Russell, Bertrand, and G. E. Moore. *The Analytic Heritage*. Cambridge MA: Harvard University Press, 1971.

Schilpp, Paul Arthur, ed. *The Philosophy of Brand Blanshard*. La Salle IL: Open Court Press, 1981.

______________, ed. *The Philosophy of G. E. Moore*. Evanston IL: Northwestern University, 1942.

Sorley, William Ritchie. *A History of English Philosophy*. Cambridge: University Press, 1920.

Sturt, Henry. *Idola Theatri: A Criticism of Oxford Thought and Thinkers from the Standpoint of Personal Idealism*. London: Macmillan, 1906.

Warnock, G. J. *English Philosophy Since 1900*. Oxford: Oxford University Press, 1920.

Welleck, R. *Kant in England*. Princeton: Princeton University Press, 1931.

III. Histories of English Religious Thought, 1901-1945

Barmann, Lawrence F. *Baron von Hügel and the Modernist Crisis in England*. Cambridge: University Press, 1972.

Brilioth, Y. *The Anglican Revival: Studies in the Oxford Movement*. London: Longmans, Green, 1933.

Clark, Henry William. *Liberal Orthodoxy: A Historical Survey*. London: Chapman's Hall, 1914.

Emmet, Cyril W. *Conscience, Creeds, and Criticism*. London: Macmillan, 1918.

Forbes, Duncan. *The Liberal Anglican Ideal of History*. Cambridge: University Press, 1952.

Horton, Walter M. *Contemporary English Theology*. New York: Harper, 1936.

Inge, William. *The Platonic Tradition in English Theological Thought*. London: Longmans, Green, 1926.

Langford, Thomas A. *In Search of Foundations: English Thought 1900-1920*. Nashville: Abingdon Press, 1969.

Lawton, John Stewart. *Conflict in Christology*. New York: Macmillan, 1947.

Lilley, Alfred L. *Modernism: A Record and Review*. London: Isaac Pitman and Sons, 1908.

Major, H. D. A. *English Modernism*. London: H. Milford, 1927.

Neill, Stephen Charles. *The Interpretation of the New Testament, 1861-1961*. London: Oxford University Press, 1961.

Ramsey, A. M. *From Gore to Temple* (American title: *An Era in Anglican Theology*). London: Longmans, Green, 1960.

Richardson, R. D. *The Causes of the Present Conflict of Ideals in the Church of England*. London: John Murray, 1923.

Reckitt, M. B. *Maurice to Temple*. London: Faber and Faber, 1947.

Shebbeare, C. J. *Religion in an Age of Doubt*. London: Robert Scott, 1911.

Spinks, G. S. *Religion in Britain Since 1900*. London: Andrew Dakers, 1952.

Sykes, Norman. *The English Religious Tradition*. London: S. C. M., 1953; rev. ed., 1961.

Vidler, Alec R. *The Modernist Movement in the Roman Church*. Cambridge: University Press, 1934.

______________. *A Variety of Catholic Modernists*. Cambridge: University Press, 1970.

Wood, H. G. *Belief and Unbelief Since 1850*. Cambridge: University Press, 1955.

IV. Histories of Other Intellectual Movements

Collins, John Churton. *The Study of English Literature*. London: Macmillan, 1891.

Greengarten, I. M. *Thomas Hill Green and the Development of Liberal Democratic Thought*. Toronto: University of Toronto Press, 1981.

Hearnshaw, L. S. *Short History of British Psychology, 1840-1940*. London: Methuen, 1964.

McPherson, Robert G. *The Theory of Higher Education in Nineteenth Century England*. Athens GA: University of Georgia Press, 1959.

Richter, Melvin. *The Politics of Conscience: T. H. Green and His Age*. London: Weidenfeld and Nicholsen, 1964.

Rothblatt, Sheldon. *Tradition and Change in English Liberal Education*. London: Faber and Faber, 1976.

Turner, Frank M. *The Greek Heritage in Victorian Britain*. New Haven: Yale University Press, 1981.

Widgery, Alban G. *Contemporary Thought of Great Britain*. New York: Knopf, 1927.

V. The Magdalen Metaphysicals

A. Robin George Collingwood (1889-1943)

A bibliography of Collingwood's published writings on philosophy and archaeology was published by T. M. Knox and I. A. Richmond in *PBA* 19 (1943): 474-75, 81-85. More complete bibliographies, including secondary literature, are in William M. Johnston, *The Formative Years of R. G. Collingwood* (The Hague: Martinus Nijhoff, 1967), and W. J. van der Dussen, *History As a Science: The Philosophy of R. G. Collingwood* (The Hague: Martinus Nijhoff, 1981).

Collingwood published his own *Autobiography* in 1939, and there is some autobiographical material in *The First Mate's Log* (1940). The best sources for Collingwood's life apart from his own writings are R. B. McCallum, "Robin George Collingwood," *PBA* 19 (1943): 464-68, and T. M. Knox in *DNB* 1941-1950, 168-70. Obituaries were published in the *Times* of 11 January 1943, the *Times Literary Supplement*, 16 January 1943, and in *Oxford Magazine*, 4 February 1943.

The most important studies of Collingwood's thought are by Alan Donagan, Louis O. Mink, and Lionel Rubinoff. A bibliography of these studies is in *HAS*, and van der Dussen gives the most complete account of the development of Collingwood's philosophy.

Most of Collingwood's papers are in the Bodleian, and a catalog that is substantially complete is in *HAS*, 454-62. Other Collingwood letters are in the Smith Papers at Magdalen, and his journals are held by his daughter, Teresa Collingwood Smith of Oxford.

B. Clive Staples Lewis (1898-1963)

Lewis's bibliography is in *Light on C. S. Lewis*, ed. Jocelyn Gibb (New York: Harcourt, Brace and World, 1965) 117-48.

The notices published at the time of his death include obituaries in the *Times*, 25 November 1963; the *New York Times*, 25 November 1963; and *Publisher's Weekly* 184 (9 December 1963); Helen Gardner, *PBA* 51 (1965): 417-28; Roger Lancelyn Green, *Aryan Path* 35 (March 1964): 98-103.

Lewis published his spiritual autobiography with the title *Surprised by Joy: The Shape of My Early Life* (New York: Geoffrey Bles, 1955). *Pilgrim's Regress* (London: Geoffrey Bles, 1933) is also important for Lewis's biography. See also W. H. Lewis, *Brothers and Friends: The Diaries of Major Warren Hamilton Lewis*, ed. Clyde S. Kilby and Marjorie Lamp Mead. San Francisco: Harper and Row, 1982.

The biographical notice was provided for *DNB* 1961-1970 (651-53) by J. A. W. Bennett, and a full-length biography was written by Roger Lancelyn Green and Walter Hooper, *C. S. Lewis: A Biography* (New York: Harcourt, Brace, Jovanovich, 1974).

For a bibliography of studies of Lewis's thought and reviews of his works to 1969, see William Luther White, *The Image of Man in C. S. Lewis* (Nashville:

Abingdon, 1969) 225-35, and especially Joe R. Christopher and Joan K. Ostling, *C. S. Lewis: An Annotated Checklist of Writings about Him and His Works* (Kent OH: Kent State University Press, 1973). Since that time there have been several important studies, among them:

Derrick, Christopher. *C. S. Lewis and the Church of Rome*. San Francisco: St. Ignatius Press, 1981.

Holmer, Paul. *C. S. Lewis: The Shape of His Faith and Thought*. New York: Harper and Row, 1976.

Howard, Thomas. *The Achievement of C. S. Lewis*. Wheaton IL: H. Shaw, 1980.

Reilly, R. J. *Romantic Religion: A Study of Barfield, Lewis, Williams and Tolkien*. Athens: University of Georgia Press, 1971.

C. S. Lewis's manuscripts were deposited at Wheaton College, Wheaton, Illinois, by Major Warren Lewis through his friendship with Professor Clyde Kilby of Wheaton. Copies and some additional material is in BLW. A few letters are in Magdalen College Library.

Portions of Lewis's letters were published in Warren H. Lewis, ed., *The Letters of C. S. Lewis* (New York: Harcourt, Brace and World, 1966). See also Walter Hooper, ed., *They Stand Together: The Letters of C. S. Lewis to Arthur Greeves (1914-1963)* (New York: Macmillan, 1979); Clyde S. Kilby, ed., *Letters to an American Lady* (Grand Rapids MI: William B. Eerdmans, 1967); Lionel Adey, *C. S. Lewis' "Great War" with Owen Barfield* (Victoria B. C.: University of Victoria, 1978).

C. John Alexander Smith (1863-1939)

Smith's bibliography, for several entries in which I am indebted to Peter Johnson, includes the following:

"On Proving the Existence of God." *Papers Read Before the Synthetic Society (1896-1908)*. London: Spottiswoode, 1909, 414-20.

"On Religious Sympathy." *Papers Read Before the Synthetic Society (1896-1908)*. London: Spottiswoode, 1909, 556-60.

"Edward Caird." *Oxford Magazine* 27:5 (12 November 1908): 71-72.

Knowing and Acting: An Inaugural Lecture Delivered Before the University of Oxford, 26 November, 1910. Rpt. *Oxford Lectures on Philosophy, 1919-1923*. Oxford: Clarendon Press, 1924; rpt. New York: Books for Libraries Press, 1966.

Introduction to *The Ethics of Aristotle*. Trans. D. P. Chase. London: J. M. Dent and Sons, 1911, i-xxviii.

"On Feeling." *PAS* 14 (1913-1914): 49-75.

"On Some Fundamental Notions of Economics." *Economic Review* 23 (1913): 366-81.

"Further Notes on Some Fundamental Notions of Economics: Capital." *Economic Review* 24 (1914): 48-64.

"Further Notes on Some Fundamental Notions of Economics: Labour," *Economic Review* 24 91914): 283-97.

"The Contribution of Greece and Rome." Francis Sidney Marvin, ed. *The Unity of Western Civilization*. London: Humphrey Milford, 1915; 2d ed., 1922; 3d ed., London: Oxford University Press, 1929; rpt. Freeport NY: Books for Libraries Press, 1970, 69-90. Read at a summer school at the Woodbrooke Settlement, near Birmingham, August 1915.

"Philosophy and Theism." *Quarterly Review* 225 (April 1916): 291-312. A review of *Naturalism and Agnosticism* (2d ed.) by James Ward; *The Realm of Ends*, by James Ward; *The Principle of Individuality and Value*, by Bernard Bosanquet; *The Value and Destiny of the Individual*, by Bernard Bosanquet; *Theism and Humanism*, by Arthur James Balfour.

"Progress in Philosophy." Francis Sydney Marvin, ed. *Progress and History*. London: Humphrey Milford, 1916; rpt. Freeport NY: Books for Libraries Press, 1969, 273-94.

"Progress as an Ideal of Action." Francis Sidney Marvin, ed. *Progress and History*, 295-314.

"General Relative Clauses in Greek." *Classical Review* 31 (1917): 69-71.

"Are the Materials of Sense Affections of the Mind?" *PAS* 17 (1916-1917): 445-52. Contribution to a Symposium with G. E. Moore, W. E. Johnson, and G. Dawes Hicks.

Review of H. Wildon Carr, *The Philosophy of Benedetto Croce: The Problem of Art and History*. *HJ* 16 (1917-1918): 503-506.

"Is There a Mathematics of Intensity?" *PAS* 18 (1917-1918): 121-37.

"Metonomy in Horace's Odes, Bks I-XI." *Classical Review* 33 (1919): 27-28.

Review of *The Spirit*. Ed. B. H. Streeter. *HJ* 18 (1919-1920): 614-16.

"The Philosophy of Giovanni Gentile." *PAS* 20 (1919-1920): 63-78.

"ΑΠΑΠΕΜΦΑΤΟΕ." *JTS* 21 (1919-1920): 329-31.

"Aristotelica." *Classical Quarterly* 14 (1920): 16-22.

"Morals and Religion." *HJ* 19 (1921): 621-24. A Contribution to a Symposium with F. von Hügel, J. Chevalier, L. P. Jacks, and H. Wildon Carr.

"ΤΟΔΕ ΤΙ in Aristotle." *Classical Review* 35 (1927): 19.

"Language as a Link." Francis Sidney Marvin, ed. *Western Races and the World*. London: Humphrey Milford, 1922, 27-46.

Review of *A Faith that Enquires*, by Sir Henry Jones. *HJ* 21 (1922-1923): 387-95.

"Aristotle, Poetics, c. xvi, par 10." *Classical Quarterly* 18 (1924): 165-68.

The Nature of Art: An Open Letter to the Professor of Poetry in the University of Oxford. Oxford: Clarendon Press, 1924.

"Philosophy as the Development of the Notion and Reality of Self-Consciousness." *CBP* (2).

"F. H. Bradley." *Oxford Magazine* 43:2 (23 October 1924): 30-32.

"Professor Alexander's Notion of Space-Time." *PAS* 25 (1924-1925): 41-60. Read 1 December 1924.

"The Economic Doctrine of the Concept." *PAS*, suppl. 5 (1925): 103-22. A Contribution to a Symposium with F. C. S. Schiller and A. D. Lindsay, 25 July 1925.

"Benedetto Croce." *Encyclopedia Britannica*. 14th ed.

"Is the Mind a Compound Substance?" *PAS* 26 (1925-1926): 255-62. A Contribution to a Symposium with G. Dawes Hicks and James Drever, 31 May 1926.

Preface to *Benedetto Croce: An Autobiography*. Trans. R. G. Collingwood. Oxford: Clarendon Press, 1927, 5-18.

"The Place of Mind in Nature." *PAS* 6, suppl. 5 (1926): 127-31. (1926) A Contribution to a Symposium with L. T. Hobhouse and G. C. Field.

"The Nature of Mind and the Reality of Genuine Intercourse Between Minds." *Proceedings of the Sixth International Congress of Philosophy*. London: Longmans, Green, 1927, 128-36.

"Address." *Proceedings of the Sixth International Congress of Philosophy*, 705-707.

"The Nature of 'Objective Mind.' " *PAS* 7 (1923-1924): 45-54. A Symposium with H. Wildon Carr and A. A. Bowman, at Bedford College for Women, London, 15-18 July 1927.

Review of *Whither Mankind: A Panorama of Modern Civilization*. Ed. Charles A. Beard. *HJ* 27 (1928-1929): 744-49.

"The Meaning of ΚΥΡΙΟΣ." *JTS* 31 (1929-1930): 155-60.

Artificial Languages. Society for Pure English, Tract No. 34, Oxford: Clarendon Press, 1930, 469-77.

"The Influence of Hegel on the Philosophy of Great Britain." *Internationaler Hegelbund Verhandlungen des Hegelkongresses, 1930*. Ed. B. Wigersma. Tübingen: J. C. B. Mohr, 1931, 57-66.

"Great Thinkers: (III) Aristotle." *Philosophy* 9 (1934): 434-49; 10 (1935): 15-26.

"Words As Separate Entities in Ancient and Modern Languages." *Philological Society Transactions*, 1931-1932, 19-38. Read at the meeting of 1 May 1931.

"H. H. Joachim, A Contribution to his Obituary." *PBA* 24 (1939): 417-20.

Smith's intellectual biography is "Philosophy as the Development of the Notion and Reality of Self Consciousness," *CPB* (2), 227-44.

Obituary notices were published by W. D. Ross in *DNB* 1931-1940, 818-20; by G. Dawes Hicks in "Survey of Recent Philosophical Literature," *HJ* 38 (1939-1940): 401-402; in *Oxford Magazine*, 8 January 1940; The *Times*, 22 December 1939; and *The Scotsman*, 20 December 1939.

D. Clement Charles Julian Webb (1865-1944)

Clement Webb's bibliography through 1945 is in his *Religious Experience*, ed. L. W. Grensted (Oxford: University Press, 1945). His writings after 1945 include:

Review of *The Idea of Nature*, by R. G. Collingwood. *JTS* 46 (1945): 248-51.

Review of *Theology in an Age of Science*, by Leonard Hodgson. *JTS* 46 (1945): 244-48.

"A Comment on 'Surgery and Sin.' " *HJ* 45 (1946-1947): 144-47.

Review of *The Christian Faith: Essays in Explanation and Defense*, by W. R. Matthews. *JTS* 46 (1945): 114-18.

Review of *Does God Exist?* by A. E. Taylor. *JTS* 47 (1946): 124-27.

Review of *Groundwork of the Philosophy of Religion*, by Atkinson Lee. *JTS* 47 (1946): 251-53.

Review of *The Idea of History*, by R. G. Collingwood. *HJ* 45 (1946-1947): 83-86.

Review of *Le Dualisme dans l'Histoire de la Philosophie et des Religions*, by Simone Pètremont. *JTS* 47 (1946): 248-51.

Review of *The Word as Truth: A Critical Examination of the Christian Doctrine of Revelation in the Writings of Thomas Aquinas and Karl Barth*, by Alan Fairweather. *JTS* 47 (1946): 123-24.

"The Revolt Against Liberalism in Theology: A Study, in This Respect, of E. L. Mascall's *Christ, the Christian, and the Church*." *JTS* 48 (1947): 49-56.

Review of *The Elements of Moral Theology*, by R. C. Mortimer. *HJ* 46 (1947-1948): 184-86.

Review of *Selected Writings of William Law: Edited with Notes and Twenty-Four Studies in the Mystical Theology of William Law and Jacob Boehme*, by Stephen Hobhouse. *HJ* 46 (1947-1948): 91-93.

Review of *Philosophical Understanding and Religious Truth*, by Erich Frank. *JTS* 49 (1948): 245-47.

"The Metaphysical Society: Comment by C. C. J. Webb." *HJ* 47 (1948-1949): 207.

Review of *The Christian Understanding of History*, by E. C. Rust. *JTS* 50 (1949): 109-13.

Review of *F. H. Bradley*, by W. F. Lofthouse. *JTS* 50 (1949): 252-53.

Review of *The Glass of Vision*, by Austin Farrer. *JTS* 50 (1949): 117-23.

Review of *God Was in Christ*, by D. M. Ballie. *JTS* 50 (1949): 113-16.

Review of *Religion*, by Nathaniel Micklem. *JTS* 50 (1949): 253-55.

Review of *The Theology of F. D. Maurice*, by Alec R. Vidler. *JTS* 50 (1949): 247-51.

Review of *The City of God: A Study of Augustine's Philosophy*, by John H. S. Burleigh. *JTS*, n.s. 1 (1950): 212-13.

Review of *A Study of the Summa Philosophia of the Pseudo-Grossteste*, by C. K. McKeon. *Medium Aevum* 19 (1950): 70-72.

Review of *The English Utilitarians*, by Leslie Stephen. *JTS*, n.s. 2 (1951): 119-21.

Review of *Faith and Duty*, by N. H. G. Robinson. *JTS*, n.s. 2 (1951): 228-31.

Review of *Is God Evident? An Essay Toward a Natural Theology*. *JTS*, n.s. 2 (1951): 121-23.

Review of *Sir S. Radhakrishnan: Comparative Studies in Philosophy Presented in Honour of his Sixtieth Birthday*. *JTS*, n.s. 2 (1951): 235-39.

Review of *The Life of Baron von Hügel*, by Michael de la Bedoyère. *JTS* 3 (1952): 143-48.

Review of Berkeley, *Alciphron ou le Pense-Menu*, trans. Jean Pucelle. *HJ* 51 (1952-1953): 403-404.

Review of *Christian Faith and the Scientific Attitude*, by W. A. Whitehouse. *JTS* 4 (1953): 142-43.

Review of *L'Expérience chrétienne*, by Jean Mouroux. *JTS* 4 (1953): 285-87.

Review of *The Fullness of Time*, by John Marsh. *JTS*, n.s. 4 (1953): 142-43.

Review of *The Language of Morals*, by R. M. Hare. *JTS*, n.s. 4 (1953): 142.

Review of *Interpreting Theology*, by Daniel Day Williams. *JTS*, n.s. 4 (1953): 88-90.

Review of *La Dottrina Trinitaria di S. Anselmo*, by Ranato Perino. *JTS*, n.s. 4 (1953): 141-42.

Review of *The Meaning of Existence*, by Mark Pontifes and Illtyd Trethowan. *JTS*, n.s. 4 (1953): 287-88.

Review of *Nature and Man in Biblical Thought*, by E. C. Rust. *JTS*, n.s. 4 (1953): 282-83.

Review of *Reason and Revelation: A Question from Duns Scotus*, by Nathaniel Micklem. *JTS*, n.s. 4 (1953): 283-85.

"Gilbert Crispin, Abbot of Westminster: Dispute of a Christian with a Heathen Touching the Faith of Christ." *Medieval and Renaissance Studies (III)*. Ed. Richard Hunt and Raymond Klibansky. London: Warburg Institute, 1954, 55-77.

"William Ralph Inge." *JTS*, n.s. 5 (1954): 188-94.

"Science and Human Nature." *Philosophy* 30 (1955): 3-6.

Obituaries were published by Sir David Ross in *PBA* 41 (1955), and in the *Times*, 6 October 1954.

Biographical notes are L. W. Grensted's preface to *Religious Experience*; G. N. Clark in *DNB* 1951-1960; and in *CBP* (2), 336-40. The autobiography Webb began, which was used by W. D. Ross in *PBA*, is in the Ross Papers in Oriel Library.

Clement Webb's journals, which are substantially complete from 1888 to 1954, are in the Bodleian, and are a unique source for Webb's biography and for the careers of his friends. The Bodleian has letters from Webb to his father and mother, to Hastings Rashdall, Gilbert Murray, J. M. Thompson, and others.

• INDEX •

MUP *The Magdalen Metaphysicals*

Binding designed by: Alesa Jones
Interior typography design by: Margaret Jordan Brown

Composition by MUP Composition Department

Production specifications:
text paper—60-pound Warren's Olde Style
endpapers—Gainsborough Silver Text Printed PMS 539
cover—(on .088 boards) Holliston Kingston Linen #24449
dust jacket—Gainsborough Silver Text Printed PMS 539

Printing (offset lithography) by Omnipress of Macon, Inc., Macon, Georgia

Binding by John H. Dekker and Sons, Inc., Grand Rapids, Michigan